COMPLEX POLITICAL VICTIMS

COMPLEX POLITICAL VICTIMS

Erica Bouris

Kumarian
Press, Inc.

Complex Political Victims

Published 2007 in the United States of America by Kumarian Press, Inc.
1294 Blue Hills Avenue, Bloomfield, CT 06002 USA

Copyedit by Bob Land
Proofread by Beth Richards
Design and production by UB Communications, Parsippany, NJ.
The text of this book is set in 11/13 Adobe Sabon.

Printed in the USA on acid-free paper by Thomson-Shore, Inc.

Library of Congress Cataloging-in-Publication Data

Bouris, Erica, 1980-
    Complex political victims / by Erica Bouris.
        p. cm.
    Includes bibliographical references and index.
    ISBN-13: 978-1-56549-232-5 (pbk. : alk. paper)
    1. Political persecution. 2. Political violence. 3. Political atrocities. 4. Victims of state-sponsored terrorism. 5. Human rights. 6. Civil rights. I. Title.
    JC 571.B6725 2007
    323.4'9—dc22

                                        2006032244

Contents

For George

Preface

I am preparing this book for publication at a time when brutal ethnic, civil, and religious conflicts rage. Darfur, Israel-Palestine, Iraq, Sri-Lanka—all are areas where people are fighting people, and a stable and lasting end to the suffering seems far removed. In the context of these conflicts, violence is creating hundreds of thousands of victims. These victims have suffered torture, murder, rape, beatings, and the destruction of their families, homes, and communities. It is simply impossible to overstate the victimization of people in the context of modern conflict.

This project emerged out of a deep commitment to better recognizing and responding to these political victims. The international community has too many moments of shame in regards to political victims—times when we could not or would not identify those who are suffering as victims, as a people deserving of our attention and assistance. Perhaps we instead saw them simply as rebels or militants or ethno-nationalists in their own right. Other times, the international community was able and willing to recognize a group of people as political victims, but we were unable to develop and implement a comprehensive set of assistance policies for these victims, limiting our actions to perhaps a few well-publicized trials of human rights abusers or an underresourced truth commission.

This project is founded on the idea that more can be done to effectively recognize and respond to political victims, and that in order to do so, we must be willing to undertake a critical reflection on the very concept of the political victim. This approach means questioning assumptions about how we stereotype victims, what assumptions we make about their identity, the role they play in conflict, and their needs in the peacebuilding and postconflict period. Such a critical reflection is rife with moral hazards. Unpacking what it means to be a political victim, and what role such individuals play in conflict and during peacebuilding, is treacherous in part because political victims are, by their very nature, so vulnerable and so desperately in need of support. As such, this project, while critically engaging the question of the political victim, aims never to lose sight of the underlying ethical commitments that launched this project. Political victims need more and better support. The international community has an ethical obligation to provide such support, but also a practical obligation. If we cannot adequately recognize political victims in instances of suffering, and if we cannot effectively assist these individuals during and after the conflict, a stable and lasting peace will likely remain elusive.

Acknowledgments

I am deeply grateful for the support I received in writing this book. My time as a graduate student at the Graduate School of International Studies at the University of Denver was characterized by numerous engaging, stimulating, and rewarding experiences that opened up the terrain from which the ideas in this book emerged. I thank also my current colleagues at Rollins College for their support of this project and for providing a hospitable climate in which to think and write.

Jim Lance from Kumarian Press deserves thanks for his early and patient support of this project. His comments, in addition to those of the anonymous reviewers, were always thoughtful, constructive, and demonstrative of a genuine interest in the project. Erica Flock was most helpful in making sure the project emerged as a book in a smooth and timely fashion.

A very special thanks is owed to George DeMartino. He served as my dissertation advisor and professor, but that role was perhaps not the most significant contribution he made to this project. Rather, it was the tremendous and delightful way in which he fostered my intellectual development by serving as a tireless point of engagement and a reminder of the precision and ethical sense that must inform any good scholarship. His careful thoughtfulness and genuine enjoyment of thought are practices that continue to inform my work, and for that I am deeply appreciative.

Finally, a special thanks to my family for their support. Gratitude is owed to my parents for sharing with me a life of generosity and integrity and to Karim, Ella, and Oscar for making the journey not just possible, but thoroughly enjoyable.

1

Political Victim Discourse

Adequate for the Twenty-First Century?

Germany, 1944

It was winter, the end of 1944. A contingent of children were brought in.
They were from Shavel, Lithuania, where German patrol cars had picked
them up from their homes. In broad daylight, six hundred Jewish boys,
aged twelve to eighteen, were brought in wearing down-at-heel shoes or
wooden clogs. The children looked so handsome, so radiant, so well-built,
that they shone through their rags. It was the end of October 1944. They
arrived in twenty-five trucks guarded by heavily armed SS men. They got
out in the yard of the crematorium area. The Kommando leader gave an
order: "Take your clothes off in the yard!" The children saw the smoke
from the chimney and instantly realized that they were being led to their
death. Crazed with fright they started running around the yard, back and
forth, clutching their heads. Many of them broke into frightful crying.
Their wailing was terrible to hear. The Kommando leader and his aide hit
out ferociously at the children. He whacked so hard that his wooden club
broke in his hand. He got himself another club and flailed at the children's
heads. Brute strength prevailed. The children, panic stricken though they
were, with death staring them in the face, undressed. Stark naked, they
pressed against each other to shield themselves from the cold, but they
would not go downstairs [into the gas chamber]. A bold little boy went up
and begged the Kommando leader to spare him. He would do any kind of
work, no matter how hard. The answer was a tremendous whack on the
head with the club. Many of the boys darted off frantically to the Jews of
the Sonderkommando, threw their arms around their necks, imploring
"Save me!" Others raced about the yard, naked, running from death. The
Kommando leader called in the SS Unterscharfuhrer with his rubber baton
to help.

The boys' high-pitched voices grew louder and louder in a bitter lament.
Their keening carried a great distance. One was completely deafened and
overcome by this desperate weeping. With satisfied smirks, without a trace
of compassion, the SS men triumphantly hailed savage blows on the chil-
dren and drove them into the gas chamber. On the stairs stood the Unter-
scharfuhrer, still wielding his club and giving a murderous crack at each

1

child. A few lone children were, all the same, still running back and forth in search of a way out. The SS men chased after them, lashing out at them and forcing them at last into the chamber. The glee of the SS men was indescribable. Did they never have children of their own? (Eisenberg 1975, 41–42)

Former Yugoslavia, 1992

Among the prisoners there were women and old men, men of over sixty and one who was 73. Prisoners were not being brought from the battlefield as captives but from their homes. Practically all of them had to go through various kinds of torture: beatings, being kept in closed, hot, suffocating premises, denied drinking water and denied use of the toilet, as well as poor nutrition.

The beatings were at the beginning done by special forces, from Serbia. Later the job was taken over by policemen who guarded us. They were local Serbs who carried out their jobs far more brutally than the special units men. They beat us with iron bars, wooden two-by-fours and truncheons, iron and rubber devices for beating, with their feet, and they were wearing military boots, with their fists and hands.

The victim was beaten over the head, neck, shoulders, back, chest, hips, feet, arms, and that is, over the entire body. Sometimes he was beaten by one man, sometimes by three, and sometimes even 10 policemen at the same time. They usually beat us during the daytime, sometimes in the room where we were housed and sometimes in the yard. After torture like this, the victim was covered with blood, over the head and back, and his back was blue and red from the blows.

Special forces would beat us during the day outside in the yard. Police guards usually beat us at night. They would take the victims out one by one, and three or four of them would throw themselves on him in the dark. And sometimes up to 10 policemen. They beat him with anything and everything, so that the victim's screams were horrible to listen to for us. Each of us feared we would be the next one they would beat.

A victim who could still walk would be thrown back into the room like an animal. . . . Apart from beating us, they tortured us by preventing us from going to the toilet as the need arose; from having drinking water, and in other ways. . . . In their tortures they went so far as to make a prisoner eat sand. And they forced one prisoner to swallow his own feces, another to perform sex acts on a fellow prisoner. . . . It was a terrible scene when one Special Force man from Serbia decided to show us, as he put it, how Chetniks slaughter their victims. While he selected his victim with a knife in his hands, every one of us thought he was going to be the victim. We stood there terrified while he made his choice. He selected as his victim one of two Albanian brothers, the younger of the two. He ordered him to crouch down on all fours and to spread out as far as he could in the middle of a circle that we were made to form around him. He tortured us and the victim horribly, psychologically by drawing his knife around on all sides of his neck but without cutting. Then he began to kick the victim with his feet and fists on the head and all other parts of his body. . . . We kept the terrible story of what we saw there from the other prisoners and we did not even talk about the horrible night among ourselves. (Gutman 1993, 56–58, quoting a former death camp prisoner)

Descriptions of political violence such as these are powerful narratives of victimization. Both the description of the death of children in Auschwitz and the description of life in Serb-run concentration camps provide tangible images of the horror of political conflict; they also articulate images of victims—victims who are helpless and fearful, pawns in a tremendous act of evil. The two images detailed above—the children being bludgeoned during their descent into death and men stripped of their humanity as they are beaten and slaughtered—are nearly interchangeable. In both instances we have a narrative of nearly incomprehensible evil and terror: "did they never have children of their own?" This inhuman evil and terror is juxtaposed next to an image of the most innocent of victims. The young, naked children, the old men, the women, stolen not from the battlefield but simply from their homes.

Yet the international community responded differently to these images of atrocity. As the realities of Auschwitz emerged in 1944–45, a stunned and shocked international community struggled to understand a level of atrocity and violence seemingly foreign to humanity.

The Holocaust, when it took place, was beyond the belief and the comprehension of almost all people living at the time, Jews included. Everyone knew that human history had been scarred by endless cruelties. But that thousands, nay millions, of human beings—men, women, and children; the old and the young; the healthy and the infirm—would be killed, finished off, mechanically, industrially so to speak, exterminated like vermin—that was a notion so alien to the human mind, an event so gruesome, so *new*, that the instinctive, indeed the natural, reaction of most people was: it can't be true (Jong 1989).

The international community grappled with the evil of Nazism, and many were ashamed that we had not done more to stop the millions of innocent deaths. During the course of the Bosnian conflict, but particularly after instances such as the Sarajevo marketplace bombing, the international community was, indeed, saddened by the violence and revolted by the attacks on civilians. Yet throughout the conflict, questions were raised about whether there were really any innocent victims, as at times it seemed like a messy civil war where "all parties were responsible" (Cigar 1995). Indeed, within hours of the Sarajevo marketplace bombings, which killed scores of civilians, questions of possible victim (for example, Bosnian Muslim) responsibility emerged (Cigar 1995). Weeks later, even after the Serbs had been heavily bombed into submission, the *New York Times* ran a headline that questioned the true role of Bosnians in the bombing: "Bosnian Army Said to Shell Own Territory" (*New York Times*, 11/10/1995). Was it possible that the Bosnian Muslims had shelled their own people, caused the carnage of women and children simply to draw attention to their cause and elicit international sympathy? What else might they have done in the conflict? Was the blood spilled tainted blood? Were the Bosnian Muslims not innocent victims of Serb cruelty but rather calculating participants in conflict? This issue became one of intense international controversy as I show shortly, but at this point I raise these differing reactions to similar images of victimization to introduce a point that motivates this project.

First, images of the political victim are powerful, gripping, and integral in helping us makes sense of conflict, particularly in making moral calculations, determining who is "good" and who is "evil." These images, and the discourse of victimization that surrounds them, inform the international community when deciding to recognize certain individuals as victims and play a role in shaping response policies. These policies in turn contribute to the potential for long-term, stable peace after episodes of political victimization.

The idea that images of conflict, and particularly victims, matter in attracting international attention is certainly not new; much political scholarship has focused on how the "CNN effect" has contributed to international engagement in conflict and humanitarian crisis (see, for instance, Gowing 1997 and Jakobsen 2000). Jakobsen articulates the supposed functioning of the CNN effect as follows,

> Media coverage (printed and televised) of suffering and atrocities leads to journalists' and opinion leaders' demands that Western governments "do something," which leads to the (public) pressures becoming unbearable, which leads to Western governments doing something (Jakobsen 2000, 132).

These visual and descriptive images of the victim matter profoundly, and yet at times they have a tendency to oversimplify (Moeller 2002). It is no coincidence that the images we see on the nightly news are that of the starving child, the maimed grandmother, the child on his way to school riddled with gunshot fire. These images are gripping because of the tremendous way in which they juxtapose the extreme innocence of the victim with the often incomprehensible violence and evil of those who can harm children and the elderly. Such images can focus international attention and lead to policies of assistance for political victims. Indeed, they have been credited with contributing to interventions, most notably in Somalia and Bosnia (Jakobsen 2000).[1] In an interview with Richard Holbrooke, British aid worker Tony Land notes, with frustration, how it took "a few pictures of people being held behind barbed wire" for the international community to respond to the Bosnian genocide, despite written reports and evidence of Serb atrocity for months (Holbrooke 1998, 36). Journalistic coverage of atrocities and particularly these victim images continue to be important, and arguably with the increasing media exposure and globalization of media their importance will only increase.[2]

Yet the twenty-first century has brought something else with it as well: increasingly complex ethnic and civil conflicts. Though we see these simplistic images of conflict, dichotomies of innocence and aggression, political scholarship tells us that modern conflicts are complex. There are often overlapping spirals of aggression, multiple parties with differing aims, some groups and at times all groups making use of horrific violence and crimes against humanity. Despite knowing that conflict and political victimization is often quite complex, the way we continue to capture and "know" victims of political violence is often through simplistic images of victimization. They provide the hook, the entryway into motivating a response to end political victimization, and in many instances inform the architecture of the final peace.

On the one hand, this is not problematic. Indeed, in many cases it has worked to bring much-needed attention to human suffering. In 1992, journalist Roy Gutman began reporting on the horrific rape and concentration camps in Bosnia. These camps, run by Serb militia, were imprisoning and abusing thousands of Bosnian Muslims and other non-Serbs—torturing, raping, and killing them in a greater plan of genocide. In part because of Gutman's and other's coverage of these camps, the United States as well as several Western European countries significantly increased their attention to the Bosnian conflict, and in particular began to discuss ways to stop the ethnic cleansing of Bosnian Muslims. Gutman's images were simple; indeed, they were not so different from narratives of Auschwitz and the Holocaust, which contributed to their power in rallying U.S. and European attention to the conflict. But, as the international community knew, this conflict was not quite as simple as the Holocaust. Without question, a policy of genocide could only be attributed to the Serbs, but crimes against humanity were occurring on all sides (though at notably disproportionate rates, with a UN report finding that 90 percent of atrocities were committed by the Serbs). Allegiances between Bosnian Muslims, Croats, and Serb state and nonstate actors were complex and overlapping, and the ethnic, religious, and territorial aspects of the conflict made for a particularly complicated conflict.

One of the questions this project asks is what are the implications of the juxtaposition of simplistic images of the victim in the context of complex political victimization? Is it in any way problematic to rely on simplistic images of the victim in representing complex instances of political victimization? Perhaps one could argue that these simple images of the victim are simply a product of a media prone to sensationalize and simplify in search of a compelling headline. To a certain extent this is true. The reliance on a simple image of the innocent victim is arguably most pronounced in media representations of conflict. But what this project also shows is that this simple image of the victims, what Smyth (2002) calls the "ideal victim," also informs peacebuilding scholarship and characterizes many attempts by the international community to engage political victims during peacebuilding. In short, the reliance on the ideal victim image is not just a problem for headline-hungry evening newscasts; it is a problem for thoughtful scholars of peacebuilding as well.

There are three primary ways in which relying on this simple image of the victim is problematic. First, insofar as the international community and peacebuilding scholarship relies on this image to represent victims (and subsequently cue a response from others), we may be considerably less likely to recognize other, more complicated images of victimized individuals as *victims*. This in turn may prevent or delay our decision to respond to and assist these harmed individuals. In cases where the international community does respond to political victimization, the policies of response are likely to be shaped by this simple image of the victim, and as such these policies may be either unavailable or ineffective for the engagement and healing of more complex victims. Third, and obviously related to the first two issues, the creation of a stable peace can be undermined by a reliance on a simple image and discourse of the victim.

This project aims to demonstrate each of these claims by unpacking the discourses and images of victimization that informed recognition and response policies in modern episodes of political victimization. Further, this book investigates the role of victimization discourses in shaping the institutions and practices of the postconflict society as it strives for a lasting and stable peace.

This is a methodology first of illustration; these episodes of political victimization and their attendant responses and efforts at peace are being used to demonstrate connections between discourses of victimization and the development of concrete policies of recognition, response, and peacebuilding. But this approach aims to do more than simply illustrate the discourse of the victim and its performativity. It is also an inquiry that Campbell has articulated as a "political criticism constituting an ethos" (Campbell 1998, 4).

Undertaking a critique involves an intervention or series of interventions in established modes of thought and action. Such interventions are thus positioned in a particular relationship to those practices they wish to critique. They involve an effort to disturb those practices that are settled, untie what appears to be sewn up, and render as produced that which claims to be naturally emergent. The positioning of the interventions means that there is an ethico-political imperative inherent to them, not a predetermined or established politics, but a desire to explore and perhaps foster the possibilities being foreclosed or suppressed by that which exists or is being put in place. Intervening necessarily involves questioning of that which is established, and that questioning betrays a concern or dissatisfaction with what is settled and creates the conditions of possibility for the formulation of alternatives (Campbell 4, 1998).

Such a methodology allows for the unpacking of a "givenness" of the victim identity and the victimization discourse that emerges from peacebuilding scholarship. As Campbell emphasizes, such an intervention is necessarily meant to disrupt, and it is in the denaturalization and the disruption that the space emerges for the creation of an alternative discourse of political victimization, a task taken up in the latter part of this project. In the context of political victimization, the need to "untie what appears to be sewn" emerges from a deep normative commitment to broadening the types and numbers of political victims that the international community recognizes and by a parallel commitment to more effective responses to these victims—responses that ultimately lay the groundwork for a stable and lasting peace.

The two episodes of political victimization explored in this project are the victimization of Bosnian Muslims during the Balkan conflict and the victimization of South Africans during apartheid. These episodes of political victimization have been chosen for several reasons. First and foremost, they have been tremendously well studied. This allows for a broad and deep range of materials from which to piece together a discourse of the victim. How have scholars and the broader international community engaged and framed these episodes of political victimization? Second, both episodes of political victimization contain many of the "typical" aspects of modern ethnic and civil conflicts. Between the two conflicts, issues of ethnicity, race, religion, class, autonomy, sovereignty, self-determination, and failed states emerge. These conflicts, without a doubt, qualify as "complex." Yet interestingly (and importantly), the analysis of both, and the more popular coverage of both, have at times drawn quite heavily on a strikingly simple discourse of political victimization. Third, both Bosnia and South Africa have moved enough past the most acute episodes of political victimization to allow a consideration of the development and establishment of institutions and practices during the postconflict period.

Teasing out discourses of victimization and illustrating how they inform actions of victim recognition, response, and peace is a critical part of expanding our understanding of complex political victims. But in order to begin to formulate effective response policies, in order to use nuanced victim discourses to contribute to peace, it is necessary to embark upon a sustained theorization of such a complex victim. As such, the second component of this project is developing a theory and discourse of the complex political victim. A discourse of the complex political victim challenges the simple, reductionist image of the innocent victim to show more precisely the nuance and complexity of those suffering political victimization. Yet in so doing, a discourse of the gray victim *never denies the victim status of the individual*. It reaffirms the humanity of all victims. Rather than hold the victim up to a nearly unreachable standard of pure good and pure innocence (and fault her when she does not), a discourse of the complex political victim embraces the complexities and contradictions of the victim identity in order to better recognize her, better respond to her, and better contribute to peace.

DEFINING POLITICAL VICTIMS: AN INITIAL ATTEMPT

Certainly before proceeding much further into this project, it is necessary to define the term "political victim." This is not, as might be expected, a particularly easy task; indeed the term is often used quite loosely in peace and conflict studies to describe individuals and/or groups who have suffered harm in a political context. It is also noteworthy that the term often appears in a dyad—for example, victims and perpetrators. Further, it is applied to a range of actors, only some of whom experience direct physical harm, with many others being indirect (though no less serious) victims. Nonetheless, a more precise definition is important for this project, and some measure of clarity can be found in the work of Huyse (2002), who articulates how political victims are defined both by official internationally accepted definitions of "victim" but also by complex social and individual processes. The UN Declaration of Basic Principles of Justice for Victims of Crime and Abuse of Power, the UN Commission on Human Rights, and the International Criminal Court all have developed specific definitions of the victim.

> ... persons who, individually or collectively, have suffered harm, including physical or mental injury, emotional suffering, economic loss or substantial impairment of their fundamental rights, through acts or omissions that do not yet constitute violations of national criminal laws but of internationally recognized norms relating to human rights. (UN Declaration of Basic Principles of Justice for Victims of Crime and Abuse of Power, General Assembly Resolution 40/34)

> ... a person is a "victim" where, as a result of acts or omissions that constitute a violation of international human rights or humanitarian law norms, that person, individually or collectively, suffered harm, including physical or mental injury, emotional suffering, economic loss, or impairment of the person's fundamental legal rights. A "victim" may also be a dependent or a member of the immediate family or household of the direct victims as well as a person who, in intervening to assist a victim or prevent the occurrence of further violations, has suffered physical, mental or economic harm. (Declaration on the Right to Restitution for Victims of Gross Human Rights Violations)

> (a) "Victims" means natural persons who have suffered harm as a result of the commission of any crime within the jurisdiction of the Court; (b) Victims may include organizations or institutions that have sustained direct harm to any of their property which is dedicated to religion, education, art

or science or charitable purposes, and to their historic monuments, hospitals and other places and objects for humanitarian purposes. (International Criminal Court)

As Huyse (2002) argues, however, these are but one component of the process of defining political victims. In addition to legal definitions of "victim," sociopolitical factors, culture, and the victim's own perception of whether he or she is a victim all contribute to the definition of "who is a political victim" in any given context. Some important nonlegal influences in postconflict societies' attempts to define victims include work done by an official agency or institution such as truth commissions, reparations boards, and so forth; local and international NGOs and civil society groups; cultural understandings of justice, conflict, and reconciliation; and the degree to which individual victims are present and active in articulating their identity as victims.[3]

In short, "political victims" cannot be defined in a purely legal, abstract manner. The definition of the political victim is necessarily embedded in the broader context of the postconflict society. In part, this project may be understood as an attempt to articulate the way in which images of the victim and victimization discourses, particularly the discourse of peacebuilders, contributes to the definition of political victims in conflict and postconflict situations. By focusing on the manner in which these victimization discourses contribute to a particular definition of who is a political victim and who is not, I am not rejecting Huyse's (2002) argument that a combination of factors contributes to the definition of the political victim in any given context. Rather, this project complements his argument that the definition of the political victim is in large part socially constructed, and in focusing on victimization discourse I aim to highlight a critical and underdeveloped aspect of this process of construction.

PROJECT ORGANIZATION

This book is organized as follows. First, peacebuilding scholarship is reviewed in order to tease out images of the victim that emerge from the various approaches to peacebuilding. Despite tremendous variation in peacebuilding approaches, what emerges is a dominant image of the victim as one who is simple, uncomplicated, and innocent—the "ideal victim." Indeed, the victim that emerges from peacebuilding scholarship is one who is attended by a certain constellation of characteristics that include innocence, purity, lack of responsibility, and moral superiority. At times this constellation of characteristics functions even more strongly as a chain of equivalence; to be recognized as a victim is to automatically be recognized as an innocent, to be exalted to a high moral ground. This constellation is explored in chapter 3, with particular attention to its staying power: why have these characteristics attended the victim for so long, and what are the risks of fracturing this constellation? Why has this constellation largely retained its representation as "naturally emergent" and not "produced"?

To better understand this image of the innocent victim, and particularly to illustrate the difficulties with fracturing this image in a political context, I turn to a consideration of the Holocaust. Arguably no image of the political victim is invoked more frequently in characterizing atrocities, particularly those of a genocidal nature. Hence, a consideration of this image of the victim is important for numerous reasons. First, it is the political image of the ideal victim referenced in much peacebuilding scholarship. Second, its shadow reaches far into the future; we see men behind barbed wire in Bosnia, and we cannot help but think of Auschwitz. This image of the victim will continue to inform policies and public opinion for decades to come. Third, particularly by engaging the scholarship of Hannah Arendt, it is possible to see what happens when a critical voice begins to dissect this image of the ideal victim. Arendt's work complicating the widely accepted image of the Holocaust victim had tremendous repercussions and begins to illuminate the difficult areas that must be crossed in order to successfully develop a discourse of the gray victim that helps victims instead of tarnishing them. In short, by considering Arendt's work on Holocaust victims, we are reminded of the serious political and moral implications that must guide any and all critical reflection on the notion of the "political victim."

Following Arendt's initial attempts to bring nuance to victimization is a theorization of the complex political victim. The complex political victim is a victim who is no longer chained to characteristics of complete innocence and purity, but remains a victim nonetheless. In particular, the discursive responsibility of victims is considered, as is a rethinking of political victim "interests." What emerges is a victim who may bear some discursive responsibility for her or his victimization, a victim who may have a contradictory set of "interests" and as such would have difficulty fitting into the traditional script of the ideal victim. The analytical and ethical arguments for retaining the victim identity despite this complexity are considered. Further, I address the very real concern that such a conceptualization of victimization could foster an overuse of the notion of political victim and as a result a decrease in its political, social, and moral efficacy.

Turning to the victimization of Bosnian Muslims, it will be possible to articulate the effects that different victim discourses have on victim recognition and response. How did a simple discourse of the innocent victim influence who the international community saw as victims in this conflict, and perhaps as importantly, when these individuals were recognized as victims? How did this same discourse then shape decisions about intervention and peacebuilding? How could a discourse of the complex political victim have helped the international community in recognizing victims in this conflict and in designing more effective policies of peacebuilding and assistance? Could a discourse of complex political victimization have better informed the international community's understanding of and engagement with the conflict? What does applying a theory of complex political victimization to the Bosnian conflict tell us about critical issues in securing a long-term and stable peace?

The rest of the project is devoted to the postconflict period of peacebuilding—the period in which conflict parties must grapple with truth, justice, healing, and reconciliation. In what ways can a theory of the complex political victim inform these practices and pursuits? Theoretically this involves a discussion of Foucaultian and Deleuzian practices of the self and subjectivation, both of which provide ritualistic but largely unscripted opportunities for the beginning of healing, and the construction of an individual with agency to act on herself as well as in her community to confront the challenges of postconflict life.

To further explore the way in which victimization discourses can inform these practices of truth, justice, healing, and reconciliation, consideration is given to postapartheid South Africa with a focus on the Truth and Reconciliation Commission (TRC). Here in particular we see the way in which a discourse of victimization influences the architecture of postvictimization institutions and practices. This architecture in turn influences who is identified as a victim; who is eligible for the most practical of victim services, such as reparations, health care, and counseling; and who narrates victimization and reconciliation. The discussion of the South African TRC illustrates the wide-ranging and important ways that victim discourse influences "on the ground" engagement and support of victims. In the case of the TRC, at times it was an image of the ideal victim that was drawn on and produced, and victims who did not fit this image of the ideal victim were marginalized in their access to community truth, justice, healing, and reconciliation. However, certain institutions and practices in South Africa, including parts of the TRC, were hospitable to the personal and political practices of complex political victims— hospitable to self-subjectivation and a nurturing of the self for the benefit not just of the individual, but of the broader postconflict community. Some initial arguments are made about the way in which the failure to fully engage a complex discourse of victimization has hindered both social and political development in postapartheid South Africa.

The project both carries out and encourages the practice of political criticism constituting an ethos. It represents one attempt to unpack a "given" in peacebuilding studies, the political victim, and puts forth a more nuanced understanding of the victim. This new understanding of the victim aims to advance the cause of the political victim by reclaiming the victim's spot among the messiness of humanity and rallying for the victim's right to recognition and response. Ideally, this new understanding will encourage broader reflection among peacebuilding scholars and practitioners, reflection upon the "givens," but perhaps even more critically, how these "givens" inform the tremendously important work we do.

NOTES

1. Though as Jakobsen argues, receiving "attention" and some level of policy assistance from the CNN effect does not necessarily mean that these policies will be adequate to truly end victimization. However, in the context of this discussion, I am highlighting the fact that the CNN effect does bring attention and often has compelled leaders to "do something" even if this attention is fleeting and the "something" is inadequate.

2. Though it should be noted that increased media coverage and/or the globalization of media will not necessarily lead to a stronger CNN effect—for example, more policies designed to alleviate political and humanitarian suffering. This may be argued from the position that the CNN effect is not that strong to begin with, and only in certain contexts (see, for instance, Natsios). Alternately, some argue that increasing media coverage may well lead to either numbness or cynicism, both of which can be thought to decrease the strength of the CNN effect (see for instance Moeller 2002).

3. For an excellent and expanded discussion, see Huyse (2002).

2

Peacebuilding and Victim Discourse

Before articulating the image(s) of the victim that emerge in specific instances of political victimization, it is useful to consider in general what sorts of images of the victim inform peacebuilding scholarship. As such, this chapter begins by briefly defining peacebuilding and exploring the "peace vs. justice" debate that shapes approaches to peacebuilding, and then considers how particular strategies of interest-based conflict resolution, social psychology–based conflict resolution, and a rights-based approach to peacebuilding both rely on and construct an image of the victim. In part, the argument is made that the conceptualization of the victim that attends particular peacebuilding approaches influences states and the broader international community when recognizing certain individuals or groups as "victimized," when deciding to take action to stop this victimization, when determining whether and how to help these victims heal, and when assisting in the rebuilding of postconflict society. Moreover, and this introduces a theme at the heart of this book, this scholarship (despite its many other disagreements and conflicts) tends to portray the victim as a simple, unsophisticated identity and one that hinges on a chain of equivalence that runs from innocence and purity, to unwarranted harm, to a rather simplistic account of responsibility and interests.

APPROACHES TO PEACEBUILDING: PEACE VS. JUSTICE

Traditionally, many foreign policy practitioners and scholars have perceived of justice and peace in conflicting terms. The choices are often cast in terms of either working toward peace and ignoring justice or seeking justice at the price of jeopardizing any chance for peace. (Williams and Scharf 2002, 29)

While Williams and Scharf go on to qualify this statement as an overly artificial characterization of the tensions in peacebuilding scholarship, the fact remains that these two concepts, and the perceived conflict between their mutual pursuit, reappeared in nearly every peacebuilding effort in the twentieth century.

Peace

The pursuit of peace is generally characterized by a commitment to establishing a "negative peace," which simply refers to the absence of violence (see
Galtung 2001 for a discussion of negative peace). In order to achieve this negative peace, there is typically a willingness to deal with all parties deemed critical to the peace process, even if some of those parties are known to have
committed grave crimes against humanity. Richard Holbrooke, one of the
chief negotiators in the Balkan conflict, is (in)famous for his willingness, even
insistence on dealing with Serbian leader Milosevic despite his role in the commission of genocide and other crimes against humanity, but did so because
"the highest goal here was to avoid war, bring peace" (Senate Confirmation
Hearings, June 24, 1999). Such a perspective on the role of peacebuilders is
perhaps even more strongly captured in the title of his memoirs of the Bosnian
negotiations, *To End a War*.

The pursuit of peace often explicitly ignores the aims of justice and instead
is driven by the ethical imperative of "saving lives" (Williams and Scharf
2002, 31). This commitment takes precedence over the immediate pursuit of
justice and supports the accommodation, and at times appeasement, of
aggressor parties in order to move more swiftly towards the cessation of violence. The practice of accommodation "instructs a negotiator to end the conflict by meeting as many of the objectives of each party as possible, thereby
accommodating their interests and satiating their appetite for more conflict"
(Williams and Scharf 2002, 24). Appeasement goes a step further in actively
meeting aggressor demands, even if these demands are met due to coercive
tactics, provided doing so is thought to improve chances at peace.

A focus on the establishment of a negative peace often leads to what
Cousens (2001) identifies as "political peacebuilding."[1] She defines political
peacebuilding as

> the construction or strengthening of authoritative and eventually legitimate
> mechanisms to resolve internal conflict without violence... Peacebuilding
> is not designed to eliminate conflict but to develop effective mechanisms by
> which a polity can resolve its rival claims, grievances, and competition over
> common resources. (Cousens 2001 4, 12)

In this understanding of peacebuilding, the goal of peace is achieved (perhaps
through the aforementioned practices of accommodation/appeasement) and
the only additional immediate goal is the establishment of mechanisms to
nonviolently resolve conflict and maintain the negative peace (see also
Cousens 2001, Harris and Reilly 1998, and Brown 1996).

An emphasis on "getting to peace," or what Cousens identifies as political
peacebuilding, lacks an explicit discourse of the victim. Indeed, as we will see

shortly, in comparison to justice or reconciliation approaches to peacebuilding, political peacebuilding has very little to say about victims per se. Such an approach is seemingly not focused on identities such as "victim" or "aggressor"; indeed, time spent wrestling with these complex questions is assumed at times to be outside the scope of political peacebuilding and an impediment to the overriding goal of achieving a peaceful settlement.

Some critics, such as Williams and Scharf, suggest that a fixation on peace, especially when accompanied by practices of appeasement, does not simply result in the glossing over of questions of justice and victimization, but actually leads to a discourse of moral equivalence and moral duplicity between victim and aggressor: "Moral duplicity...entails declarations and actions designed to create the perception of moral equivalence among the parties, thereby eroding the distinction between aggressor and victim and spreading culpability among all parties" (Williams and Scharf 2002, 27).

From this perspective, it is not just that "getting to peace" fails to directly engage issues of victim identification and aggressor identification, but in fact it can falsely lead to equating the two groups as combatants on the same moral platform. By "eroding the distinction between aggressor and victim," peace negotiations can circumvent issues of injustice and, it is argued, move more swiftly toward the establishment of peace.

While the erosion of the victim is certainly a risk in this approach to peace, the eroded victim is arguably not the only possible image of the victim within this discourse. Such an approach may also be understood at least in part as a recognition of the complexity of victimization—a recognition that not only is it likely to be contested, but it is also likely to be genuinely complicated, such that even a "neutral" third party would have difficulty effectively managing its introduction into peace negotiations and peacebuilding and rather should focus solely on ending violence and building capacities that limit the likely recurrence of violence. Finally, there is evidence that some advocates of this approach actually retain a strong commitment to recognizing victims. For instance, during the early 1990s when many in the international community were still referring to the Bosnian conflict in terms of a civil war, Holbrooke, despite his goal of reaching peace as quickly as possible, frequently highlighted the victimization of Bosnian Muslims. In particular, he highlighted the genocidal acts of the Serbs against Bosnian Muslims, and the high number of innocent civilians being targeted by the Serbs (see, for instance, ongoing coverage in *Newsweek* during August 1992, as well as his journal entries in Holbrooke 1998).

> ...if the war continues, and the Serbs succeed in permanently reducing the Muslims to a small state or "cantonment" within a Bosnia that has been divided by Croatia and Serbia, the immediate consequences will be terrible—and

> the long-term consequences even worse. In the short run, the Muslims will
> have been removed from areas in which they have lived for centuries, with
> countless thousands butchered, often by their longtime neighbors.....
> [N]othing is likely to deter the Serbs except actions that raise the costs of
> their genocidal policies to an unacceptable level. (Holbrooke 1999, 39)

While his negotiating tactics did not engage the discourse of victims and
aggressors as explicitly, it is by his own admission a continued desire to help
these conflict victims that motivated his strong push for peace.[2] This image
of the victim is not one that is "morally equivalent" to the aggressor. Further, Holbrooke is voicing an acceptance of the notion of a distinct victimized group.

On a preliminary level we can see multiple images of the victim emerging
from this approach to peacebuilding: a victim eroded as a result of a platform
of moral equivalence; a discourse that recognizes some degree of victim complexity though purposefully does not develop this in the context of peacebuilding; and lastly a strong, moral commitment to the victim that can motivate movement toward peace even if it does not feature prominently in the
peace negotiation dialogue.

Justice

There are many, however, who understand peacebuilding as a much more
expansive endeavor than merely creating a negative peace and the development of structures to handle conflicts without violence. An alternative
approach to peacebuilding argues that in addition to the cessation of violence,
peacebuilding must also address issues of justice arising from the commission
of political violence. Indeed, even while focusing on the narrow goals of political peace, Albin (2001) argues that incorporating the principles of justice and
fairness is critical:

> The design of workable agreements can rarely rely on hard-nosed bargain-
> ing and the promise of mutual benefits alone. In order to win the respect
> and voluntary approval of the parties and their constituencies, the provi-
> sions must be seen as worth honoring partly by appealing to their sense of
> fairness. (Albin 2001, 215)

Albin is suggesting that even in the most basic step of negotiating and
enforcing a negative peace, issues of fairness, justice, perceptions of victimization, and so on, must be addressed; otherwise the agreement is likely to perform poorly, because those involved in the conflict likely want basic principles
of fairness and justice addressed, if only in the context of securing negative
peace. What precisely "justice" and "fairness" mean is, of course, contested
and often context-specific, but Galtung (2001) provides a working definition:

> Justice can be interpreted as "to each party his/her due"; the problem is
> determining what this means. As legal frameworks tend to carry the
> imprint of past injustices it is better to lean on such concepts as parity,
> equality, and equity. However, justice for slaves or for women cannot mean
> that they share the conditions of slave owners or men, but that some social
> order comes about where equality and equity (not the same) are possible.
> (Galtung 2001, 3)

In the context of peacebuilding, Williams and Scharf suggest that achieving
justice means adequately addressing the four components of justice: truth,
fairness, rectitude, and retribution/requital.

> In the context of peacebuilding, truth relates to an accurate understanding
> and recording of the causes of conflict, as well as which parties are respon-
> sible for which actions, and which parties, including individuals, may be
> characterized as the victims or the aggressors (including the possibility that
> both parties are the aggressors).... Fairness relates to an initial approach
> of impartiality—which can and must be adjusted in light of the truth about
> the conflict.... [F]airness also requires that third parties do not seek to
> apply undue pressure on the victims of a conflict in order to achieve an
> expedient political objective.... Rectitude encompasses a sense of moral
> virtue, integrity, and righteousness, requiring parties to "do the right
> thing.".... Retributions/requital comprises notions of compensation for vic-
> tims, punishment of aggressors. (Williams and Scharf 2002, 13–14)

Hence, peacebuilding informed by principles of justice entails much more
than simply reaching an agreement to end the violence. At the very least it
requires attention to truth, fairness, rectitude, and retributions/requital during
the negotiation stage, but in most instances requires attention to these matters
outside the scope of the negotiation (for example, the establishment of institutions to facilitate truth gathering and recording, funding for reparations, etc.).

As such, incorporating justice and fairness in peacebuilding does serve
much more than a tactical purpose of securing and maintaining negative
peace. Williams and Scharf (2002) articulate the following functions of justice
in the peacebuilding process:

> Within the context of creating stable, peaceful societies out of war-torn
> states, the norms and institutions of justice may serve several functions.
> These include establishing individual responsibility and denying collective
> guilt, dismantling and discrediting institutions and leaders responsible for
> the commission of atrocities, establishing an accurate historical record,
> providing victim catharsis, and promoting deterrence. (Williams and Scharf
> 2002, 16)

Further, incorporating the norms of justice into peacebuilding can allow
other peacebuilding tactics the time and public support necessary to see
progress. For instance, Williams and Scharf (2002, 92) argue that many in the
UN Security Council agreed to the establishment of the Yugoslav War Crimes

Tribunal in 1992 not because of a commitment to the usefulness of pursuing justice to achieve peace, but rather because they hoped it would convince the public that they were indeed "doing something" and help "marshal support for more aggressive responses."

Many who advocate for the inclusion of norms of justice in the peacebuilding process highlight how critical the inclusion of these norms is for long-term peace. Richard Goldstone, former chief prosecutor of the International Criminal Court and now a justice in South Africa, notes that if one wants "real peace... enduring peace" it is imperative to simultaneously address issues of justice (Goldstone 1997). Even Holbrooke, generally associated with his efforts to "get to peace" in Bosnia, noted that unless war criminals were brought to justice as a part of the peace process, whatever agreement was achieved was unlikely to last in the long term (Holbrooke 1999, 261). Further, Morphet (2002) argues for the inclusion of norms of justice as a part of peacebuilding particularly because of the way in which adhering to widely accepted, international norms increases the likelihood of the agreement, by securing a broad and continuing platform of international support. While this may be a practical reason for incorporating norms of justice into peacebuilding, others suggest that adhering to principles of justice is important for peacebuilding because they are a critical part of the human response to conflict and postconflict healing.[3] Albin offers the following on justice:

> This [incorporating principles of justice and fairness into the peacebuilding process to ensure cooperation from both sides] is not to suggest that ethical principles and behavior have no inherent value or that they are simply used tactically for narrow self interests. Arguments about justice and fairness would not carry any weight, and could therefore not be instrumental in promoting an agreement, unless parties saw them as genuine and compelling. (Albin 2001, 219)

Not only is incorporating justice into the peacebuilding process important, but the *highlighting* of the "justness" of the peacebuilding efforts can assist both victims and society. Kritz (2001) describes the effects of one such justice-based practice, that of holding war criminals accountable:

> In many countries, prosecutions for abuses committed during the conflict can serve several functions. They provide victims with a sense of justice and catharsis—a sense that their grievances have been addressed and can more easily be put to rest rather than smoldering in anticipation of the next round of conflict. In addition, they can establish a new dynamic in society, an understanding that aggressors and those who attempt to abuse the rights of others will be held accountable. (Kritz 2001, 809)

In other places, an emphasis on justice has led not to the courtroom but rather to the establishment of truth commissions and reparation efforts. While truth commissions and reparations do not offer formal avenues for justice, they do recognize the legitimacy of victim narratives, promote principles of restorative justice, and at times make perpetrators "pay" their victims in a variety of ways (all of which are components of justice as defined by Williams and Scharf 2002). While there is much debate as to whether these practices really provide "justice" (see, for instance, Van Der Merwe 2001), their appearance in the peacebuilding process is generally motivated at least in part by a desire to provide some justice for the victims of political violence.

One of the most notable features of the justice-based approach to peace-building is the discreet, delineated conception of the victim (and, indeed, per-petrator) identity. Whether institutionalized in war crimes tribunals, truth and reconciliation commissions, or reparations boards, there is a strict delineation between victims and perpetrators (on the group or individual level). We see this in the very structures that often attend justice-based peacebuilding. The courtroom has its defendants and victims; the truth commission has separate boards for victim testimony and perpetrator amnesty; reparations boards have a separation between those who are due compensation (victims) and those who must make contributions (often perpetrators, though funding comes from other sources as well). Indeed, we might recall Williams and Scharf's articulation of one of the main functions of justice in peacebuilding: to iden-tify who is responsible for which actions and which groups or individuals are victims and which are perpetrators.

This is not to suggest that a justice-based approach to peacebuilding is blind to the potential complexity of conflict and victimization. Rather, a jus-tice-based approach to peacebuilding often assumes that the victim, while empirically difficult to identify in complex situations of violence, is, once found, something of a "given" identity. Victims are those who suffer injustice, those who bear no responsibility for this injustice, and those who are without guilt. Even in situations where one individual is recognized as having multiple identities (for example, victim and perpetrator), these identities themselves are not seen as complex, though the individual on the whole may be described as complex.

> We are victims, or affiliates of victims, of some wrongs; perpetrators or affiliates of perpetrators of others, and bystanders with regard to others. In the Canadian situation for instance, one might be a Holocaust survivor or child of a Holocaust survivor and in this respect a victim, and nevertheless one might also be a beneficiary and, through affiliation with a church or state institution a perpetrator with regard to Canadian social wrongs against Aboriginal peoples. (Govier 2003, 69)

A justice-based approach does not ignore that we may be constituted as victims and perpetrators in different situations of injustice, and as such, need to participate in multiple processes of justice. Yet insofar as a justice-based approach to peacebuilding does recognize an overlap of injustices—the generation of multiple identities—it does not investigate the complexity of a singular process of victimization. The above situation might be described as "complex" because the individual is both a victim and a perpetrator, but it does not manifest any complexity in regards to the victimization that occurred—for instance, during the Holocaust.

In any one instance of victimization, the victim is one who has suffered; one who is not responsible for the violence and has no guilt; one who, most importantly, needs and deserves justice; one who needs to see the perpetrator responsible for her victimization identified and held accountable in some way. Indeed, a focus on justice encourages the dividing up of conflict participants into two mutually exclusive categories: those who need justice (the victims) and those who must be held accountable for fairness and justice to prevail (the perpetrators). These neat and discreet identities allow little room for a more nuanced consideration of the role of the victim and perpetrator in violence and peacebuilding.

Reconciliation

Particularly in the last two decades, approaches to peacebuilding that have incorporated principles of justice and fairness have also included a goal of reconciliation. These are distinct goals, with "justice" referring to "each getting what he/she deserves" and "reconciliation" referring to a more holistic process.

> Reconciliation [is] the process of healing the traumas of both victims and perpetrators after the violence, providing a closure of the bad relation. The process prepares the parties for relations with justice and peace. (Galtung 2001, 3)

The argument for reconciliation in peacebuilding, beyond simply achieving political peace and justice, is identified by Borris:

> If hatred, bitterness, and other psychological issues are not also addressed agreement will be weak at best. Since there are important psychological and emotional components to all protracted conflicts, there will also be equally important psychological and emotional components to their resolution. These are the issues reconciliation addresses. (Borris 2001, 161)

Reconciliation clearly recognizes that violence causes much victimization and that these victims need to undergo healing and/or closure. Conceptually, there are still clear distinctions between the victim and the perpetrator; that these are two distinct groups is taken as a given. However, many advocates of reconciliation are in favor of it in part because of a belief that perpetrators are victims, too; they also need to participate in a process of healing and closure (see, for instance, Minow 1998). Govier and Verwoerd (2002) note that reconciliation often scripts the identities of victims and perpetrators further. The perpetrators must come clean with the truth and articulate their full responsibility for the commission of violence. The victims, as the harmed but innocent group, have the unique power of forgiveness, a power that they should exercise during the reconciliation process. They and they alone can forgive the perpetrators for the awful acts of violence committed upon them. Reconciliation, when it is attended by such a script of roles (as Govier and Verwoerd argue it was in South Africa), can be seen as furthering the construction of the victim and perpetrator identities both as opposites in the relation of violence and as defined by innocence and responsibility respectively.

A justice-based approach to peacebuilding, at times incorporating the additional goal of reconciliation, emphasizes the victim identity much more so, and in different ways, than an emphasis on "getting to peace." Arguably, advocates of justice-based approaches emphasize the need for justice precisely because an injustice has created victims. Further, justice-based approaches, and reconciliation as well, tend to conceptualize victims and perpetrators as distinct groups and/or individuals; there may be many and overlapping groups of victims and perpetrators, but these identities are themselves uncomplicated. The victim identity is, quite simply, the identity of the one who has suffered injustice, the one who needs to see the perpetrator accept full responsibility for the wrongs that have occurred. Further, in the process of reconciliation, this innocent victim with a moral superiority in relation to the perpetrator is capable of the critical process of forgiveness, whether or not justice is fully done. Williams and Scharf in particular highlight the salience of these identities. It is critical for justice-based approaches to peacebuilding to identify and name those who are victimized and those who are responsible, lest the process of justice remain incomplete and peace elusive.

PEACEBUILDING STRATEGIES AND THE IMAGE OF THE VICTIM

Though peacebuilding activities that are strongly informed by a goal of an expeditious political peace on the whole might be expected to look quite different than peacebuilding activities informed by a deep commitment to justice, in reality, these two concepts often jointly inform the peacebuilding process. Though they have at times been articulated as conflicting goals, current peacebuilding scholarship and practice suggests that some justice-based strategies (e.g., war crimes tribunals) can be pursued alongside or perhaps after a political peace has been hammered out (e.g., the Dayton Accords and the subsequent trials of war criminals). Certainly neither a stable peace nor full justice are likely to be achieved in the short term (and in terms of justice, perhaps never). Yet it is possible for peacebuilding to be informed by attention to securing peace and providing at least limited justice.[4] It remains the case, however, that understanding the images of the victim that emerge from a "peace"-based approach to peacebuilding and a "justice"-based approach to peace-building are critical for this project. As has been shown, on the broad, conceptual level, both approaches draw on an impoverished understanding of the victim—perhaps simple and innocent, perhaps swept under the rug in an attempt to secure peace. Further, these images of the victim are instrumental to the success of a peace-based approach and a justice-based approach. Securing a relatively expeditious negotiated political peace would be difficult if all victim claims had to be sorted through and taken account of; similarly, pursuing justice would be difficult if a clear and accepted distinction between innocent and guilty were absent, particularly if such a strategy were pursued in a formal, juridical process.

However, to further understand the images of the victim that inform various approaches to peacebuilding, it is necessary to delve into specific peace-building strategies. The following section gives consideration to conflict resolution strategies, including interest-based conflict resolution and social psychology–based conflict resolution. Consideration is also given to a rights-based approach to peacebuilding. Again, these approaches are not always mutually exclusive, and at times two or more of these strategies may inform peacebuilding in any given situation. The purpose of considering these strategies, then, is to articulate what image(s) of the victim they draw on and to assess whether these specific strategies of peacebuilding invoke a more nuanced discourse of the victim.

Conflict Resolution

> The field of conflict resolution is oriented toward changing conflicts so that they can be conducted constructively, even creatively in the sense that violence is minimized, antagonism between adversaries is overcome, outcomes are mutually acceptable to the opponents and settlements are enduring. (Kriesberg 2001, 407)

In light of the previous discussion of peace vs. justice, conflict resolution is generally associated with a primary interest in peace. In characterizing conflict resolution, *Human Rights Dialogue* notes that conflict resolvers are "'characterized as willing to compromise rights or avoid sensitive discussions of abuses altogether to satisfy the interests of the parties and secure a political deal' and further that conflict resolvers are 'cooperative' and 'pragmatic'" (*Human Rights Dialogue* 2002, 1).

Conflict resolvers demonstrate a willingness to prioritize resolving conflict as opposed to strict adherence to, for instance, international norms on human rights.[5] The form that this conflict resolution takes, however, is varied. Schirch (2004) identifies three primary strategies of conflict resolution: rational, relational, and symbolic. Lederach (1997) characterizes conflict resolution as necessarily different than the realpolitik interest-based approaches and instead argues that conflict resolution is a strategy informed by social psychology and reaching for a much deeper social reconciliation (see also Kriesberg 2001). And certainly there are numerous debates about specific tactics employed during the process of conflict resolution (such as the use of force). The discussion that follows articulates two strategies in conflict resolution and their attendant discourses of the victim. While this review of strategies of conflict resolution is not exhaustive, the two strategies addressed are appropriate and useful in so far as they represent common strategies with important differences.

Conflict Resolution: Interest-Based[6]

An interest-based strategy of conflict resolution views conflict parties as having differing interests that are either perceived as, or perhaps actually, opposed to one another. For instance, an ethnic minority group may desire a greater degree of political autonomy, whereas the majority ethnic group may desire the maintenance of a centralized political structure to protect their ability to politically capitalize on their demographic superiority. An interest-based approach to resolving such a conflict would focus on how each party can secure their interests in a way that is acceptable to the other party in a context of peace and stability. An underlying assumption of this conflict-resolution strategy is that as long as conflict parties have their interests met in a way that they perceive as satisfactory (which may well be less than their initial demands), steps can be made toward peace and stability.

What sort of victim discourse informs such a strategy of conflict resolution? Certainly, it is a concern with human harm, often of the most atrocious sort, that motivates a concern with resolving conflict.

> Whole generations have no other experience than war. The resultant size of the cumulative death toll is difficult to comprehend while the overall tally of material destruction, psychological suffering and human misery... dwarfs any gains by particular conflict parties.... This provides the main impetus for the central aim of conflict resolution... to find non-violent ways of achieving structural and political goals. (Miall, Ramsbotham, and Woodhouse 1999, 33)

And yet, despite the motivational force of human harm, there is infrequent reference to victims per se; rather the neutral, even sterile, term of "conflict parties" predominates. Much like in the discussion of "getting to peace," there

is a clear normative commitment to ending harm, but neither the conceptualization nor achievement of this end to harm requires the naming and foregrounding of the victim. The term "victims," when it appears, occurs most
frequently in discussions of postconflict tasks—for example, "attending to the
psycho-social needs of victims"—and is here used in a rather generic and
"given" sense (Miall, Ramsbotham, and Woodhouse 1999). It is not that an
interest-based strategy of conflict resolution is unconcerned with the notion of
political victims; indeed this motivates most conflict-resolution efforts and
helping those harmed by conflict is generally assumed to be within the scope
of conflict resolution, but sustained attention to the victim as an identity and
victimization as a process is absent.

Crocker, Hampson, and Aall (2004) also note that at times there is public
pressure on conflict mediators/resolvers to engage a discourse of "good guys"
vs. "bad guys," even though most conflict-resolution practitioners prefer to
avoid such identities and labels:

> The public tends to applaud mediators who moralize publicly and define
> every conflict in terms of good guys and bad guys, even if such posturing is
> counterproductive to the task of ending a conflict; and the public has a low
> tolerance for the uncertain, hard slogging often required to achieve an
> agreement and bring about substantive change on the ground. (Crocker,
> Hampson, and Aall 2004, 39)

They further note that conflict-resolution practitioners avoid such labels and
identifications, as they "cannot easily select which parties to talk to in a hot
conflict: ignoring the men with the guns or with the capacity to block a deal will
not work" (Crocker, Hampson, and Aall 2004, 29). Such comments suggest
that from a conflict-resolution perspective, if one assumes that an acceptable
"deal" is the goal, it is simply not feasible to identify the good from the bad
(or, we might suggest, the aggressors from the victims) because first, conflicts
are complicated, and second, such tactics are likely to interfere with a movement toward reaching an acceptable agreement where conflict parties feel that
their interests have been met.

Conflict Resolution: Social Psychology

There is another strategy of conflict resolution, however, that deeply and purposefully engages a discourse of victimization. Lederach (1997), Montville
(1993), and Fisher (2001) illustrate that one of the most powerful tools of conflict resolution can in fact be to help the parties develop a discourse of *mutual
victimization*. This emphasis on mutual victimization is partially due to the
reality of some of the most difficult and enduring conflicts in the world today.

> Unilateral or reciprocal atrocities committed by one generation become the
> basis for retributive, vengeful atrocities perpetrated by the next generation.

> Over decades or centuries, it often becomes unclear, if not irrelevant, as to who the original persecutor was, or who is most responsible for a condition of mutual victimization. . . . It is important here to recognize that while the physical reality of victimization is seldom equal or balanced, it is very often shared to some degree. This creates a social-psychological reality of mutual victimization which third-party consultants must accept and attempt to work with. (Fisher 2001, 26, 37)

The problem for conflict resolvers is to move conflict parties away from a simple aggressor-victim model and toward one of a "conflict spiral model" that enables the conflict parties to see themselves as both victims and perpetrators (Fisher 2001; see also Rubin, Pruitt, and Kim 1994). The fact that both sides have been victimized and that both are perpetrators does not lead Fisher to suggest that typical acts of "victims" and "perpetrators" should be ignored; indeed, this strategy of conflict resolution encourages the taking of responsibility by the aggressor: apology to the victim, and so forth. It is interesting, and critical from the perspective of this project, that while such a strategy of conflict resolution initially seems to draw on a more nuanced discourse of victimization, it simultaneously does not problematize the simplicity of these categories when suggesting, for instance, that "aggressors must acknowledge grievances," "accept responsibility," and "express contrition" (Montville 1993).[7]

What explains this dual tendency in social psychology–based strategies of conflict resolution? Why, in one sense, is the victimization discourse one that hints at nuance and complexity, while at the same time the policy prescriptions for "victims" and aggressors" seem to draw on underdeveloped or "given" notions of these identities? Arguably part of this tension can be explained by understanding that this conflict-resolution strategy is employing a discourse of mutual victimization for instrumental purposes; that is, it is understood as a functional platform from which aggrieved and hostile parties can begin to build peace. From this perspective, unpacking the victim identity (or indeed even the perpetrator identity) is not necessary to reach the goal of resolving conflict.

In this strategy of conflict resolution we can characterize the image of the victim as one that is, first, important to peacebuilding. Further, the emphasis on mutual victimization indicates that this approach accepts that political victimization as a process is complex. However, the victim identity is relatively undeveloped. Her wants, for instance, are treated as a given; she wants apology, justice, peace. The possibility that these wants are complexly interwoven with her experiences as a perpetrator (if this was the case) is unexplored. The notion that "victim identities/roles" can be acted out simply, as can "aggressor identities/roles" even in a situation of complex conflict and spirals of victimization, is not problematized. The discourse of victimization associated with this strategy of conflict resolution is one that foregrounds the victim identity and recognizes the complexity of the social process of political victimization, but does not investigate the possibility of the complexity of the victim identity itself.

Rights-Based Approaches

> *Human rights advocates are seen as idealistic and uncompromising in seeking redress for individual violations. . . . The typical human rights organization's position is that there can be no peace without justice, in the form of criminal prosecutions for past abuses, and that impunity cannot be tolerated, even if the pursuit of justice prolongs the conflict. (Human Rights Dialogue 2002, 1)*

A rights-based approach to peacebuilding is, essentially, a quest for peace informed by a deep commitment to justice. Specifically in regards to political victimization, a rights-based approach advocates for a timely and legitimate prosecution of those who have committed human rights violations, for several reasons. First, as indicated above, pursuing justice is seen as critical for long-term peace. Second, the prosecution of human rights violators is in accordance with international norms, and the strengthening of these norms of human rights requires the prosecution of those who violate them. Third, the pursuit of justice is generally understood as beneficial to the victim, providing among other things a "sense of closure" and restoring confidence in society and the government (Kritz 1995). A rights-based approach has informed recent peacebuilding activities such as the trial of war criminals in Bosnia, Rwanda, Iraq, and Sudan. In none of these cases was a rights-based strategy the only, or even the dominant, strategy in peacebuilding activities (for example, many compromises and negotiations were made in an effort to "get to peace"); nonetheless, the high-profile trials of individuals such as Slobodan Milosevic, Saddam Hussein, and Hutu Power members from Rwanda are evidence that a rights-based approach actively informs peacebuilding efforts today.

What image of the victim informs a rights-based strategy to peacebuilding? As the previous discussion of justice as a path to peacebuilding indicated, any strategy of peacebuilding that is embedded firmly within a legalistic framework necessarily engages the concept of the victim. The victim/perpetrator dyad is critical to the articulation of claims against the perpetrator; put simply, there could be no charges of war crimes against the perpetrator without a clear and identifiable victim(s). However, here again we see the reliance on a rather "given" conception of the victim and, indeed, perpetrator. The distinction between the perpetrator and the victim(s) is rarely problematized even in conflict situations that are widely recognized as having cycles of mutual violence. The portrayal of the victim as "innocent" in contrast to the "evil" of the perpetrator can be of instrumental importance in securing a guilty verdict. The selection of victims to testify can of itself often reify this image of the innocent victim.

Even outside the courtroom, the practice of a rights-based peacebuilding strategy often draws on a simple and innocent conception of the victim. Organizations informed by a rights-based strategy explicitly and purposefully engage a particular image of the victim. Moeller (2002) notes that human rights and relief organizations such as Amnesty International purposefully select children in their marketing campaigns because they effectively capture the innocent, simple, and compelling victim; their image amplifies the statement of injustice. Carpenter (2005) further suggests that calls for humanitarian assistance are often made with reference to "women and children" precisely because "women and children" denotes "innocent civilian victim." Regardless of who is being victimized most severely (and in many instances it is in fact young men of draft age), Carpenter argues that the only victim image that is sufficient in attracting broad international attention and support is that of the "innocent victim," most easily connoted through pictures of children, mothers, and grandmothers. Carpenter quotes a UNICEF official as articulating just how important these images of the "simple" and "innocent" victim are for the practice of human rights interventions. Such imagery allows for the protection of the "objectively innocent" and the simplification of the conflict:

> We simplify the issue, simplify the scenario, "we are just here to help innocent civilians, innocent women and children. . . . So bringing it down to a very fundamental level—in that sense the simplistic nature of the analysis is meant to reduce controversy and *make it easier to work*. (UNICEF official quoted in Carpenter 2005, 315, emphasis added)

Further, evidence suggests that human rights workers on the ground also rely on an idealized image of the innocent victim (Eisenman, Bergner, and Cohen 2000). Indeed, even though mental-health workers have found that relying on such an image of the victim increases the likelihood of posttraumatic stress disorder, the dominance of this image of the victim for human rights workers remains:[8]

> [Victim] idealization has another side that serves many of our broader purposes: changing foreign policy, enlisting political support, or fundraising to name a few. This is because human rights workers function in a milieu where many factors—political, economic, and moral—routinely press for attention. There are usually multiple agendas competing for limited resources. Human rights agendas may depend upon a narrow, idealized view of the victim that helps justify a claim for scarce resources. We may feel constrained by the overall political context to view or present the victims' predicament in dichotomous terms, in which there are only purely innocent victims and utterly evil perpetrators. (Eisenman, Bergner, and Cohen 2000, 113)

In sum, a rights-based strategy to peacebuilding, enacted by human rights workers as well as those in the courts, certainly draws on a particular image of the victim: simple and innocent. This image of the victim is instrumental to the functioning of a rights-based strategy, playing a role in the prosecution of war criminals as well as enabling the continued work of rights advocates at the organizational and individual level.

ASSESSING THE IMAGE OF THE VICTIM IN APPROACHES TO PEACEBUILDING

From the discussion of peacebuilding and the victim thus far, it is apparent that no singular image or discourse of the victim emerges. In addition, these discourses are first and foremost discourses of political violence *in service to peacebuilding*. That is, there is a certain instrumental quality to these discourses. They do not necessarily represent a general understanding of how and why political victimization occurs or who political victims are, but rather represent a way for understanding and representing political victimization such that it serves as a possible starting place for ending victimization and building peace.

Approaches to peacebuilding—both broadly understood in terms of peace and justice as well as more precise strategies of peacebuilding—draw on, and through their continued enactment produce, images of the victim. In some cases, the victim identity is marginalized, as engaging competing claims of victimhood or attempting to wrestle with real redress for victims of political violence is seen as an impediment to peace. Other strategies of peacebuilding foreground the victim, either in the context of mutual victimization on the road to reconciliation or perhaps as a pivotal image that enables the pursuit of even limited justice in the difficult postconflict period. In general, peacebuilding scholarship is doing an increasingly good job engaging the complexity of modern conflicts. Whether highlighting the diverse causes of any one conflict (scarce resources, ethnicity, weak states, etc.) or recognizing that political violence is rarely a one-sided affair but more often fits the cyclical model of aggression and retaliation, peacebuilding scholarship is developing methods of analysis and policies to respond to these complex and multifaceted political conflicts.[9]

However, while the complexity of modern political conflicts is being unpacked, the political victim remains theoretically underdeveloped in a particular way: the exclusion of a notion of complexity of the victim identity. It is treated and invoked as if it is a settled-upon concept. The "complexity" that is being recognized, unpacked, and engaged is a systematic level of complexity and for the most part does not engage the complexity of individuals in conflict. To be sure, there are some exceptions here—for instance, feminist scholarship on the multiple roles that women play in conflict (see, for instance, Marshall 2000) or elite theory that engages the multiple roles those elites can play in negotiating and building peace. However, even given this attention to the multiple roles that any one individual can have in a conflict (for example, a woman who functions as an insurgent but is also sexually victimized by an opposing force), this scholarship does little to unpack the nuance of any one of these identities. And for the purpose of this book, the victim identity is still assumed to be a "given," even as it may be only one of many identities experienced by an individual. Again drawing on feminist peacebuilding scholarship, it is critical, certainly, that such scholarship challenges the image of women as only, and naturally, innocent victims.

> In public media and state discourses of the situation [Northern Ireland] women have often been characterized as "apart from" the conflict, frequently as victims belonging to an innocent space, apart from the evil men who have perpetrated the violence. This politically constructed "innocent" woman-only space has certain conditions of entry to which some women may have access at certain times. (Rooney 2003)

Authors such as Moser and Clark (2001), Enloe (1999), Marshall (2000), and Carpenter (2005) have challenged this image of the woman as only an innocent victim in conflict, but divorcing "woman" from a simple identity as "innocent victim" does not challenge the conceptualization of victim as "innocent" and given. The contribution of this book, then, is to build on the tradition of peacebuilding scholarship that increasingly recognizes the complexity of modern conflict, and that individuals may have many identities and roles within conflict. Building upon this scholarship, this book poses the following questions: Might we reconsider the tendency to assume that modern political victims, while empirically difficult to sort out in complex conflicts, are, once found, something of a given? And how might such a project help the international community recognize and respond to political victims more effectively—even contributing to a lasting peace? Before embarking on such a task, it is useful to consider the work of two authors whose recent work has begun to unpack the nuance and construction of the political victim in the context of peacebuilding.

UNPACKING THE VICTIM: A BEGINNING

Though more simplistic discourses of the victim certainly pervade peacebuilding scholarship, there have been recent attempts to challenge such discourses.

One of the most focused efforts to counteract the "givenness" of the victim identity can be found in the work of Borer (2003). Borer creates a taxonomy of victims and perpetrators, drawing on the South African case but suggesting the need for more careful consideration of victims and perpetrators throughout conflict studies. As she explains, the motivation for her study is to contrast several incorrect assumptions that inform most human rights scholarship. These include:

> 1) Most often they [victims and perpetrators] are referred to as two distinct groups: in situations of Gross Violations of Human Rights you have victims and you have perpetrators.
> 2) Implicit in this approach is the assumption that both groups are homogenous: victims and perpetrators are referred to as if they are all the same. The victims. The perpetrators.
> 3) In the worst case, the two are set up as diametrically opposed—for example, victims vs. perpetrators. (Borer 2003, 1088–89)

Borer creates a taxonomy that shows that the separation and givenness of victims and perpetrators is often an inappropriate understanding of victimization. She contends that victims can be perpetrators and vice versa. Moreover, she contends that each "group" is heterogeneous—that there are important distinctions between types of victims and types of perpetrators, particularly in relation to their level of direct participation and responsibility. Some of the categories she identifies are perpetrators who become heroes, heroes who become perpetrators, perpetrators who were victims, victims who were heroes, individual vs. group perpetrators, and beneficiaries (Borer 2003).

For Borer, these distinctions are important in deciding such critical political issues as who can or should apply for amnesty? Who is eligible for reparations? Must a narrative of apartheid attempt to distinguish between varying levels and types of perpetration, responsibility, and victimization? She explores how the functioning of the TRC depended upon individuals identifying in a particular way, either as victims or perpetrators (even if they may have felt they were both, or neither), in order to partake in the "official" process of healing and social reconstruction.

> Whether one was a victim—or a perpetrator for that matter—it became clear, was often a function of self-identity.... [I]n order to be eligible for any reparation money, one had to be officially certified by the TRC. This could only happen if a person came forward and identified him or herself as a victim. Whether one identified with the term perpetrator also had consequences. Many would-be applicants for amnesty never applied because they could not identify with the process—they were not perpetrators, they were defenders of the nation. (Borer 2003, 1114–15)

Borer (2003) has demonstrated three critical issues in relation to the victim. First, the category is not a "given": different individuals experience different types and levels of victimization, and some may not identify as victims at all. Second, responsibility is often complex among perpetrators (see also Crocker 2003). Who should we hold more accountable: the soldier or the one who ordered the soldier's actions? Last, self-identification as a victim carries tremendous political significance. Such identification influences the extent to which individuals partake in official healing and social reconstruction processes, which in turn may very well have significant effects on the overall course of the postconflict society.

Marie Smyth has also contributed important work in the area of political victims and their role in the postconflict period. Among the issues addressed in her work are the issues of victim definition, contested views of victimhood, and the tension between "real" victims and others asserting some status as victims. She embeds this discussion of political victims in the context of the challenging postconflict period. She notes the centrality of the victim identity in conflict and, importantly, in the pursuit of peace.

> The status of victim renders the victim deserving of sympathy, support, outside help and intervention by others in order to vanquish the victimizer. Victims, by definition, are vulnerable, and any violence on their part can be construed as a consequence of the victimization process and as the responsibility of the victimizer. It is a phenomenon observable elsewhere, that those who have participated in the violence of the past, particularly those who have killed and injured others, themselves lay claim to victimhood. Without such status, their violence becomes too naked, politically inexplicable, and morally indefensible. The acquisition of the status of victim becomes an institutionalized way of escaping guilt, shame, or responsibility. (Smyth 2003, 126–27)

The ability to legitimately claim the victim identity in conflict could not be more consequential. It is the pathway to assistance, sympathy, and the shedding of responsibility for violence, and indeed critical for the very moral justification of a people and a cause. Given its consequential nature, then, it is not surprising that there is abundant controversy surrounding who gets to claim the victim identity, this tragic yet hallowed identity that deeply shapes the process of transitioning from conflict to the postconflict environment. Smyth (2003), drawing on her work in Northern Ireland, notes that a range of methods can be used to ascertain who is a victim in conflict. Largely objective measures such as "human suffering" have been used, but these are often politically controversial as they result in "the inclusion of those from the community that had harmed them in the same "victim" category as themselves" (Smyth 2003, 128). In response to these "inclusive" approaches, Smyth notes that many in Northern Ireland began to articulate "exclusive" categories of victims, particularly as the competition for victim-assistance resources increased.

The ability to legitimately claim the victim identity is also important in the postconflict period for reasons that Smyth (2003) drawing on Thomas (1999) identifies as a perception that victims can and should serve as "moral beacons" in the postconflict period. This role as a "moral beacon" can be particularly important during attempts at reconciliation and postconflict norm development, as the perception that "suffering results in accelerated moral development" can give tremendous weight and moral authority to those who were political victims. Here too, however, Smyth (2003) and Thomas (1999) articulate the controversy surrounding the identification of "real" victims who are "legitimate moral beacons" in the postconflict period. It is not a given that all who are victimized will emerge as moral beacons; "suffering per se is not a sufficient qualification."

> This tendency to elect some and not others is manifest in Northern Ireland's Troubles. The widow of an alleged informer, the victim of punishment beatings, or the wife of a prisoner are unlikely to qualify as moral beacons, in spite of their suffering. One of the criteria of qualification seems to be that the suffering must be "undeserved" (according to dominant values). . . . This has been manifest in Northern Ireland in the attempt to qualify some victimhood as "innocent" or "real" in order to discount the suffering of certain bereaved or injured parties. (Smyth 2003, 142)

Such scholarship reports on how the image of the victim is often constructed and articulated in the postconflict period and further explains the contours of this "ideal victim," showing the importance of legitimately claiming this ideal victim image. In the postconflict period, who gets to legitimately claim this identity is critical in terms of peace, access to resources, local and international perceptions of the conflict, and fundamental assessments of the righteousness of each of the conflict groups. Closely associated with this image of the ideal victim is a certain constellation of characteristics, including innocence, lack of responsibility, purity, and moral superiority. These characteristics resonate with some of the images of the victim that have emerged in the analysis of peacebuilding approaches as well—for instance, justice-based approaches that draw heavily on an image of the innocent victim/guilty perpetrator. Even in strategies of peacebuilding that marginalize the victim identity, such as an interest-based conflict-resolution strategy, we might appreciate that part of the reason such approaches do not engage the victim identity is that there is no clear "victim," or at least not one that matches the ideal victim image.

From this point, then, this book is poised to embark upon two critical tasks. First, the next chapter is devoted to fleshing out the contours of this ideal victim. What are the meanings of these characteristics that attend the victim identity, and why do they sometimes function not simply as a constellation helping to define the victim but sometimes more strongly as a chain of equivalence where to be a victim automatically means one is, for instance, morally superior? But in the broader scope of this book, what this chapter has aimed to demonstrate is that the political victim is theoretically underdeveloped. Much peacebuilding scholarship has had a tendency to treat the victim as an agreed-upon concept, some strategically foregrounding it, others sweeping it under the rug on the route to an expeditious peace. Even when the constructed and politicized nature of the "ideal victim" has been exposed, not enough has been done to develop a nuanced and complex account of the political victim—an account that can ultimately contribute to more effective recognition, response, and peace.

NOTES

1. The literature on peacebuilding is characterized by the use of multiple terms addressing similar concepts. For instance, what Cousens refers to as "political peacebuilding" (and Galtung refers to as the creation of a negative peace) is captured by Ropers (1995) by the term "peacemaking." He then differentiates the term "peacemaking" (which is primarily about reaching a peace agreement) from "peacebuilding," which is a considerably more expansive project dealing not just with political peace but also issues of justice, reconciliation, community reconstruction, and the like. For my purposes here, I use the term "peacebuilding" in its broadest sense, encompassing activities ranging from the basic establishment of a negative peace through approaches to peacebuilding that incorporate principles of justice, reconciliation, reconstruction, and the like. Conceptually, I delineate the spectrum of peacebuilding activities, but maintain that they all reside under the general concept of peacebuilding. See Hamber and Kelly (2004) for further (and alternate) discussion on the conceptual delineation of peacebuilding.

2. This issue is explored in more depth in subsequent chapters.

3. "Healing" is a term often used quite loosely in this scholarship. Precise definitions of what it means for an individual (or, for that matter, a community) to "heal" are often absent. Some, such as Montville (1993), emphasize that healing requires the individual to regain a sense of security, move beyond a space of "moral vulnerability," and regain a sense of self-control and efficacy in regards to their relationship with their victimizer (or the victimizing structure). Throughout this project we will see the term take on other characterizations as well; for instance, for many leaders in South Africa individual healing demanded reconciliation with aggressors. My use of the term "healing" will be more closely aligned with Montville's (1993) use of the term, emphasizing a decreased sense of moral vulnerability and the reemergence of the self both as an identity apart from the victim and as an efficacious agent in the previously victimizing relationship.

4. Williams and Scharf (2002) develop a model in *Peace with Justice?* that serves as one example of how recent scholarship aims to draw on both peace and justice in articulating a peacebuilding approach. Biggar (2003) provides another model for integrating these two ideas in the peacebuilding process.

5. This is not to suggest that conflict resolution has no interest in norms of human rights, international law, etc. Certainly, employing a strategy of conflict resolution does

not indicate disagreement with these norms. As we will see shortly, some approaches to conflict resolution do in fact emphasize the importance of recognizing and accepting responsibility for, for example, grave violations of human rights and other forms of political victimization.

6. I use the term "interest-based" here, though much of what I am characterizing is also referred to as "rational" strategies of conflict resolution. The term "interest-based" seems, however, to better capture the focus on the peacebuilding activities and processes (for example, a negotiation that ultimately leads to conflict parties having their interests met) as opposed to the concept of a "rational" strategy of conflict resolution, which highlights the cognitive nature of the decision-making and resolution process.

7. These themes can be seen most prominently throughout the work of Montville, but also in the work of subsequent authors in this tradition (Fisher 2001; Borris 2003).

8. Eisenman, Bergner, and Cohen begin to question the merits of this commitment, an issue I return to later in the book.

9. While certainly there is not the space here to engage in a comprehensive review of the myriad ways in which peace and conflict scholarship is engaging the complexity of conflict and building peace, even a cursory review of the literature provides evidence of the many dimensions of conflict and challenges for peace in complex conflicts.

3

Fleshing Out the Ideal Victim

The previous chapter took aim at sketching out what images of the victim inform and emerge from various peacebuilding discourses. Here the image of the ideal victim is developed much more carefully to emphasize that while the image of the victim in peace and conflict is often underdeveloped, there are a set of important and relatively constant characteristics that attend the victim identity. These characteristics are innocence, purity, lack of responsibility, the absence of guilt, and moral superiority. In what follows, I define these characteristics and demonstrate how they attend the image of the ideal victim often invoked, aspired to (for example, competing claims of victimhood), and produced during peacebuilding.

INNOCENCE

Descriptions of political victimization ranging from the Holocaust to the Rwandan genocide to the terrorist attacks of September 11, 2001, all make frequent use of the phrase "innocent victims." To be sure, these descriptions of political victims do not always come from peacebuilders per se, but are generated through the interplay of media, politicians, and on-the-ground peacebuilders and humanitarian workers. As such, we may be inclined to dismiss the notion of innocent victims as media sensationalization or mere political rhetoric—in other words, not a substantive component of the peacebuilding discourse on the victim. In a certain sense this is true. No doubt the nightly news reports which are eager for viewers are more prone to hyperbole and a sensationalized account of innocent victims and evil perpetrators. And certainly political actors, particularly leaders, may at times adopt sweeping and simplistic moral language in order to accomplish some discreet political goals (such as rallying support for increased military spending). But as shown in the previous chapter, certain approaches to peacebuilding draw heavily and explicitly on an unquestioned notion of the innocent victim. We see this concept emerge after the Holocaust as well as postvictimization Bosnia and South Africa. Further, it should not be forgotten that "on-the-ground peacebuilding" almost always transpires in the context of politics and, more broadly, media. In other words the image and discourse of the victim in peacebuilding is necessarily linked to and constrained by these other images and discourses. For the purposes of this book, we must ask precisely what this phrase "innocent victim" means.

Civilian vs. Combatants

In the first instance, we may recognize that the phrase "innocent victims" is often used to describe the noncombatant status of the victimized. Noncombatant status in international law was progressively defined through the Geneva Conventions and currently is defined according to the following standards:

> First, not civilian or military status as such but whether the person is functioning as a combatant is the deciding factor, whatever the reason for this. Second, no theoretical definition is provided or even attempted; rather, classes of persons are simply listed as deserving certain considerations and protections from belligerent parties. Third, the restrictions and protections laid out, as well as the classes of people to whom they apply, are represented as generally accepted in the law and customs of war—that is, they are not innovations in the practice of war or conceptions of restraint derived from another sphere (that is moral philosophy or religion), but internal to what war itself is about. (Johnson 2000, 431)

Noncombatant status is thus a functional definition; one is a noncombatant provided one is not functioning in such a capacity (see also Palmer-Fernandez 1998). Carpenter (2005), however, notes that both opposing militaries and the international community often use nonfunctional methods of ascertaining who is a combatant and who is not, most often assuming that women and children are noncombatants and that adult males are active or likely combatants. This use of nonfunctional identification methods to identify a category of people that is functionally defined is noteworthy, especially when recalling Carpenter's earlier arguments about the association of "innocence" with the category of "women and children." Hence what emerges is a chain of equivalence running from noncombatants to women and children, and from women and children to innocence. So while the functional definition of noncombatant status suggests a limited innocence (for example, innocent in regards to carrying out combat), the way in which "noncombatants" are generally identified suggests a broader form of innocence, one that, as we shall see shortly, takes on a moral significance.

Johnson (2000) argues that the historical concern with noncombatant status can be traced to early Christian and medieval warfare, with Thomas Aquinas articulating the difference between "evildoers" and the "innocent," the first of whom were legitimate targets in a just war, the latter of whom were not. This sort of innocence is both a descriptor of the victim's role (as a noncombatant) but also a descriptor of moral status as well. Insofar as the rules of war distinguish between appropriate targets of aggression (combatants) and inappropriate targets of aggression (noncombatants), an aggressor's targeting of noncombatants indicates a deviance from the accepted practices of war.

> The. . . fundamental moral issue is that, both within and outside the reach of the law, it is quite simply wrong to make non-combatants targets in an armed conflict. It is their status as non-combatants that endows them with this moral immunity. (Johnson 2000, 433)

Hence, when the term "innocent" is used to signal "noncombatant," it is first functionally descriptive, but also contributes both to the construction of the perpetrator as morally evil (deviating from just practices of war) and the victim as morally good. The identification of noncombatant "innocent" victims is intended to widen the moral gap between the perpetrator and victim, to assist in moral calculations that make it easier to recognize and sympathize with the victim and condemn the perpetrator.

Innocence of Wrongdoing

Innocence can also be conceptualized more broadly in the context of peace and conflict, suggesting not just noncombatant status but also the absence of wrongdoing. That is, not only is the victim innocent in the sense that she is not functioning as a combatant, but she is also innocent in the sense that she has not done anything wrong or to invite or deserve her victimization. In memorial speeches commemorating the victims of the September 11 terrorist attacks, this form of innocence was highlighted, as in the following examples:

> . . . terrorist attackers orchestrated four acts of pure evil on innocent Americans *going about their daily lives*. (Everett 2003, emphasis added)

> Those who died represented each of us, for they came from every walk of life. They were stock brokers and bond traders, busboys and clerks, maintenance workers and accountants. They were pilots, flight attendants, business travelers; families on holiday. . . . *The victims of September 11 did nothing to bring death upon themselves.* They died in a savage assault on the symbols of America. (University of California Chancellor Robert Berdahl, 2002, emphasis added)

In this context, victims of September 11 are innocent in part because their activities were not provocative; these victims were doing nothing wrong by simply "going about their daily lives" and hence are innocent. This conception of innocence, though related to the previous conception of innocence, transcends combatant/noncombatant distinctions as it emphasizes more than an individual's function in a conflict, but frames the activities, and indeed the identity, of the victim as normal, right, and acceptable. Here we might also recall the opening narrative of the Bosnian concentration camp survivor, in which the author took pains to note that the victims were "not from the battlefield as captives, but from their homes" (Gutman 1993, 56). Rony Braumann, former head of Doctors Without Borders, further articulates this concern with the victim as wholly innocent, particularly in the context of recognizing and assisting victims.

> ... the symbolic status of "victim," which can in effect only be granted in cases of unjustified or innocent suffering. It matters little whether the subject is the victim of mother nature's cruelty, of a senseless war (other people's wars are always senseless), or ruthless armed gangs, or of an evil tyrant—the point is that he must be 100 percent victim, a non-participant. (Braumann 1993, 154)

Susan Moeller (2002) argues that the need to present political victims as wholly innocent of any wrongdoing, as "good" people doing "normal" things in contrast to "evil" people doing "evil things," is exemplified by the widespread use of the image of the child in journalistic coverage of modern conflict:

> Children dramatize the righteousness of a cause by having their innocence contrasted with the malevolence (or perhaps banal hostility) of adults in authority. . . . [C]hildren [were] portrayed as "angels." Their innocence blackened the villains' evil or misdeeds especially when the depicted innocent child was an infant. In that case the debauchery of the villain was painted most darkly, for what possible threat is a babe in arms, what kind of human is capable of harming those so obviously helpless? (Moeller 2002, 40–42)

The image of the "babe in arms" is perhaps most telling, for what could be a more "normal," more "natural" a behavior than a mother holding her child? Moeller's arguments also include reference to the "hierarchy of innocence," in which victims are prioritized in relation to their presumed innocence. At the top of this hierarchy are children. They most perfectly match the "innocent victim" image, and all other victims are recognized in varying degrees depending upon their conformity to this image of the innocent victim—the victim who is doing nothing wrong, who perhaps, like a child, is not even capable of doing anything morally wrong.

Moeller's argument suggests another important point: the attachment of innocence to the victim, particularly when understood as the "freedom from wrongdoing," is often used to simultaneously vilify the perpetrator. In this sense, the innocence that attends the victim serves two purposes: it signals to the outside world that (1) the victim has done nothing wrong, and is a good and righteous individual, and (2) not only has the perpetrator done something wrong, but he is also evil in character. In effect, the innocence of the victim also demonizes the perpetrator (a fact emphasized in the description of the September 11 narratives). Moeller suggests the media in particular draws upon and reinforces the innocent victim/evil perpetrator dichotomy in regards to political victimization, by "pigeonholing all situations into a good guy–bad guy dichotomy" (Moeller 1999, 314). The characteristic of innocence helps to divide the episode of victimization into two opposing and distinct sides and morally affirms the side of the victim as the good and righteous one.

Smyth (2002) notes the increased reliance on the terms "innocent victim" and "real victim" in the aftermath of the Good Friday Agreement in Northern Ireland. In part because of differing attitudes toward the Good Friday Agreement, victim groups began to express their dissatisfaction through a discourse that drew clear distinctions between legitimate and illegitimate victims.

> [L]obbying to disqualify certain categories of people from legitimate victimhood intensified alongside the activities of the anti-Agreement lobby. The use of the terms "innocent" or "real" as qualifications for victimhood began to appear (8–9).

This use of terms is noteworthy for several reasons. First, it shows the central place that the politics of political victim identity can play in peacebuilding efforts. Second, it shows the chain of equivalence between "innocent victim" and "real victim." To be a real victim is to be an innocent victim, and anything less than innocence problematizes being recognized as a "real victim." Further, Smyth (2002) notes that this is not just an issue of semantics or political posturing in the difficult peacebuilding period. Such semantics have real bearing on allocation of resources for victims and the role of victims in the postconflict society.

The innocence that attends the victim is a critical and multifunctional characteristic of the political victim. It widens the moral gap between good and evil, legitimizes the claim to resources and assistance, and as we shall see shortly, plays a role in the construction of the conflict narrative, particularly in regards to responsibility.

PURITY

Closely related to the concept of innocence is the notion of victim purity. The term "purity" can suggest many things, including "unpolluted," "free from anything that debases," and the "freedom from guilt or evil, innocence" (*Oxford*

English Dictionary). The concept of purity is at times used as a synonym for the innocence of the victim, but often it is used in particular to emphasize the victim's unpolluted morality. A pure victim may be thought of as wholly good and beyond reproach.

Braumann, again commenting on the tremendously high standards the international community holds in regards to the "100% victim," writes with exasperation that in this day and age, precious few victims can really achieve this exacting standing of purity.

> The high point in this lunatic requirement for purity of victim status was provided by two great communicators of the 1980s, Presidents Ronald Reagan and Mikhail Gorbachev, with the rescue of the two ice-trapped whales off the coast of Canada in October 1988. Little attention has been drawn to the significance of this spectacular race's success. It was the prototype for other rococo events, an object lesson in the unexpected capacity of an emotionally-charged scenario to anaesthetize the critical faculties of the population at large. Here we had a hostile environment in the polar ice, innocent victims in the whales, a spectacular rescue with the giant helicopters and the blessing of authority in persons of Misters Reagan and Gorbachev, no less. Whilst all this was going on, and the front pages of the world's press were acclaiming the "rescue of the century," in southern Sudan an organized famine was killing Dinkas by tens of thousands, in the silence of general indifference. (Braumann 1993, 154)

So great is this standard of victim purity, Braumann suggests, that only whales can qualify as true victims deserving of assistance; modern humanity, in the eyes of the international community, are simply too impure, housing certain moral imperfections that disqualify them from assistance. While Braumann discusses this "cultural requirement" of purity in regards to humanitarian and conflict victims, we can further appreciate its significance through a consideration of the way in which purity is a requirement for other victims as well. For instance, victims of sexual assault are often subject to these same pressures. In order to be recognized as a true victim, they must be seen as "unpolluted," which historically has meant anything from virginal (up until the early twentieth century in the United States) to, at the very least, "free from promiscuity."[1]

If it could be shown, in a courtroom, that a sexual assault victim was not "free from anything that debases" (which, in this context referred to socially inappropriate interest in sexual encounters), she was very often not seen as a victim.

> Case reports were filled with examples of hapless victims subjected to abusive and demeaning cross-examination. Defense attorneys routinely asked victims whether they used birth control or attended bars unescorted, and victims were required to enumerate their prior sexual experiences. (Schulhofer 1998, 28)

Indeed, though rape shield laws developed in the 1970s which protected women from being interrogated about their sexual history (and hence limited defense attorneys' ability to demonstrate whether the victim was "free from that which debases"), it is interesting to note that these same laws actually can be seen as reinforcing the idea of a pure victim. Insofar as they encourage a strategy of isolating the episode of the assault in order to effectively prosecute without having to engage the victim's sexual history, they are, in effect, reifying the idea that a victim must be pure. In other words, rather than incorporating the potential "impurity" of the victim (for example, sexual history), sexual assault prosecutions have isolated the victim/perpetrator moment such that the victim can retain her purity; her ideations of helplessness and innocence can be juxtaposed to the aggression and perversion of her attacker *at the moment of the attack*. This is mentioned not as a criticism of such laws, as they have been and continue to be critical in the prosecution of sexual assaults. Rather, it is demonstrated to show what a fervent link there is between notions of "purity" and "victim." This example illustrates that rather than attempt an unlinking of the two, we see victim advocates retaining this image of the pure victim through a strategy of isolating the moment of assessment, the moment of determining what ideations can be assigned to the victim (helplessness, fear) as opposed to the perpetrator (aggression, perversion). Similar tactics reemerge in our discussion of Bosnian Muslim victimization.

According to Braumann (1993), purity serves as a moral fulcrum around which outsiders determine whether or not a harmed individual is truly worthy of victim status. Part of this determination is made through an assessment of whether the victim was a participant and/or combatant, but clearly, a moral and subjective criteria of purity must also be met in order to see harmed individuals as victims. When Smyth (2002) notes that the wife of a prisoner does not function publicly as an ideal victim we might understand this in part by recognizing that her husband's activities have left her with a taint—she is no longer pure, no longer an ideal victim. Smyth, Moeller, and Braumann each introduce an important point that is addressed throughout this book—namely, that the decision to recognize an individual or group as a political victim draws on important and preexisting images of victimization. When looking at a conflict situation, we look for images of the victim that match our own preconceived images of victimization, which frequently are heavily biased toward the innocent and pure. This is indeed related to Huyse's (2002) argument about the manner in which what he deems "cultural" ideas about victims influence who is recognized as a victim and who is not. Victims are not defined simply by their adherence to a particular legal or official definition; they are, in a sense, interpolated through the interplay of existing victim discourse(s), relatively stable legal norms, and the specificities of a given political context.

MORAL SUPERIORITY

Victims, in part because of their innocence and purity, are often bestowed with a mantle of moral superiority. In the previous chapter we encountered Smyth's (2002) and Fisher's (2001) arguments as to why this may be the case. In essence, the extreme suffering of the victim is thought to lead to accelerated moral development. Victims, by virtue of their suffering, become moral beacons.

On what grounds might the innocence and purity of victims lead to their characterization as morally superior? In regards to innocence, the noncombatant status of victims—the fact that they have not taken up arms—may be one reason that these victims are characterized as morally superior.[2] Even when victims engage in some form of violence in order to defend themselves, the purity of the political project—the fact that it is portrayed and understood as self-defense and not as a project based on facism, ethnic cleansing, and so on—also contributes to a sense of the moral superiority of victims. Indeed, without a claim to victimhood, the "nakedness" of conflict participant actions are exposed and their righteousness is lost (Smyth 2002). The corruptions of the "pure" and "good" human spirit belong with the perpetrator, morally debasing him while morally protecting, even exalting, the victim who is only acting in self-defense.

Smyth (2002) also articulates how whether or not victims actually possess some objective measure of moral superiority, their community and the media in particular often put them on the spot to draw out a spectacle of moral superiority and righteousness.

> [Victims] have been put in the spotlight at key moments to pronounce on new political development or initiatives. Media representations of those bereaved and injured in Northern Ireland's Troubles have sometimes probed in a rather crude and insensitive manner. In interviews with the newly bereaved, broadcasters have asked immediate family members if they forgave the perpetrator or if they wanted revenge—often within hours or days of the death. The bereaved person's response is held up as a moral benchmark by which others could gauge their degree of entitlement to desire revenge or retaliation. (Smyth 2002, 11)

Moeller (2002) notes an interesting phenomenon regarding the moral superiority of victims. Responding to these victims makes the responders feel morally righteous (Moeller 2002, 47). Arguably, part of the reason that moral superiority attends the victim image is precisely because of its effect on responders. Moeller quotes Malcolm Browne, former foreign correspondent for AP, ABC, and the *New York Times*, as saying:

> Especially in America, we like to think of things in terms of good guys and bad guys. . . . If one of the partners in a conflict is one that most people can

identify with as a good guy, then you've got a situation in which it's possible to root for the home team.... [W]e love to see everything in terms of black and white, right and wrong, truths versus lies. (Moeller 1999, 13–14)

Smyth (2002) also notes how the moral superiority of victims can help the broader community:

> Such figures are often used as examples of moral behavior or some accomplishment of self-governance of which they set an example. If, in spite of their great suffering, they can forgive, then the rest of us can also forgive.... Conciliatory in political attitude and forgiving of those who cause bereavement, injury, or hurt, the moral beacon is a de-escalator of conflict. (Smyth 2002, 11)

Seeing victims as morally superior can simultaneously help motivate others to take the high road and reassure them that this is indeed the righteous path; after all, it is what the moral beacons are choosing. As such, there is a self-reinforcing tendency both for victims and those who assist them to occupy a platform of exalted morality. Research into human rights workers and victim images bears out this argument as well, suggesting that regardless of "objective" moral superiority, a perception of moral superiority is critical for responders to go about their work in recognizing and assisting victims.

Further, the moral superiority of the victim has been identified as critical in the victim's own healing as well. As Eisenman, Bergner, and Cohen (2000) articulate, victim healing often requires a strong and clear declaration (by the victim and her advocate or interviewer) of the location of the "evil" that contributed to the victimization as outside the moral sphere of goodness inhabited by the victim.

> To name the perpetrators' actions as evil is to take a moral stance... to declare, forcefully and unambiguously, that the evil that has been recognized and named is located outside of the survivor-interviewer pair... against the backdrop of such a pact, which is felt to be representative of moral good.... [U]pholding an alliance in the face of what is thought of as pure evil is the interviewer's job, and it is natural to want to counteract the presence of pure evil with proof of the presence of the opposite, pure good. (Eisenman, Bergner, and Cohen 2000, 110)

By still inhabiting the sphere of uncorrupted human goodness, by locating evil as outside of herself and good within, the victim can lay claim to an exalted sense of morality. Gobodo-Madikizela (2004) argues that we see evidence of this moral superiority in understanding the act of victim forgiveness.[3] In exploring the practice of victim forgiveness in the context of the South African TRC, she notes how some victims felt that they could forgive and wanted to forgive, but others could not. In either case, though, Gobodo-Madikizela attributes the decision to forgive or not as one that related to which option, from the perspective of the victim, would keep safe their identity as the morally superior one. For some, this stance meant refusing to forgive, as forgiving would be to acknowledge that the perpetrator was human too. It would allow the perpetrator to reenter the hallowed and moral ground of humanity for understanding, and forgiving perpetrators is seen as akin to "lowering the entry requirements into the human community" (Gobodo-Madikizela 2004, 120). But for others, the act of forgiveness is the way to preserve their moral superiority in relation to perpetrators.

> [T]he decision to forgive can paradoxically elevate a victim to a position of strength as the one who holds the key to the perpetrator's wish. For just at the moment when the perpetrator begins to show remorse, to seek some way to ask forgiveness, the victim becomes the gatekeeper to what the outcast desires—readmission into the human community. And the victim retains that privileged status as long as he or she stays the moral course, refusing to sink to the level of evil that was done to her or him. . . . [F]orgiveness does not overlook the deed: it rises above it. "This is not what it means to be human," it says. "I cannot and will not return the evil you inflicted on me." And that is the victim's triumph. (Gobodo-Madikizela 2004, 117)

Such a reflection on the victim and the act of forgiveness demonstrates how tremendously important this issue of moral superiority is for the victim identity; the victim often must feel a sense of moral superiority in order to protect the sanctity not just of themselves but of humanity. Moral superiority is a characteristic that enters the constellation of the victim in large part because of the presence of innocence and purity, but its presence extends beyond these characteristics and helps the victim achieve a moral footing instrumental in the postvictimization period. This moral superiority serves an important purpose for victims as well as external actors engaged in the postvictimization period.

Finally, at least some within the peacebuilding community are particularly insistent on identifying and acting in accordance with an understanding of victims as morally superior. Those who advocate for a justice-based postvictimization strategy often, though not necessarily, do so because of a belief in and respect for the moral superiority of victims.[4] Here, we might recall Williams and Scharf's repeated concern with how "getting to peace" might create a platform of moral equivalence—an equivalence of which they are highly critical. A justice-based strategy is seen as superior in part because it emphasizes the moral separation of victims and perpetrators.

LACK OF RESPONSIBILITY

The question of responsibility has already implicitly appeared in the discussion of innocence and purity. For instance, when innocence is standing in to signal noncombatant status, the very distinction between combatants and noncombatants suggests two groups with differing roles and responsibility. Moeller also argues that part of the power of using children as the image of the victim for modern conflicts comes from the fact that they are conceived of as being too young to be responsible for their actions or situations in any way.

> . . . images of Kosovo orphans, young Ethiopian famine victims, Sierra Leone amputee survivors, preadolescent Thai prostitutes, or shantytown urchins in Brazil, for example. . . the children seem, evidently, to be innocent victims of situations *beyond their control.* (Moeller 2002, 49, emphasis added)

Clearly, having characteristics of innocence and purity in the constellation of the victim identity are related to the issue of responsibility, namely, a conception of the victim as wholly irresponsible for her victimization. But more needs to be said about the notion of responsibility. First, in certain traditions outside of political science, the absence of responsibility is definitive of the victim. Victimology is perhaps the most prominent discipline to define the victim in this way:[5]

> The term victim has evolved to one commonality, which can be applied to all victims: Victims are individuals who have suffered injury and harm by forces beyond their control and not related to their personal responsibility. (Karmen 1990, 2)

An alternative definition, also coming from mainstream victimology, can be found in the work of Bayley (1991):

> People are victims if and only if (1) they have suffered a loss or some significant decrease in well-being unfairly or undeservedly and in such a manner that they were helpless to prevent the loss, (2) the loss has an identifiable cause, (3) the legal or moral context of the loss entitles the sufferers of the loss to social concern. . . . *Victims must be innocent, they must not be guilty of having contributed to their loss.* (Bayley 1991, 53–54)

In each of these definitions, we see the lack of responsibility—what Bayley calls "contribution to loss"—as definitive of the victim identity. While Huyse (2002) correctly argues that official definitions are but one part of defining victims, the fact that these definitions of victims explicitly emphasize lack of responsibility is important. For instance, as we will see shortly in a discussion of the *Judenrat* (Jewish council leaders who helped carry out Nazi policy) the issue of responsibility emerges as a central issue in deciding whether or not to consider these individuals as victims. Braumann (1993) too notes how victims must be seen as entirely without responsibility for their victimization.

But what does it mean to say that a victim is not responsible? Answering this question requires a consideration of the various types of responsibility. First, there is the question of legal responsibility; that is, in a court of law, what party would be held responsible for the act of violence? Responsibility for criminal activity is generally placed squarely on the perpetrator(s), though this may include a divvying up of responsibility between both direct and indirect participants (for example, officers at the Srebrenica death camp as well as Serbian leader Slobodan Milosevic). Victims in legal proceedings are generally not seen as legally responsible for their victimization. Indeed, in discussing victim behavior in the context of an episode of victimization, most victimologists persist in distinguishing between victim precipitation and victim provocation. Precipitation and provocation carry two separate, though related, meanings in legal discourse. Precipitation refers to the victim engaging in behaviors that may help to foster criminal activity (such as violent verbal arguments preceding an assault) but are not, in themselves, criminal acts, whereas provoking a crime means that a victim engages in *criminal acts* that result in her victimization (such as selling drugs and subsequently being assaulted). From the perspective of the victim, a victim is thought to be without legal responsibility for her victimization if she did not *provoke* the episode of victimization (for more on victim precipitation vs. victim provocation, see Sgarzi and McDevitt 2002).

Broadening the discussion of responsibility, we might think about other forms of responsibility. To say that a victim has "no individual responsibility" for her victimization is to go a step beyond considerations of whether she might be held legally culpable for her victimization and to address whether her actions may have contributed to her victimization—in effect, to consider acts of precipitation. French (1998) argues that individuals may be held responsible for their contributory role in events, including their own victimization. Further, he argues that identifying an individual as responsible necessarily means to blame that individual for its occurrence, but here the notion of blame is applied only to signal causation and not necessarily to morally judge a person as blameworthy. Hence, here we have a form of responsibility in which individuals may play a causal role in what happens to them, but certain additional conditions must be met before they are to be held morally responsible.[6]

French (1998) argues that the conditions for moral responsibility (of any individual, including victims) are as follows:

> The types of judgments which signal the practice of moral blaming are first, "should haves" of a particular kind; for example, moral judgments based on our moral standards, and second, "could haves.". . . [M]oral blame is justifiable when no mitigation or exculpation is demonstrable in the secondary "could have" evaluation of an individual already to blame for failure to meet a moral standard. (French 1998, 19–20)

In effect, individuals can only be held morally responsible when they have transgressed socially agreed-upon moral standards and when it is determined that the individual could have done something differently.

In the first instance, it would seem that many political victims, certainly most civilians, would rarely be held morally responsible for their own victimization. Even if they could be understood as "provoking" their victimization (such as the Bosnian vote for independence in 1992), such actions certainly do not transgress agreed-upon moral standards. As such, while we might identify this action as "causal" and hence indicative of some degree of Bosnian responsibility for the ensuing conflict, Bosnians would not be understood as having any moral responsibility.

Yet the frequency with which moral responsibility of victims tugs at the minds of political victims is interesting. Gobodo-Madikizela, writing in reference to South Africa, begins to wrestle with the issue of the moral responsibility of victims, bystanders, and the blended category of victim/bystander. She quotes a black South African woman from Mlungisi, an Eastern Cape township devastated by apartheid, and in particular the "necklace" killings of blacks suspected of collaborating with the apartheid security forces.

> We failed our children. . . . [W]e failed to protect them, not just those who were burnt by the necklace, but those who did this terrible thing. We sat here and watched. We did or said nothing. The whole community. We sat here hoping somebody will do something, to break this cycle of insanity. It has left us with this terrible unhealable scar, knowing that we could have, but we didn't. (Gobodo-Madikizela 2004, 75)

Gobodo-Madikizela does not respond definitively to this question of moral responsibility of the victim/bystanders, yet she finds herself asking a question not unlike Arendt: was there time and space to stop the killing? Gobodo-Madikizela is engaging a particular question of the moral responsibility of victims, namely whether they should have fought harder to end the victimization; this question is critical and tremendously controversial.[7]

A final form of responsibility is one that can be called discursive responsibility. Discursive responsibility, in the context of political victimization, refers to the participation of individuals and groups in discourses that create space for episodes of political victimization; it is, then, a specific manifestation of French's individual responsibility. This form of responsibility clearly does not refer directly to physical actions of victimization, nor does it necessarily refer to explicit provocation, but rather is a considerably more nuanced idea of responsibility that considers the ways in which individuals—including, but not limited to, victims—often participate in the creation and maintenance of discourses that create the space for their victimization. Whether this form of responsibility can be understood as moral responsibility is a critical and controversial question, and arguably one that must be carefully investigated in the context of specific cases of political victimization.[8]

So now we can ask more precisely: when the ideal victim is characterized as lacking responsibility, what form of responsibility is lacking? Certainly legal responsibility, though perhaps of even greater significance in regards to the image of the victim is the presumption of the absence of moral responsibility. The image of the ideal political victim arguably draws heavily on an image of the victim that is not morally responsible. To be sure, in telling the story of political victimization, victims are sometimes articulated as having some degree of individual responsibility, but this narrative of individual responsibility falls short of the conditions necessary for holding these victims morally responsible.

WHY THE VICTIM HAS THE CONSTELLATION THAT IT DOES, AND WHY IT PERSISTS

The above discussion suggests that victims, and in particular the ideal of the political victim, have an identity that is attended by a constellation of characteristics: innocence, purity, moral superiority, and lack of responsibility. To invoke a "constellation" is to suggest that these characteristics often attend the victim; at times they help us recognize her, and they help us to fill in answers to her character, and importantly, whether she is worthy of our attention and response. A stronger argument could be made that at times there is a chain of equivalence between the victim identity and these characteristics. That is, when an individual is recognized as a victim, she automatically assumes the characteristics of innocence, purity, moral superiority, and lack of responsibility, whether or not these characteristics were central to assessments of her character before. In discussing the Troubles in Northern Ireland, Smyth (2002) argues that a "stereotype" of victims emerged, and that this stereotype of victims came with a specific set of characteristics that victims, by virtue of their victimhood, were assumed to possess:

> Certain myths and stereotypes of those bereaved or injured in the Troubles have developed during the period of the Troubles. Many of these have been developed by the kind of media coverage given to tragic events, and the myths that had developed by the 1994 ceasefires tended to project certain characteristics on to those in close proximity to events: resilience, forgiveness, forbearance, courage, anger at perpetrators, a desire for reconciliation. These stereotypes represent victims as grief-stricken rather than angry, forgiving rather than blaming, passive rather than active, heroic rather than fearful, peace-loving rather than violent, innocent rather than guilty. (Smyth 2002, 139)

What Smyth is articulating in the context of Northern Ireland resonates with the arguments made here. Not only is there an ideal image of the victim, but this image of the victim is wedded to a set of specific characteristics. The argument developed here builds upon Smyth's argument in two respects. First, this notion of the ideal victim and her characteristics is applicable across episodes of political victimization, and this same image of the ideal victim with similar characteristics is drawn on, invoked, and produced in diverse postvictimization peacebuilding efforts. Second, these characteristics do not simply attend the image of the ideal victim—they are not merely in the same constellation—but in many cases the characteristics function as a chain of equivalence.

Now we might ask, why? Why is it that the image of the victim must be attended by characteristics of innocence, purity, moral superiority, and lack of responsibility? Certain answers to this question have already emerged; consider, for example, the importance of morally superior victims for human rights workers. Smyth responds to this question by highlighting the needs of society in the postvictimization period: "The stereotypes through which victims were perceived were based on how the wider society needs victims to be, rather than on any real data about actual victims" (Smyth 2002, 140).

Arguably, there is another compelling reason that the image of the political victim clings so tightly to this particular constellation of characteristics: victim blaming, the tendency to blame victims for the harm done to them, usually because of provocative behaviors that suggest that they were "asking for it." Precisely because of a deep and real concern with victim blaming, much scholarship on political victimization does not simply overlook or oversimplify issues of, for instance, victim responsibility, but rather such issues are purposefully suppressed. Victim blaming has made the lives of victims and their advocates tremendously difficult. Perhaps one of the most familiar instances of victim blaming is the case of the sexual assault victim who attempts to prosecute a rapist and who instead finds herself on trial for her dress, manner, and behavior. Such cases lead us to realize how tightly linked issues of perceived victim innocence, purity, moral superiority, and responsibility really are. The slippery slope of victim blame can be equally dangerous in the context of political violence as well, for a discourse of victimization that blames the victim does little to aid in the recognition and assistance of victims and often revictimizes them, to say nothing of its detrimental effects on postsettlement peacebuilding. Insofar as unlinking victim innocence, purity, moral superiority, and lack of responsibility is seen as a gateway to blaming the victim, it is certainly justifiable to refrain from tampering with the constellation of the victim that protects her from such assaults.[9]

In addition to concerns about blaming the victim, another reason this particular constellation of the victim remains intact is because of the need to simplify the actors in a conflict—to demonize the aggressor and exalt the victim in order to make policy. Berton, Kimura, and Zartman (1999) note how "Demonization and dehumanization of the enemy are strong psychological motives that help countries clarify their purpose and demarcate their goodness from others' badness" (Berton, Kimura, and Zartman 1999, 319).

Berton, Kimura, and Zartman (1999) argue that for individuals as well as governments, the stark and unequivocal distinction of good from bad, victim from aggressor, is often critical for positive self-perception as well as the formation of foreign policy. Such logic suggests that in addition to concerns about blaming the victim, a more nuanced discourse of the victim has also been underdeveloped because individuals and governments need clear-cut, demarcated identities in order to be confident in their self-perception and policy actions. As such, there are both normative concerns with fracturing this constellation (it can easily lead to victim blaming) and practical considerations (it may be necessary for the formation of policy and broader community needs).

Given the contentious and problematic nature of investigating or even fracturing this constellation, one may rightly question the purpose of embarking upon such a project at all. Why navigate the murky space between sweeping such issues under the rug in the name of "progress towards peace," or decisively identifying victims and granting them their righteous place among the innocent, the pure, and the morally exalted? Such a project is critical for the following reason: simplistic conceptions of the victim identity limit our ability to recognize many individuals who suffer unwarranted harm as victims. This, in turn, influences decisions about if, and how, to respond to political victimization. Smyth (2002) rightly identifies this issue in the context of Northern Ireland:

> [P]rojected characteristics and public 'pseudo knowledge' about victims of the Troubles may also contribute to the fragmentation of perception about the Troubles and the situation of victims. Through existence of stereotypes of how victims ought to be, the variety and diversity of actual feelings and experiences of those who were bereaved or injured are silenced. Where their feelings do not conform to these stereotypes, the bereaved and injured must struggle with the 'illegitimacy' of their non-conforming feelings, thus compounding feelings of isolation. The perception that suffering due to the Troubles is short-term, for example, illegitimizes long-term suffering—particularly psychological suffering—pathologising the individual as having some kind of weakness or predisposition to suffering, a lack of resilience or an inability to adjust to loss. (Smyth 2002, 140)

From the perspective of peacebuilding, this investigation is necessary because oversimplifying the victim identity may fail to address the complexity of victimization, to the detriment of long-term peace in postconflict societies. It may well lead to too many marginalized victims—victims who may be ignored and silent today, but whose simmering sense of injustice, dissatisfaction, or isolation may lead to renewed violence in the future. The constellation of the victim identity that includes innocence, purity, moral superiority, and lack of responsibility must be critically considered. A tendency to use this constellation as a platform, and at times a chain of equivalence, to recognize and respond to victims and to build peace is, in many instances, detrimental to all three of these tasks. In addition, it is necessary to consider more precisely both how victim recognition and response are shaped by images of the victim and victimization discourse, and further, to understand that there is a significant connection between victim recognition and response and a successful journey toward long-term peace.

In short, this project of developing an alternate, more complex discourse of victimization allows for more effective recognition of victims and a more diverse set of peacebuilding strategies that enhance the prospects for achieving long-term peace. The discourse of the victim developed here is certainly, in the context of peacebuilding, an instrumental discourse. It is important not because it is the one best way to understand the process of victimization and the contours of the victim identity, but rather because in many contexts such a discourse may do a better job of recognizing certain political victims and of contributing to peacebuilding efforts. This alternative discourse of victimization deserves a place among conceptualizations of the victim in the international community. It should not always *supplant* the rather simplistic discourses of victimization that exist in current peacebuilding scholarship, as these discourses may still have a role to play, but instead should *supplement* these discourses and bring nuance to the way in which the international community thinks and acts towards political victims.

NOTES

1. See *Sex without Consent* (ed. Merrill Smith) for a good discussion of these purity requirements for victims of sexual assault throughout history.

2. Such a statement draws on the idea that nonviolence is seen as the better, and indeed more moral, manner in which to respond to conflict and injustice. This is not a universal norm, to be sure, though particularly among Western democracies nonviolent response to conflict is seen as preferable to violence (and arguably this norm extends beyond Western democracies too, as in the politics of Mahatma Gandhi).

3. See also Govier and Verwoerd (2002) on the victim and forgiveness.

4. Certainly, support for justice-based strategies cannot be reduced simply to a desire to morally differentiate between victims and perpetrators. Other reasons include a desire to respect and strengthen international legal norms and the belief in the instrumental value of a justice-based approach in terms of contributing to rule of law, democracy, and peace. See Kritz (1995) for an expansive defense of a justice-based approach.

5. Here I am drawing from mainstream victimology; other approaches to victimology (including critical and feminist approaches) do, at times, define the victim in alternate ways.

6. There is an abundant literature on moral responsibility in regards to political victimization. The majority of it focuses on how to understand perpetrator responsibility (consider as an example Borer [2003] and the discussion of whether direct or indirect

perpetrators during the apartheid period were more responsible). Additional questions in considering moral responsibility often include the potential responsibility of outsiders (neither the victims nor the perpetrators; often understood to be the international community broadly speaking) in preventing and/or stopping political victimization. A related issue is that of bystanders; what moral standards should we have of the Afrikaners and the Germans who did not actively participate in acts of victimization but also did not actively fight against victimization? Finally, Arendt introduces another important question (to be discussed shortly): do victims have any moral responsibility for their victimization, perhaps because of their efforts (or lack thereof) to resist victimization? For a good collection of essays on responsibility, particularly collective vs. individual responsibility and the dimensions of moral responsibility, see French, ed., *Individual and Collective Responsibility* (1998).

7. This question of whether victims have a moral responsibility to resist more is, as suggested, highly controversial and handled through various existing literatures (most notably Arendt). When I return to this question later in the book, it is in fact not this conception of victim responsibility in which I am most interested. Arguing for more nuance and complexity in understanding victims is, I contend, a separate conversation from whether victims should have done more. This book is primarily interested in the first issue.

8. This form of responsibility, insofar as it is critical to arguments made later in this book, is developed more thoroughly in subsequent chapters.

9. Although conversely (and an idea that motivates much of this book), allowing attacks on these characteristics of the victim to also be viewed as attacks on victim status is equally problematic and a source of injustice for the victim.

4

The Ideal Victim in the Political

The Holocaust, the *Judenrat*, and Hannah Arendt

Few episodes of modern political victimization produced images more horrify-ing than that of the genocide of Jews in Europe. The story of the Holocaust emerged as a devastating spectacle of unfathomable evil and doomed innocence. This victimization took center stage in a world war and brought the term "genocide" into modern use. In each of the subsequent cases in this book, the genocide of the Bosnian Muslims and the apartheid regime in South Africa, there were frequent references and comparisons to the Holocaust. The Holo-caust has served as one of the most defining moments of political and human victimization; its aftermath shaped, and continues to shape, international think-ing about political victimization, human rights, genocide, and totalitarianism.

Arguably, without recognizing the way in which the victims of the Holo-caust shape our perception of political victims, we cannot understand the frame of reference for future instances of victimization, such as in Bosnia and South Africa. Later on in the book, when considering these cases, we will see how the narrative of mass political victimization that emerged from the Holo-caust became a critical reference point. In understanding the violence in Bosnia and South Africa, world leaders, activists, journalists, and victims often invoked the Holocaust narrative to communicate to the international community a particular sort of horror, one that demanded a certain type of swift and decisive international response. The narrative of victimization during the Holocaust was premised on the ultimate evils of Nazi Germany, the incomprehensible inhumanity of the Final Solution. Indeed, such a conception of unambiguous evil was important in leading Europe and the United States to take action against the Nazis. As we will see shortly, the story of the Holo-caust did not necessarily begin by foregrounding the innocent Jewish victim, but rather such a victim emerged as the counterpart to the ruthless, evil Nazi. The narrative of the Holocaust, at least in regards to the identity of Nazi Ger-many and its victims, is one that lacks nuance or complexity. There were no discussions of this victimization as a "civil war," as we will see in Bosnia. For most, the Holocaust is the quintessential and horrifying story of the slaughter of millions of innocent victims by a ravaging and evil force—entire families ripped from their homes, deported to concentration camps, and killed for no other reason than their religious ancestry. It provides an image of the victim that is innocent and pure, devoid of responsibility—the political representation of the victim sketched in the previous chapter. The Holocaust provides an image of the victim whose engagement with the discourse of her victimization is limited to horror, disbelief, and abhorrence. The point in making this demonstration is not to contest the historical accuracy of this image. Rather it is to draw attention to the lasting imprint of this conception of victimization, and its transposition onto other historical cases. After the Holocaust, it becomes impossible to consider political victims without its influence, which arguably complicates the recognition of more complex political victims in future atrocities.

Even when considering the Holocaust, some people argue that this image of the ideal victim may be problematic and may not adequately capture the entire story of Holocaust victimization. Perhaps nowhere do we see this more prominently than in the work of Hannah Arendt. Her intervention into the narrative of the Holocaust and the Jewish identity was a departure from a simple script of the evil victimizing the innocent. Instead, she endeavored to ask probing questions about responsibility, both among the many perpetrators and among the many victims. She worked to create a much more complicated script of political victimization, a script where good and evil were not diametric opposites but rather were tightly woven together in the functioning of individuals and society. This intervention, in the context of this book, forces us to consider why, when Arendt challenges the responsibility of victims or suggests that some are not wholly innocent, pure, and morally righteous, this viewpoint is taken by many as a challenge to their status as victims.

From the perspective of rebuilding community after victimization, it is also critical to understand the divisiveness of these contending victimization discourses. Rebuilding community refers not just to the physical rebuilding of conflict-ridden societies, but also to the development of community norms that recognize the injustice of violence and embrace the flourishing of human development. Rebuilding community also suggests that these norms emerge as community values—not merely that individuals within a community embrace such norms, but that the community in part defines itself along such norms. Though Arendt writes two decades after formal reconstruction efforts, she clearly sparked such divisiveness among the Jewish community that many accused her of undermining the healing and rebuilding of that community. Indeed, during the time of Arendt's writing, Israel was in the international spotlight, working hard to justify its aggressive actions against its Arab neighbors. Many in the Jewish community, particularly Israelis, clung strongly to the narrative of the grave injustices that Jews had innocently suffered and held strongly to the belief that Jews still held a moral high ground because of their status as victims. This moral high ground was critical in legitimizing the actions of Israel during the Six-Day War, as well as that nation's ensuing foreign policy. Morris (2001) notes that Israeli Prime Minister Golda Meir bristled at the notion that Israel's actions in the Six-Day War, and particularly the occupation, were anything less than righteous. In response to such concerns she commented that "the supreme morality is that the Jewish people have a right to exist. Without that there is no morality in the world" (Meir, quoted in Morris 2001, 343). Facing stiff criticism for Israel's preemptive attack of its Arab neighbors from the Soviet Union, Europe (particularly France), and to a considerably lesser extent the United States, Israel desperately needed to be identified as the untarnished victim, an identity that emerged in large part from the Holocaust script.[1] For many Jewish leaders and scholars, Arendt's discourse of Jewish victimization represents an assault on this narrative of the innocence and morality of the Jewish people. It not only challenged the narrative that was critical for the reconstruction of the Jewish identity postvictimization, but it had the potential to undermine the perception of the righteousness of the Jewish people during a time when Israel could ill afford such a perception. Arendt challenged the reconstruction of community premised on a pure community with a unique claim to the moral high ground, but also argued passionately that only by embracing a more complex understanding of evil and victimization could the Jewish community and human community truly be rebuilt.

THE HOLOCAUST VICTIM AS THE IDEAL VICTIM

Sketching out an image of the Holocaust victim as innocent requires that one look no further than the most visceral images of the era. Images of Nazi occupation and victimization are rife with displays of concentration camps full of innocent civilians, slaughtered and abused in grotesquely inhumane ways. Six decades since the Holocaust, images of the Holocaust victim still appear frequently in media and scholarship as a reminder of the terror and victimization that transpired during one of humankind's most horrid experiences. Below is an exploration of how this narrative of the Holocaust emerged during the 1930s and 1940s in the international community, with particular attention to the allied powers of Britain and the United States. In addition, consideration will be given to how this narrative reemerged in 1967 during and after the

Six-Day War in the form of Holocaust theology. Such a narrative will serve as a baseline for understanding how the Holocaust helped shape the international discourse on political victimization.

International Community: Churchill and Roosevelt

During the late 1930s and into the 1940s, as information about Nazi aggression and Jewish victimization spread worldwide, there are many indicators that the international community did in fact see European Jews as innocent victims of unchecked Nazi hatred and violence. Perhaps no world leader articulated the innocent and profound suffering of the Jews, in comparison with the atrocities of the Nazis, as eloquently as Winston Churchill. In his June 1941 speech to the Allied delegates, Churchill paints a telling picture of the war.

> What tragedies, what horrors, what crimes has Hitler and all that Hitler stands for brought upon Europe and the world! The ruins of Warsaw, of Rotterdam, of Belgrade are monuments which will long recall to future generations the outrage of unopposed air bombing applied with calculated scientific cruelty to helpless populations. . . . But far worse than these visible injuries is the misery of the conquered peoples. We see them hounded, terrorized, exploited. Their manhood by the million is forced to work under conditions indistinguishable in many cases from actual slavery. Their goods and chattels are pillaged or filched for worthless money. Their homes, their daily life are pried into and spied upon by the all-pervading system of secret political police which, having reduced the Germans themselves to abject docility, now stalks the streets and byways of a dozen lands. Their religious faiths are affronted, persecuted or oppressed in the interest of a fanatic paganism devised to perpetuate the worship and sustain the tyranny of one abominable creature. Their traditions, their culture, their laws, their institutions, social and political alike, are suppressed by force or undermined by subtle, coldly planned intrigue. (Churchill 1941)

In Churchill's speech we see a clear identification of a cold, calculating, evil aggressor. And we see the victims, Jews and Germans alike, reduced to "abject docility," relentlessly persecuted and suppressed. Throughout this speech, and much of Churchill's commentary on the war, we encounter images of victimization where the aggressor is identified and condemned as evil, and the victim is portrayed as weak, helpless, and cruelly subject to inhumane treatment. Churchill's sympathy for the Jewish victims of the Holocaust is rarely contested; against a background of relentless military opposition to the Nazis, a rallying of the international community against Hitler, and demonstrations of sympathy for Jews (such as by leading prayer sessions in Parliament for the salvation of Jews), it is clear that Churchill recognized Jews and other Holocaust victims as victims of a great injustice.

American President Franklin D. Roosevelt also singled out the evil, aggression, and violence of the Nazis, and condemned their discourses of racial superiority. Heuvel (1996) notes that Roosevelt was "disgusted" by the discourse of Nazism, and that well before the United States entered World War II, he was convinced of Hitler's "irredeemable evil." Heuvel (1996) notes how some have criticized Roosevelt for not doing enough to help European Jewry, but he defends Roosevelt in identifying a combination of actions, such as partially relaxed immigration for fleeing Jews beginning in the 1930s, as well as a commitment to liberating the Jews through a swift and forceful victory.[2] Indeed, it seems that even where we might be inclined to criticize the United States for passivity or late entry into helping the Jews, this passivity can be traced to the perception that Europe's problems were not our own, and not ambiguity about whether the Jews were truly being victimized by Nazi aggressors.[3]

Even Lipstadt (1986), one of the harshest critics of the American and European response to the Holocaust, does not suggest that the reason for the delayed response was an unwillingness to recognize innocent victims. She cites many reasons for the delayed response, including an unwillingness to believe that such atrocities could actually be occurring, a media that often cast doubt about the extent or nature of the atrocities, American isolationism, and a general anti-immigration sentiment that made accepting refugees difficult. As Hilberg (1992) notes:

> It was hard enough to explain to a Briton or an American why the war was being fought, hard enough to make clear to an American why it was being fought in Europe. For all the emphasis on One World or the admonition that no man was an island, the ordinary Briton was very conscious of being on an island, albeit for a brief period in 1940 an endangered one. The American, on a much larger island, was an ocean away. Accordingly Britain and the United States fought a carefully controlled war, minimizing their casualties and simplifying their words. (Hilberg 1992, 255)

That the Jews were perceived as victims was not contested even among the harshest critics of the Allies. Whether this victimization was sufficient to motivate a policy of engagement and rescue is a separate (though important) question. Indeed, even as Lipstadt argues that Americans in particular were not as engaged as they should be, for many of the reasons above, she notes that 94 percent of Americans in 1944 did not approve of the German persecution of Jews (Lipstadt 1986, 127; see also Heuvel's 1996 discussion of surveys that indicate that the majority of Americans did see the Jews as "wrongful victims"). And for all her criticism of Roosevelt, Lipstadt notes how he was "genuinely repulsed by Nazi behavior." Lipstadt's argument suggests that Americans did recognize the Jews as innocent victims, yet were mitigated in pushing for a strong response because of other concerns.

The above discussion highlights American and British perceptions of both the Nazis and their Jewish victims, and in both instances, there seems little conflict over recognizing the Jews as victims, the Nazis as aggressors. Further, British and American sentiment indicates sympathy for these victims, in part because of a recognition of the atrocities they were enduring, and in part because of a recognition of their helplessness. Finally, there is a clear sense of conviction about the evil of the Nazis. Nazi Germany is described in the press as a "nation possessed," and Nazis are described as "fanatics" headed toward "sadistic lowness" (Lipstadt 1986, 102–3). Indeed, this conviction of evil appears first and most strongly in much of the international rhetoric surrounding the European and later American decision to challenge the Nazis. Churchill, Roosevelt, and others rallying support to oppose the Nazis focus most clearly on the pure evil of the aggressors; as counterpart to this pure evil is an image of an innocent and suffering Europe. Hilberg notes that there was a concern among Allied leaders that emphasizing that the war was being fought on behalf of these innocent Jewish victims might sound like the Allies were "mercenaries in a Jewish cause," but it also is importantly not contested. At no point do we see any suggestion of victim responsibility, victim blame, or victim support of the discourse of victimization. Neither Churchill nor Roosevelt suggests that the Jews were in any way responsible for their genocide, nor that they were responsible for maintaining a discourse of racial superiority, hatred, and violence.

It is not being argued that no one within either the British or American government or public held anti-Semitic views that encouraged viewing the Jews as somehow responsible for their genocide; certainly such individuals existed. Rather, legitimate political discourse, as well as political and military action, presented first an image of unimaginable hatred and aggression, and from this an image of European Jews (and indeed Europeans as a whole) as helpless and innocent victims, unfortunate pawns in the strategy of unfathomable evil. In upcoming cases we will see that ambiguities about the behavior and attitudes of victims of genocide and state-sponsored violence have delayed or discouraged the international community's willingness to recognize these victims *as victims*; not so in the case of Jewish victims of the Holocaust.[4]

The Jewish Community and Holocaust Theology

Much like the international community, the Jewish community is also inclined to narrate the Holocaust from the perspective of Nazi evil and innocent suffering. But Ellis (1990) notes that this narration did not begin immediately after the war; it was left "unnamed" by Jewish thinkers as the pain was too fresh and the practical needs of rebuilding Jewish life too pressing.[5] However, during the 1960s, with high-profile trials of Nazi war criminals in Israel, as well as the tremendous victory of the Six-Day War, the Jewish narration of the Holocaust began in earnest. What emerged during this time was Holocaust theology, as much an ethical and political platform for Israel and Jews as it was a narration of the Holocaust.

Ellis argues that Holocaust theology has three dominant themes: suffering and empowerment, innocence and redemption, and specialness and normalization (Ellis 1990, 2). The story of the Holocaust is one of unparalleled Jewish suffering, which necessitates Jewish empowerment such that this type of victimization can never occur again. The story of the Holocaust is a story of Jewish innocence—an innocence that destines the Jewish people for redemption. The Six-Day War offered a new context for the Holocaust:

> For Holocaust theologians the victory in the Six Days War was a miracle, a sign that an innocent people so recently victimized might be on the verge of redemption. That is, a subtheme of Jewish suffering in the Holocaust is the total innocence of the Jewish people and thus the innocence of those who defend the lives of Jews in Israel. (Ellis 1990, 3)

Holocaust theology emphasizes Jewish innocence and purity. In fact, the third theme of Holocaust theology takes this innocence a step further, suggesting a "specialness" of the Jewish people, a moral high ground connected to their innocence and suffering. Indeed, this argument is not unlike Morrissey and Smyth (2002) and Fisher's (2001) discussion of the victim as "moral beacon," a victim whose suffering has led to an accelerated moral development. Frequent references to the good/evil, innocent/guilty dialectic surface in Holocaust theology. For instance, noted Holocaust theologian Elie Wiesel describes the trials of Nazi war criminals as "the eternal dialogue between the Jew and his murderer, good and evil, between man and the devil" (Wiesel 1985, 179). Holocaust theology is characterized by foregrounding the innocence and purity of the Holocaust victim.

> The classic Jewish self-image—the innocent, sinned against sufferer... the traditional Jewish conviction of being morally superior which has sustained our self-respect throughout centuries of persecution. (Greenberg 1988, 1)

Holocaust theology takes this identity further; however, it is not merely a self-image, but it places this identity at the forefront of Jewish and Israeli politics. In other words, for Holocaust theologians, narrating the Holocaust became one and the same with crafting the Jewish identity. The innocence and vulnerability that characterize the Holocaust victim also characterize modern Jews. Such an identity demands the presence of a Jewish state (to protect the Jews) but also justifies the actions of the state as righteous because they are being carried out by such a "pure" people and for the protection of the vulnerable, the victimized.

Holocaust theology was the dominant voice in narrating the Holocaust for the Jewish community; indeed, Ellis (1990) notes that one of the remarkable aspects of Holocaust and Jewish scholarship during this time period is the tremendous success in stifling dissent. Holocaust theology became the narrative of the Holocaust for Jewish people; Jews were "acquainted for the first time" with the Holocaust, the Jewish identity of purity, and the need for empowerment.

INTERJECTING ARENDT

Against this backdrop the work of Hannah Arendt stands out as a provocative attempt to rethink the Holocaust and Jewish victimization. Much of Arendt's work, both before and after the Holocaust, engaged "the Jewish question," yet her 1964 coverage of the Eichmann trial in Israel was certainly the most controversial. In "Eichmann in Jerusalem: The Banality of Evil," Arendt put forth an exceptionally controversial account of victims and perpetrators. This discussion was not long, but generated vehement criticism from Jews around the world, as well as many scholars. In these pages, Arendt discusses both Eichmann and the *Judenrat*, the Jewish council leaders who played a role in carrying out Nazi policy.[6] Arendt treats the *Judenrat* harshly. She questions whether they were truly coerced into committing the atrocities they did, and whether they could not have done more to resist. Numerous passages demonstrate her seeming lack of sympathy, as follows:

> Wherever Jews lived, there were recognized Jewish leaders, and this leadership, almost without exception, cooperated in one way or another, for one reason or another, with the Nazis. The whole truth was that if the Jewish people had really been unorganized and leaderless, there would have been chaos and plenty of misery but the total number of victims would hardly have been between four and a half and six million people. (Arendt 1964, 125)

And again:

> To a Jew this role of the Jewish leaders in the destruction of their own people is undoubtedly the darkest chapter of the whole dark story. (Arendt 1964, 117)

Such statements instigated a furious controversy over whether Arendt was attempting to hold Jews responsible for their own victimization, or whether she was blaming the victim, maybe even denying that the *Judenrat* were legitimate victims at all. One of her leading critics, Gershom Scholem, expressed outrage that she was abandoning the *Ahabath Israel*, the love of the Jewish people, in her "malicious" treatment of Jews. Further, he questioned whether she was in any position to be making the sorts of judgments that she was.

> Which of us can say today what decisions the elders of the Jews—or whatever we choose to call them—ought to have arrived at in the circumstances?. . . There were the *Judenrat* for example; some among them were swine, others were saints. I have read a great deal about both varieties. There were among them also many people in no way different from. ourselves, who were compelled to make terrible decisions in circumstances that we cannot even begin to reproduce or reconstruct. I do not know whether they were right or wrong. Nor do I presume to judge. I was not there. (Scholem 1978, 243)

Other critics admonished Arendt's lack of exploration of the coercive measures used to get the *Judenrat* to assist the Nazis (indeed, her description of how they cooperated "for one reason or another" could certainly be read as a rather euphemistic description of the pressures on the *Judenrat*). Laqueur (1965) criticized Arendt for blatant historical error, noting that she "did not have that essential minimum of factual knowledge," and Robinson (1965) labeled her work as "amateurish." Other criticisms suggested her work should have considered the numerous acts of resistance from the *Judenrat* and other Jews. Arendt suggests mostly acts of compliance; many called for a celebration of the acts of protest. Scholem references this early on in his response to Arendt's work:

> There is a question thrown at us by the new youth of Israel: why did they allow themselves to be slaughtered?. . . At each decisive juncture, however, your book speaks only of the weakness of the Jewish stance in the world. I am ready enough to admit that weakness; but you put such emphasis upon it that, in my view, it ceases to be objective and acquires overtones of malice. (Scholem 1978, 241)

One strand of criticism is of particular important for this book, and it too is found in the work of Scholem. In assessing "Eichmann in Jerusalem," Scholem asserts that, fundamentally, Arendt is attempting to discredit the status of the Jew as victim, particularly the Jew who participated in any way in Nazi atrocities (as the *Judenrat* did). He accuses her of attempting to blur the line between victim and perpetrator.

> [Y]our thesis that the machinations of the Nazis served in some way to blur the distinction between torturer and victim . . . seems to me wholly false and tendentious. In the camps, human beings were systematically degraded; they were, as you say, compelled to participate in their own extermination, and to assist in the execution of fellow prisoners. Is the distinction between torturer and victim thereby blurred? What perversity! We are asked, it appears, to confess that the Jews, too, had their "share" in these acts of genocide. (Scholem 1978, 243)

Scholem's criticisms were written as part of an ongoing exchange of letters between himself and Arendt, and as such, we have the opportunity to explore whether Arendt really was attempting to discredit the status of the *Judenrat* as victims. Indeed, I consider this proposal shortly, but for now, I wish to focus attention most strongly on the fact that this issue, of responsibility and its implications for victim status, became the center of controversy during this discussion of the Holocaust. For those victims who were not seen as entirely innocent, for those victims whose role in the Nazi atrocities was complex, their status as victims was immediately problematized; fracturing the constellation of victim characteristics meant attacking the very identity of victim. For Scholem, allowing some degree of victim responsibility (which is what he believed Arendt was doing) was equivalent to the denial of victim status altogether. If Arendt was painting a picture of the *Judenrat* as, on some level, practically or morally responsible for their cooperation with Nazis, this was interpreted as an attempt to assault their victim status.

The Banality of Evil

In addition to problematizing the victim status and responsibility of the *Judenrat*—indeed, the entire image of the Jews as the ideal victim—Arendt's work also probed the broader process of such horrific political victimization. In particular, her efforts to understand how such atrocities could occur led her to develop the concept of the banality of evil. The precise meaning of the term "banality of evil" has itself been the subject of much debate. For our purposes we restrict ourselves to Arendt's attempts to explain this concept; many years after initially introducing the concept, she still labored to explain it:

> I spoke of the "banality of evil" and meant with this no theory or doctrine but something quite factual, the phenomenon of evil deeds, committed on a gigantic scale, which could not be traced to any particularity of wickedness, pathology, or ideological conviction in the doer, whose only personal distinction was perhaps an extraordinary shallowness. However monstrous the deeds were, the doer was neither monstrous nor demonic, and the only specific characteristic one could detect in his past as well as in his behavior during the trial and the preceding police examination was something entirely negative; it was not stupidity but a curious, quite authentic inability to think. (Arendt 1978, 417)

Responding to the concept of the banality of evil, many of Arendt's critics thought that she was attempting to remove responsibility from those who had committed atrocities during the Holocaust. Bearing in mind that these writings came out as a direct result of her observance of the Eichmann trial, many critics interpreted her discussion of the banality of evil as a statement about the lack of responsibility of Eichmann in committing horrendous acts against humanity. Critics such as Scholem thought Arendt's refusal to recognize the "doer as neither monstrous nor demonic" was the invocation of a society without morals, leading directly toward seeing Eichmann, and other perpetrators, as somehow not responsible for the atrocities committed. Indeed, some of Arendt's writing also suggests that she may be trying to spread the blame for the moral conditions of society, these conditions of evil, onto the victims (Arendt 1964).

As in the previous section, I consider the merits of this interpretation of Arendt shortly, but here the focus is again on the way in which responsibility and the victim identity relate. In criticizing the "banality of evil," Arendt's critics rejected the way in which spreading responsibility away from the perpetrator (and perhaps in the direction of the victim) minimized the Jewish claim to the victim identity (see both Scholem and Laqueur). Indeed, when Scholem criticizes Arendt for being "flippant" and "malicious," he is articulating what he sees as attempts either to minimize the trauma and victimization of the Jewish people (in the case of the banality of evil), or directly attack their status as victims (as in the case of the *Judenrat*). Arendt's work began to fracture the constellation of characteristics that attend the ideal victim, and the response of many was to argue that fracturing this constellation was in fact attacking victimhood.

Reading Arendt and her critics in the decades after World War II, we find that perceptions of Holocaust victims were premised on a notion of the ideal victim. Many of the most visceral images of these victims—the images of emaciated concentration camp victims, the gassing of women and children—both evoked and confirmed an image of the innocent victim, and certainly Holocaust theology gave prominent place to the ideal victim in narrating the Holocaust (and, indeed, Jewish identity more broadly). When Arendt, two decades later, began to wrestle with complex issues of responsibility and the dynamics of evil and victimization, her stories of victimization contrasted sharply with these previous images of innocence. It should be noted that Arendt was not only challenging the "empirical" innocence of a handful of victims (most notably the *Judenrat*) but was clearly challenging the normative conception of victims as innocent and morally superior in a much broader context. She was challenging the very idea that victims are, and must be, innocent and righteous. Arendt was reaching toward a more complex understanding of responsibility both for victims and perpetrators. Arguably, this subtlety was not appreciated by her critics, but undoubtedly this contrast is what sparked many of her critics to suggest that she was denying at least some Jews their rightful claim to victim status. Arendt's departure from the narrative of the ideal victim caused many to cast her as antivictim and anti-Jew. For many, the additional tragedy of Arendt's work included not just defaming Jews of decades past, but interjecting unnecessary controversy and slander precisely when the Jewish community was facing an immense pressure to justify itself (in the context of the Six-Day War and beyond). To reconsider Jewish victimization, identity, and responsibility in this era of a struggling Israel facing international criticism was seen by many, notably Holocaust theologians, as a particularly cruel and detrimental interjection to Holocaust survivors and the broader Jewish community.

EXPLORING ARENDT'S IMAGE OF THE VICTIM

The response to Arendt's work, particularly "Eichmann in Jerusalem," suggests that many people believed Arendt was portraying some victims of the Holocaust as partially responsible for their victimization, and perhaps even casting a shadow on whether individuals such as the *Judenrat* should really even be seen as victims. However, there is significant evidence within Arendt's work which suggests that she was not interested in denying their victim status. Rather she put forth a more nuanced map of political victimization and particularly responsibility, one that attempted to sort out how best to understand these atrocities in the face of changing social norms, knowledge, and motivation. Moreover, much of Arendt's work suggests that rather than trying to hinder the process of rebuilding community, Arendt was attempting to provide an alternative discourse of victimization that would ultimately strengthen not just the Jewish community, but the human community.

Changing Social Norms, Knowledge, and Motivation

In Arendt's definition of the banality of evil, she suggests that when a society plunges into moral depravity, committing an act of evil does not require evil motivation. In such a social atmosphere, one need not be a monster to create monstrous acts. Arendt attributes this to the "crushing of human spontaneity," by which she means that individuals are no longer engaging in spontaneous, unique acts; any independent faculty we may have thought humans possessed is gone, and distinguishing right from wrong, evil from good, is impossible for many.[7]

> The totalitarian policy, which has completely destroyed the neutral zone in which daily life of ordinary human beings is ordinarily lived, has achieved the result of making the existence of each individual in Germany depend upon committing crimes or complicity in crimes. (Arendt 1978, 228)

From this perspective, we can begin to understand what Arendt means when she comments that "Eichmann did not know what he was doing [in committing Holocaust atrocities]" (Arendt 1978). His independent human faculty was gone, and he was simply engaging in "normal" behaviors. This is in sharp contrast to the depiction of Nazi aggressors as individuals motivated by evil and hatred, "fanatics" headed toward "sadistic lows"; rather it is a picture of Nazi aggression as "normalized" behaviors in a regime of moral depravity.

One question we must pose is whether this implies that Eichmann has any responsibility for his acts, and if he does, what form of responsibility? Certainly many of Arendt's critics assumed that by arguing that he could not comprehend the wrongness of his actions, and by suggesting that his independent human faculty had been obliterated, Arendt was attempting to "exonerate" Eichmann (and other Nazis) from any moral responsibility, and perhaps even pass this responsibility onto the victims. It is not clear that Arendt herself made this leap; that is, it is not clear that she believed that Eichmann's failure to comprehend what he was doing, the horrific nature of his behavior, necessarily meant he did not bear moral responsibility for his actions. Indeed, Bernstein (1996) notes how Arendt was in total agreement with the judges of the Eichmann trial when they held him responsible for the atrocities he committed. However, it should be noted that what she found most persuasive in the final judges' report was represented in the following passage:

> [T]he extent to which any one of the many criminals were close to or removed from the actual killer of the victim means nothing, as far as the measure of his responsibility, is concerned. *On the contrary, the degree of responsibility increases as we draw further away from the man who uses the fatal implement with his own hands.* (Arendt 1978, 246–47)

As much as Arendt's critics saw her diminishing the responsibility of the perpetrators and even suggesting "universal responsibility," passages such as these indicate that Arendt still held individual criminals such as Eichmann practically and morally responsible for their actions, even if they could not possibly comprehend the horror of their acts. A similar stance is seen in her assessment of the responsibility of the "high society of Germany":

> Among the responsible in a broader sense must be included all those who continued to be sympathetic to Hitler as long as it was possible, who aided his rise to power, and who applauded him in Germany and other European countries. . . . They, who were the Nazis' first accomplices and their best aides, truly did not know what they were doing. (Arendt 1978, 228)

Clearly, for Arendt, the ability to think reflectively about what one was doing is not a prerequisite for responsibility; she insisted on recognizing personal responsibility even when this "independent human faculty" and "evil motivations" were absent. This insistence on personal responsibility, even in the context of a "morally collapsed society," is consistent throughout Arendt's work. Bernstein (1996) identifies it as a "central theme" of her scholarship.

At this point, it is worth reiterating that the very term "responsibility" is used in diverse ways—certainly among different scholars and in different contexts, but arguably in the work of Arendt as well. One of the first distinctions she makes is between political responsibility and personal responsibility. Political responsibility is succinctly defined as "every government assumes for the deeds and misdeeds of his predecessor and every nation for the deeds and misdeeds of its past" (Arendt 2003, 27). Personal responsibility, Arendt argues, must be understood in contrast to political responsibility. There is considerably more ambiguity in Arendt's understanding of personal responsibility; indeed, she makes an interesting switch in her discussion of these issues in the essay "Collective Responsibility" which suggests that though personal responsibility was of central concern to Arendt, it lacked a certain degree of precision and remained a malleable concept. Arendt does write precisely about personal guilt, and continues her discussion of responsibility by contrasting political responsibility with personal *guilt* (not responsibility). She makes a distinction between "political (collective) responsibility, on one side, and moral and/or legal (personal) guilt, on the other" (Arendt 2003, 150). In making this distinction she is advancing the notion that political communities are always, *as a community*, responsible for their actions; she even argues that they must assume responsibility for "the sins of our fathers," much as we "reap the rewards of their merits" (Arendt 2003, 150). She distinguishes personal guilt as the inappropriate and unwarranted guilt that individual members of a community may feel in reaction to recognizing this collective responsibility; "we are of course not guilty of their [our fathers'] misdeeds, either morally or legally, nor can we ascribe their deeds to our own merits" (Arendt 2003, 150).

The development of the concept of personal responsibility remains more piecemeal. At times, it relies more on negative qualifications (one does not necessarily have to be able to think critically about the consequences of what one is doing in order to be held personally responsible; individuals need not be direct participants in order to be held personally responsible) than it does on fleshing out what precisely she intends the term "personal responsibility" to mean. For Arendt, the term is also related to the condition of "independent human faculty" (which is, in effect, the process of thinking), and while much of her work can be read to suggest that at times she associates totalitarian conditions that reduce or eliminate this capacity for thinking as negating the conceptual value of "personal responsibility," this is not always the case. Such an assessment surely attended her description of the Eichmann trial, and yet she was insistent on recognizing some degree of personal responsibility. Further, she very nearly scoffs at arguments that suggest that when presented with "temptation" to do something wrong, it is obvious that personal responsibility for subsequent actions can and should be negated.

> [There is] a widespread conviction that it is impossible to withstand temp-
> tation of any kind, that none of us could be or even expected to be trust-
> worthy when the chips are down, that to be tempted and to be forced are
> almost the same. . . . And while a temptation where one's life is at stake
> may be a legal excuse for a crime, it certainly is not a moral justification.
> (Arendt 2003, 18)

Overall, Arendt's ideas about political responsibility and personal (also referred to as moral) responsibility are relatively broad. She extends political responsibility both to the past and into the future, and also notes that no person can ever escape community responsibility. One can perhaps change from one community to another, but since "no man can live without belonging to some community" this collective responsibility is a constant of the human condition. Further, her conception of personal responsibility is clearly a deep normative commitment; in some ways it is amplified as she is so often responding to critics who accuse her of downplaying the personal responsibility of men such as Eichmann.

Arendt's discussion of responsibility arguably is significant in regards to the image she develops of the political victim. At a minimum, she is articulating a more complex notion of responsibility that suggests that neither victims nor perpetrators necessarily have the simple and absolute responsibility (or lack thereof) that many may assume. Particularly in the context of this project, it merits emphasis that as Arendt challenges the chain of equivalence that links the victim identity to the absence of responsibility, she is not challenging the victim status of Jews during the Holocaust.

"Perpetrator as Victim"

As Arendt depicts a society with changing social norms that has reduced the space for independent human faculty, she also engages the idea of the "perpetrator as victim." Arendt is willing to see perpetrators of Nazi violence as victims; for her they are victims of a discourse that makes them, as humans, superfluous and victims of the moral collapse of society. It seems that from Arendt's perspective, recognizing these perpetrators as victims is quite critical, because if we do not see them as victims, we are unlikely to understand the true horror of Nazi or other totalitarian discourses. Many scholars were quite opposed to any attempt to see perpetrators such as Eichmann as victims; we have already encountered the comments of Scholem about the blurring of the victim/perpetrator distinction. Robinson (1965) also expressed displeasure at Arendt's attempt to make Eichmann "more complicated than he was," a tactic that "only serves to confuse" (Robinson, as referenced in Laqueur 1965, 255). Arendt was nonetheless committed to a more nuanced understanding of

Eichmann. In considering his trial, she was insistent that he, as well as his crimes, be viewed in the appropriate context—a context that she seems to suggest simultaneously illuminates his victimization and the horror of his actions.

> She strongly objected to what she took to be the prosecutor's melodramatic attempt to demonize Eichmann, to portray him as a "sadistic monster" who was possessed by an "insane hatred of Jews." By relying on such conventional categories, the prosecutor... obscured the character of this "desk criminal" and his crimes.... [Eichmann] was "terrifyingly normal."... *This is what Arendt thought was so unprecedented, and what needed to be confronted squarely to understand Eichmann's deeds and responsibility.* (Bernstein 1996, 160, emphasis added)

In this instance Arendt does not use the language of victim in describing what needs to be "confronted squarely." Yet recognizing an individual such as Eichmann as a victim (in addition to being a criminal) seems to be central to Arendt's understanding of the banality of evil. It speaks to the way in which the moral depravity of an "evil" society reaches, and victimizes, even those who carry out these victimizing actions.

Arendt's conception of Eichmann's responsibility for the crimes he committed against Jews has been discussed; she clearly held him responsible even if he "did not know what he was doing." But how much responsibility or interest did an individual such as Eichmann have in the discourse of Nazism? How was Eichmann situated in and engaged with the discourse of Nazism? Does she portray Eichmann as simultaneously being victimized by the discourse of Nazism, and being constituted by this discourse as something other than a victim? Arguably, she does. Arendt recognizes the way in which the insidious nature of totalitarian discourses can constitute individuals as "normal" people, even when they are engaging in otherwise unusual, violent, and even barbaric behaviors. They are accepted soldiers, managers, and mid-level leaders doing their job, fulfilling their responsibilities in a way in which society recognizes them as productive and acceptable. She asks rhetorically, "He [a Nazi war criminal] had only carried out orders and since when has it been a crime to carry out orders? Since when has it been a virtue to rebel? Since when could one only be decent by welcoming death?" (Arendt 1978, 231).

Arendt is articulating the way in which the discourse of Nazism both victimized perpetrators by denying their independent human faculty, but also constituted them as model, virtuous individuals; they were operating under conditions in which "every moral act was illegal and every legal act was a crime" (Arendt 2003, 41). Arendt cannot tease out the components of the Nazi discourse that constituted Germans as victims, as opposed to the components that constituted Germans as productive members of Nazi society. Indeed, it is not simply that Arendt cannot tease out the aspects of Nazi discourse that constitute individuals both as barbarians and as model citizens; the point is precisely that it cannot be done. One discourse, Nazism, creates many identities even within singular individuals, and in so doing, establishes itself as a social construct that is difficult for some of its victims (such as Eichmann) to oppose. This difficulty hints at the notion of discursive responsibility, an idea taken up in the subsequent chapter in theorizing the complex political victim.

Personal Responsibility and Jewish Victims

Insofar as her commitment to personal responsibility influenced her ability to see criminals such as Eichmann as responsible perpetrators despite his lack of understanding of the atrocities he committed, a commitment to personal responsibility forces us to investigate her claims about the responsibility of Holocaust victims, particularly the *Judenrat*. Arendt is (in)famous for criticizing the *Judenrat* for their role in the victimization of Jews; she holds them personally responsible despite acknowledging the unique horrors of the Holocaust. Her basis for holding the *Judenrat* responsible is quite simple; she recognizes (though at times minimizes) the coercive measures used to manufacture their participation, but notes that "non-participation" is always a choice: one can always "choose to do nothing."

> I said there was no possibility of resistance, but there existed the possibility of doing nothing. And in order to do nothing, one did not need to be a saint, one needed only to say: "I am just a simple Jew, and I have no desire to play any other role."...Moreover, we should not forget that we are dealing here with conditions which were terrible and desperate enough, but which were not the conditions of concentration camps. These decisions were made in an atmosphere of terror but not under the immediate pressure and impact of terror. These are important differences of degree.... [T]hese people had still a certain, limited freedom of decision and action. (Arendt 1978, 248–49)

It seems apparent that Arendt is holding the *Judenrat* responsible for their participation in the victimization of Jews in the Holocaust—responsible because they always could have chosen a path of nonparticipation. This, quite obviously, fractures the constellation that links the absence of responsibility, moral righteousness, and the victim identity. Yet, it does not seem fair to suggest that in articulating this responsibility, Arendt is attempting to diminish their status as victims; she is not trying to deny the victim identity, merely suggesting that the victim identity must not be understood as necessarily without responsibility. Arendt continues to recognize many victims in the Holocaust, even while raising new questions about responsibility. Arguably for Arendt, when society faces a moral collapse such as she describes in the banality of evil, all are victimized, because any hope of independent human faculty capable of thinking and reasoning in a moral manner is lost. This remains true even if the issue of responsibility is reconsidered.

Further, in this broader sense of victimization—the victimization engendered by the Nazi discourse that "makes humans superfluous"—Arendt importantly *does not* hold Jews and other victims of the Holocaust as responsible (see Kohn's introduction to Arendt 2003, xii). The Nazis (particularly leaders) are most frequently cited as "responsible" for the creation of such a discourse, with other portions of the German upper class that supported Hitler also implicated. For the creation of the Nazi discourse, *Jewish victims are not seen to bear responsibility*. She assumes that they remain righteous and innocent in this regard. For Arendt, the *Judenrat* play an integral role in the reach and continuation of Nazism, but are in no way implicated in its genesis. Eichmann has discursive responsibility; Jews do not.

Though Arendt ultimately does not hold Jews responsible for the grand totalitarian discourse that victimizes them, she importantly recognizes the *potential* for Jews, and others, to contribute to the political space necessary for the emergence of such a discourse. Arendt argues that individuals or communities who are unwilling to accept the idea of a unified humanity, because of its attendant burdens (such as being responsible for the well-being of all humans), can contribute to the political space necessary for Nazi-like discourses.

> [P]eoples have learned to know one another better and learned more and more about the evil potentialities in men. The result has been that they have recoiled more and more from the idea of humanity and become more susceptible to the doctrine of race which denies the very possibility of a common humanity. They instinctively felt that the idea of humanity, whether it appears in a religious or humanistic form, implies the obligation of a general responsibility which they do not wish to assume. For the idea of humanity, when purged of all sentimentality, has the very serious consequence that in one form or another men must assume responsibility for all crimes committed by men and that all nations share the onus of evil committed by all others.... Those who today are ready to follow this road in modern version do not content themselves with the hypocritical confession, "God be thanked, I am not like that," in horror at the undreamed of potentialities of the German national character. Rather, in fear and trembling, have they finally realized of what man is capable—and this is indeed the precondition of any modern political thinking.... This, however, is certain: upon them and only them, who are filled with a genuine fear of the inescapable guilt of the human race, can there be any reliance when it comes to fighting fearlessly, uncompromisingly, everywhere against the incalculable evil that men are capable of bringing about. (Arendt 1978, 235–36)

Arendt recognizes that those attempting to define themselves as "not like that," as incapable of victimization and violence, may in fact contribute to the political space necessary for victimization and violence. Certainly this contrasts with the image of the victim as necessarily morally superior. If these victims can also generate discourses, in the context of healing, that make space for political victimization, then they ought not be characterized as "moral beacons." This discussion of responsibility, perhaps even more than Arendt's discussion of Nazi or *Judenrat* responsibility, is particularly illuminating in terms of the victim identity. Arendt is suggesting that the very discourse of a fractured humanity that helps people constitute themselves as "good," or removed from the horrors of victimization, actually may contribute to the development of victimizing discourses. As we see later in this book, this fracturing of humanity along "good and bad" or "us and them" is often the first step in creating the political space for mass victimization, particularly genocide. Moreover, she alludes to an idea developed later on in this book: that victims may not always oppose a total fracturing of the discourse (such as a particular discourse of humanity) that contributes to their victimization. Arendt recognizes how difficult, how "burdensome" it is to participate in a discourse of humanity, and seems to realize that even if Jewish victims of the Holocaust were to understand the way in which turning one's back on the discourse of humanity can contribute to victimization, they may be unwilling to move beyond this fractured discourse of humanity, because it is precisely this discourse that allows them to recognize themselves as "not like them [Nazis]."

CONCLUSION

This chapter began with an image of the Holocaust victim as the ideal victim. The second image of the Holocaust victim, which emerges in the work of Arendt, presents the victim as more complex, particularly in the case of the *Judenrat*. Her commitments to personal responsibility, her belief in the option of nonparticipation, her understanding of totalitarianism and political victimization, and her criticism of how Jews were rebuilding community made her unwilling to conceptualize the *Judenrat* as ideal victims. She finds them to be responsible and articulated the role they chose to play in cooperating with the Nazis. Yet she did not stop recognizing the *Judenrat* as victims; she saw even Eichmann as a victim, though the case for his responsibility in victimizing the Jews was considerably stronger and of a different sort.

To simplify what is clearly a complex discourse of victimization by taking up one strand in the argument and discarding the others is tempting—tempting to state that the image of the victim who must bear personal responsibility should be the prevailing image of the victim extracted from her work. Rather we can emphasize her convictions about the widespread victimization of many, both Jews and even German soldiers—individuals who were victimized by the crushing discourse of Nazism. In this instance of victimization, they were innocent, devoid of responsibility. Alternately, we could focus most heavily on her conceptions of humanity, and the important responsibilities all people have in maintaining this discourse to prevent victimization.

At this point, it seems better to presume a complex account to which all the strands contribute. Presently, I wish to emphasize the controversy that emerged when she introduced the discussion of victim responsibility, juxtaposed as it was next to the discourse of the ideal Holocaust victim. This was a fracturing of the chain of equivalence between the victim identity and innocence, purity, moral superiority, and lack of responsibility. This controversy was thought by many to be an assault on the process of Jewish community reconstruction, though there is ample evidence within Arendt's work that her alternate discourse of victimization was in fact an interjection motivated by a desire to see the reconstruction of a human community; the only community that, for Arendt, was really capable of closing off the political space necessary for mass human atrocity. Arguably, the ideal victim discourse of the Holocaust did play a critical role in the processing of the Holocaust and the reconstruction of the Jewish community. It provided a narrative, parameters of justice, and a reaffirmation of the Jewish people as "good" rather than "evil." Yet for Arendt, this narrative of victimization obscured the complexity of victimization and potentially hindered attempts to reconstruct a human community, so reliant was it on distinguishing between us and them, good and evil. It therefore left the Jewish community in jeopardy, both because of the way in which it fostered only a limited healing in a bifurcated notion of humanity, and because it opened the door to even closer international scrutiny of the Jewish people, their righteousness and motivations.

This story of the Holocaust, and Arendt's work on the subject of victimization, demonstrates the complexities of favoring one narrative of victimization, one image of the victim, over another. One image of the victim may allow for certain important practices of justice, healing, reconstruction, yet hinder other practices. In the case of the Holocaust, the ideal victim narrative helped significantly in the condemnation of Nazism and the establishment of a Jewish community post–World War II. Yet perhaps, as Arendt suggests, the ideal victim discourse obscured critical aspects of genocide, violence, and "moral collapse"—to the detriment of our understanding of, and response to, political victimization.

NOTES

1. For an excellent discussion of the struggles Israel faced in legitimizing its actions during the Six-Day War, see Michael Oren's *Six Days of War* (2002). See also Benny Morris's *Righteous Victims*.

2. Lipstadt 1986 (discussed shortly) is one of the staunchest critics of this sort. She interprets the relaxed immigration policies for fleeing Jews as minimal (and cites several pieces of proposed but defeated legislation to help Jewish children, Hungarian Jews, the creation of "free ports," etc.) as evidence that Roosevelt did not do enough. Further, she is critical of the approach of "victory as the best rescue." She argues that rescue attempts even before/short of victory were an option that the Roosevelt administration ignored. However, for our purposes here, and as will be shown shortly, as critical as Lipstadt is regarding the response of the international community, the reasons she articulates for this inadequate response do not suggest that the international community was unwilling to see Jews as innocent victims.

3. Such a statement is supported by the fact that many of Roosevelt's speeches in 1940 focused on articulating the Nazi problem as an American problem, not on trying to convince the American public that Nazis were cruelly detaining and killing innocent Jews.

4. Again, strong arguments can be made that many factors did contribute to slow or delayed responses, but the point here is simply that it was not because of a concern that perhaps the Jews were provoking genocide, or an assessment of the situation as some sort of a civil war where all sides were committing atrocities against one another.

5. This is not to suggest that Jewish scholarship completely ignored the Holocaust prior to the 1960s, though during the 1960s widespread attention to narrating the Holocaust from the Jewish perspective began. For earlier examples of Jewish scholarship engaging the Holocaust, see Eli Wiesel's *Night* (published in 1956 in Yiddish; 1969 in English), and Primo Levi's *Survival in Auschwitz* (originally published in Italian in 1947; 1961 in English).

6. I expand on the nature of this role shortly.

7. Arendt herself only briefly considers why some individuals may be able to act morally in a morally collapsed society. Critics of Arendt often question this, particularly in understanding the true pervasiveness of the "banality of evil," but it remains an underdeveloped topic in Arendt's scholarship. See Arendt 2003, 44, for more.

5

Theorizing a Complex Political Victim

To reach "beyond" the politics of good and evil is not to liquidate ethics but to become ashamed of the transcendalization of conventional morality. It is to subject morality to strip searches. (Connolly 1993, 366)

This chapter puts forth a theory of the complex political victim. The constellation of simplicity and innocence that dominates the ideal political victim identity will be fractured so that critical questions about the complex processes of victimization and identity can be asked—questions that thus far have either gone unasked, or when asked have been understood as attacks on the victim. With such negative outcomes stemming from discussions of complex victims, one might concede that such a discussion is simply too volatile or potentially damaging to occur. But, as suggested in the introduction, there are compelling reasons that the complex political victim must be theorized. First, without an image of the complex political victim, there are many individuals and/or groups that we may be unable to recognize as victims, which may lead to a failure to act to decrease the unwarranted harm being inflicted upon them. Second, without a discourse of the complex victim, policies of response and assistance may be too narrowly conceived and fail to engage and assist this particular sort of victim, leaving her without aid, healing, and justice. Last, failing to account for these complex political victims may decrease the chance for a stable and long-term peace.

A theory of the complex political victim begins with articulating why even poststructural theorists, with their interest in "deconstructing what is assumed to be given," have not engaged in a sustained theorization of the political victim. Following this is a theorization of the complex political victim. At this point we can address two critical questions: Can such a complex victim still be considered a victim, and ought they be? Finally, what might it mean to use a theory of the complex political victim in the policy realm? Though this question is more fully answered in the case studies on Bosnia and South Africa, we must begin to think about the challenges of incorporating into the highly charged political space of peacebuilding such a radically different understanding of the victim.

POSTSTRUCTURALISM AND THEORIZING THE COMPLEX POLITICAL VICTIM

Poststructuralist conceptions of identity across disciplines reject a reductionist conception of identity. Poststructuralism challenges the idea that we can "essentialize" the characteristics of a signifier such as victim, woman, Jew. Moya (2000), in discussing concerns with essentialist identities in general, articulates the primary thrusts of this critique.

> The first problem with essentialist conceptions of identity that critics point to is the tendency to posit one aspect of identity (say, gender) as the sole cause or determinant constituting the social meanings of an individual's experience.... The instability and internal heterogeneity of identity categories (such as gender) have prompted critics of identity to point to a range of additional problems. They remind us that insofar as every woman differs from every other woman in more or less significant ways, it is impossible to determine the (racial, class, cultural, etc.) identity of the "authentic woman" and thus to unify different women under the signifier "woman."... This difficulty, in turn, gives rise to a variety of political predicaments: if no one woman can know the experiences of all women, on what authority can she speak "as a woman"? (Moya 2000, introduction)[1]

Poststructuralism challenges both the theoretical defense of essentialist identities as well as their political efficacy. As such, it would challenge both the idea of a singular experience of "victim" as well as a politics designed to recognize and assist this "victim." While deconstructing the givenness of the victim identity and the process of political victimization is in accordance with the basic tenants of poststructuralism, reclaiming the concept of a "victim identity" and theorizing this identity is less in line with poststructuralism.[2] There is a deep skepticism of the essentialism of categorical signifiers that dissuades many poststructural theorists from retheorizing these categorical signifiers, assuming such efforts are doomed to reproduce essentialisms.

Second, poststructural theorists may not have constructed an image of the complex political victim because of their methodological approach. While there is no singular methodological approach in poststructuralist theory, Milliken (2001) does flesh out the basic parameters of such research in international relations. For poststructuralists it is important to

> explain how a discourse produces this world: how it selectively constitutes some and not others as "privileged storytellers... to whom narrative authority... is granted," how it renders logical and proper certain policies by authorities and in the implementation of those policies shapes and changes people's modes and conditions of living, and how it comes to be dispersed beyond authorized subjects to make up common sense for many in everyday society. (Milliken 2001, 145, incorporating arguments by Campbell 1998)

But beyond explanation, Milliken highlights that discourse analysis, as a methodology, also has an inherent normative project of change.

> [D]iscourse analysis. . . has clear political and ethical significance: in explaining discourse productivity scholars can potentially denaturalize dominant forms of knowledge and expose to critical questioning the practices they enable. (Milliken 2001, 145).[3]

We can see an example of this sort of discourse analysis in the work of international relations scholar David Campbell. In *National Deconstruction*, Campbell (1998) challenges the discourse of the Bosnian conflict as one of "intractable ethnic conflict." Campbell critiques the dominant discourse of identity, ethnicity, and violence in Bosnia, opening up the possibility of a different understanding of ethnic identity, and indeed, the nature of the Bosnian conflict. The "political and ethical significance" of which Milliken speaks is explicit in the work of Campbell: by denaturalizing a particular discourse of ethnicity, identity, and conflict, he suggests previously unrecognized ethical considerations for the international community and is poised to criticize the politics of intervention as predicated on an "impoverished discourse of identity politics."

Having established these basic parameters of a method, we may continue to use Campbell's work to highlight an additional feature of such a methodology. In his work, Campbell deconstructs the discourse of ethnicity and identity in order to show how it may be thought to produce conflict, particularly in the context of sovereignty and contested territory. He presents a nuanced and rich narrative of the performativity of this discourse in shaping the Bosnian conflict. However, it should be noted that the object of deconstruction (the discourse on ethnicity and identity) is considered primarily as it relates to issues of conflict, violence, and state and territory. Certainly, a discourse on ethnicity and identity also constructs other relationships and identities unrelated to one's role in conflict. Campbell spends little time on the way the discourse of ethnicity and identity influences these nonconflict factors, which is understandable given that this deconstruction has specific instrumental purposes, namely to better understand how the Bosnian conflict came to be and what sorts of politics of peace were enabled by this discourse.

In focusing on how a discourse constructs one set of problems (for example, ethnicized conflict), it is likely that the critiques of this discourse will be focused on how the dominant discourse must be changed in order not to produce that particular problem (violent conflict). Campbell demonstrates convincingly that the dominant discourse on ethnicity, identity, and violence does not provide adequate politics for the resolution of the Bosnian conflict. From such a critical perspective, he suggests constructing a new discourse on ethnicity and identity that would allow for a more effective politics of peacebuilding in Bosnia. What this sort of discourse analysis may not adequately consider is how this "new" discourse on ethnicity, identity, and the state also constructs identities and relationships outside the sphere of conflict, statehood, and ethnic and political identity.

Arguably there is a tendency in this type of deconstructive methodology to artificially isolate the performativity of a discourse to allow a more focused, instrumental critique of a particular discourse. Why might this matter in regards to a discourse of political victimization? When using such an approach with a discourse of political victimization, it is considerably easier to retain a simple conceptualization of the victim—her identity as one who suffers and her interests in ending this suffering. This is because we are only looking at the victimizing discourse as it constructs the victim identity; put another way, we are only considering the discourse as a victimizing one and not considering the other manners in which this discourse constructs other identities and other relations. For instance, if we take the discourse of ethnicity, nationalism, and sovereignty that Campbell argues contributes to the victimization of Bosnian Muslims and see this only as a discourse of political victimization, we can retain a simple conception of the identity of Bosnian Muslims. As "victims" in this discourse they are presumably interested in ending their victimization, in contesting this discourse insofar as it is constructing them as victims. Yet deconstructing one discourse, such as a discourse of ethnic nationalism, necessarily disrupts many identities and relations, not just the identity of the victim, and not simply the relation between victim and sources of oppression. Shortly we will explore why this is the case.

What a Deconstructive Approach Shows Us, and What It Doesn't

Campbell's work on Bosnia will be used here again to show precisely what deconstructing victimizing narratives can do—namely, show that there are different/more spaces to resist victimization—and what it often does not do— namely, show how deconstructing the discourse contributing to their political victimization impacts them apart from their identity as victims. Campbell's work on Bosnia was identified as a project meant to denaturalize and deconstruct the discourse of ethnicized conflict that dominated the international community's assessment of the Bosnian conflict:

> [T]his book aims to demonstrate that the settled norms of international society—in particular, the idea that the national community requires the nexus of demarcated territory and fixed national identity—were not only insufficient to enable a response to the Bosnian war, they were complicit in and necessary for the conflict itself. (Campbell 1998, 13)

In the execution of this project, Campbell first demonstrates the dominance of ethnicized understandings of the conflict, particularly within the international community, media, the Serbs, and to a somewhat lesser extent, academe (Campbell 1998, chap. 3). Such a discourse of the conflict was constraining and limiting, not just in what was "seen" in Bosnia, but what solutions were imagined. In particular, Campbell argues that such an ethnicized discourse of conflict, especially in the context of the "nexus of demarcated territory and fixed national identity," led to a policy preference for partition. Campbell further notes that insofar as both the Serbs and the Croats (but not the Bosnian Muslims) shared in this dominant ethnicized discourse of conflict, the peacemakers, in putting forth a policy of partition, were in fact supporting "an alliance of political logic with some of the paramilitaries" (Campbell 1998, 14). Of the solution that resulted from this particular conflict discourse, he notes:

> [T]he international community's structural solutions for Bosnia produced the very ethnicization of politics they later criticized, furthered the nationalist project they ostensibly wanted to contest, and provided no space for nonnationalist formations they professed to support. Through the violence of conceptual determination, the international community legitimized, replicated and extended the violence of ethnic cleansing. (Campbell 1998, 225)

Hence, Campbell is critical of this ethnicized script of the Bosnian conflict because of its dominance, because of the manner in which it narrowly informed policy options, and because of the manner in which it furthered victimization. Despite the dominance of the ethnicized conflict discourse (and ethnicized peace discourse), he does demonstrate that there were important spaces where alternative understandings of the conflict led to different peacebuilding practices. Campbell identifies some Bosnian groups and individuals, often operating under the broad mantle of "civil society," that are in fact problematizing the dominant discourse of the conflict and partition plan; they are engaging in the pursuit of nonnationalist politics and the "rearticulation of nonnationalist space" (Campbell 1998, 236).

This brings us to the first point critical to understanding what a deconstructivist approach can show us about victims. Even in a very strong climate of oppression (for example, not only did Bosnian Muslims suffer tremendously at the hands of the Serbs, but also are being revictimized by a particular dominant discourse of ethnicity and nationalism), there remains space for victim agency and victim resistance. This observation, of course, relates directly to one of the main tenets of poststructural understandings of the social: meaning is never fully sutured, and a discourse may be dominant but it is never uncontestable. Laclau and Mouffe refer to this as the "unfixity of the social"; whether the meaning of conflict or ethnicity, meaning can never be fully "fixed" (Laclau and Mouffe 1985).

Using a deconstructivist approach can demonstrate the "unfixity" of discourses that are victimizing. It can begin to show the spaces, the points that are not quite sutured, where new meanings can emerge, meanings that construct a discourse that is less victimizing. This point is important, because both within peace and conflict scholarship and beyond, some argue that some situations, some discourses, are so oppressive as to offer no space for victim agency and alternatives.[4]

So a deconstructive method demonstrates that there is space for victim agency and possible victim resistance, but such an approach has yet to deeply probe the equally important question of whether victims want to do so. On the surface, this may seem an absurd question, for certainly victims, particularly the sort discussed in this project, are suffering the worst sorts of harm, and it is nearly unimaginable that they could be uninterested in contesting the discourse that enables their victimization. Campbell deals with this issue only briefly in the context of his discussion as to why many in the former Yugoslavia continued to support ethnic parties despite recognizing that this very discourse of ethnicized/territorialized/nationalized identity was what led to such horrific victimization in the first place. He argues that some of this support was tactical and quotes a refugee voter planning to vote for Izetbegovic's party (Muslim party):

> [W]e don't want a Muslim country, but we need to vote SDA to get a state. . . . Later on maybe we can have different parties but now it has to be the SDA or we will be stateless, like the Kurds. (Campbell 1998, 224)

This highlights the potential constraints on victims in challenging the dominant discourse of their victimization (in this case, it may reduce their chance of getting any political representation at all). It helps explain why sometimes political victims cannot afford to access the spaces of agency and resistance, but it does not fully engage the possibility of whether such a victim might actually want to vote nationalist, might want to reify the ethnic/national/territory nexus that contributed to such widespread victimization during the conflict. What if this refugee did "want a Muslim country," even if he was aware of the manner in which reifying this discourse could open up the space for political victimization? Another way of asking this question is: why would a victim knowingly and willingly support a propitious discourse, one that helps create the space for their own potential political victimization?

THE COMPLEX POLITICAL VICTIM: IDENTITY, RELATIONS, AND DISCOURSE

To show the complex political victim, it is necessary to demonstrate that the victim has intrinsic and conflicting wants in relation to the discourse(s) that make space for her victimization. The theory of a complex political victim must go beyond simply highlighting constraints that cause victims to engage in contradictory political behavior (for example, voting along ethnic party lines while recognizing that ethnic nationalism contributes to political victimization). Such a theory must articulate how we could make sense of a political victim who knowingly and freely supports propitious discourses that contribute to the space of her victimization. Developing such a theory requires a careful discussion of how any one discourse helps construct multiple identities within one subject. Even those discourses that might be identified as propitious discourses in relation to political victimization also contribute to the construction of valued identities.

Any one particular discourse, such as ethnicity, does not construct only one relation; it does not constitute only one identity; nor does it only construct political victims. Indeed, a discourse's web of influence, the identities it helps to constitute even in one individual, is considerably more complex. As we will see in reference to the Balkan discourse of ethnicity and the South African discourse of race, certainly these discourses contributed to political victimization, playing a role in the violent rise of Serb nationalism in the case of the Balkans and the emergence of apartheid in South Africa. And as Campbell suggests, deconstructing a discourse *can* change the victim status of those harmed by it, perhaps by disarticulating the ethnicity/nationalism/statehood nexus. However, the consequences of such a strategy are far more expansive in their reach, and as we recognize the diverse identities and relations any one discourse constitutes, the simplicity of the victim and the homogeneity of what we can assume the victim wants, how she will be impacted, is fractured.

The above discussion of identities and discourse allows us to be more precise in describing the victim identity. I have articulated how, precisely, we could conceive of victims wanting the maintenance of the discourse(s) that contribute to their victimization, while still being wholly opposed to the unwarranted harm engendered by a particular relation or identity that emerges from a specific discourse. It is not because an individual wants to be victimized but rather because the victimization is just one relation supported in part by a broader discourse that enables many more relations and many more identities, some of which are of central importance and value to the victim. What these victims may want is the continuation of these discourse(s) because of certain ways in which the discourse constitutes other relations, other contours of identity and existence. *Knowingly continuing a discourse that supports certain forms of victimization cannot be conflated with desiring victimization.* The "desires" are in fact on two different levels; desiring the continuation of the discourse may necessitate the continuation of victimization, but this cannot be understood simply as desiring victimization. The victim constructed above is a *complex* victim—complex because of ambiguities and contradictions surrounding her opinion of and constitution within a particular discourse, not complex because of ambiguities about her position in a particular moment of victimization.[5] The complexity arises because whatever we may identify as a "victimizing discourse" is not just a "victimizing discourse." That is, it does not merely create "victims" and "victimizers"; it may create multiple identities and relations in any given subject. As such, it is difficult to retain a simplistic conception of victim identity, and particularly victim wants in relation to the victimizing discourse. The victim is complex because of the many ways in which she engages and is constituted by a particular discourse.

Adaptive Preferences and Rational Agent Arguments

It would be remiss to continue without giving consideration to two existing theories that account for contradictory behavior of victims and that offer alternate explanations as to why victims might sometimes support the very discourses that contribute to their political victimization.

Adaptive Preferences

Jon Elster, an analytical Marxist, takes seriously the idea that those who are exploited or victimized sometimes justify, rationalize, or generally support the discourse that exploits and victimizes them. Indeed, he is quick to clarify that individuals choose to support the discourse of their victimization *for their own benefit*, and not because it benefits those who victimize them. Elster terms this concept "sour grapes," which can be understood as the devaluation of that which appears unattainable, a shifting of an individual's wants because of a recognition that what the individual "wants" is something that she will never be able to attain. Elster defines "sour grapes" specifically as the "mechanism for dissonance reduction that operates on the preferences by which options are graded" (Elster 1983, 123). This process is a way for victimized individuals to cope with their poor situation, not a purposeful attempt to support a victimized discourse (and those who benefit from it).

> Sour grapes may make people content with what little they can get. This, no doubt, will often be to the benefit of other people, who can get away more easily with exploitation and oppression. But this should not lead one into assuming that resignation generally is induced by those who benefit from it. . . . It is good for the rulers that the subjects are resigned to their situation, but what brings about the resignation—if we are dealing with sour grapes—is that it is good for the subjects. (Elster 1983, 115–16)

Indeed, Elster's subjects are theorized as developing adaptive preferences that allow them to rationalize, justify, and even change their perceptions of the victimizing situation such that the end result includes support for the victimizing discourse. In many ways, this depiction of the victimized may seem similar to the complex political victim, a victimized subject who nonetheless supports the discourse of her victimization. However, two substantial differences must be noted. First, Elster characterizes the support of the victimizing discourse or the "benefits to the oppressor" as "by-products" (Elster 1983, chap. 2). That is, he specifically argues that the support of the victimizing discourse is not intended; rather it is a by-product of the adaptive processes necessary for the subject.[6] As part of a process of dissonance reduction, the victim inadvertently ends up supporting the victimizing discourse. For instance, a Bosnian Muslim votes along ethnic party lines because she has developed a preference for such political representation and has lost hope in any other form of political representation. Inadvertently, this contributes to a political discourse that could once again pave the way for ethnically based political victimization. This differs from the complex political victim in that the complex political victim *intends* to support the discourse of her victimization, in part because of the multiple ways in which it constitutes her identity(ies). Continuing the above example, a Bosnian Muslim might vote along ethnic party lines because she intends to support an ethnicized political environment, perhaps because it contributes to a strong sense of self-worth, cultural uniqueness, or communal history.

A second important difference between the victimized subjects of Elster and the complex political victim relates to the notion of essential preferences. Elster distinguishes between preferences and adaptive preferences.

> In the standard theory of individual or social choice, preferences are taken as given independently of the choice situation. The alternative situation, explored here, [adaptive preferences] is to see preferences as causally shaped by the situation. (Elster 1983, 121)

Elster suggests that individuals are the holders of adaptive preferences—that is, the preferences that have been shaped by the situation and the choices available to them. Hence, when we see an individual supporting a discourse that is victimizing, this may be understood as an adaptive preference; the subject is supporting this discourse because of the relatively few alternatives available.[7] Elster's subjects are presumed to have *adapted* to behave in contradictory ways; there is no presumption of inherent nuance or contradiction within the subject. Indeed, the subject is assumed to be singularly motivated (to dislike victimizing discourses), yet continue her support of a victimizing discourse because she is responding to a set of constructed preferences.[8] Hence, Elster's representation of the subject is ultimately premised on a simple conception of the victim and her preferences, and though the behaviors of Elster's subject may at times mimic the behaviors of the complex political victim, the fundamental composition of these two subjects must be understood as radically different.[9]

Rational Agents

In depicting the complex political victim as a victim who chooses not to deconstruct the discourse that victimizes her because of other benefits, this complex political victim might sound quite a bit like a rational agent. By "rational agent," I am referring to theories that posit the subject as an actor, embedded in a particular social structure, who makes rational calculations and decisions as to how to maximize her happiness. Hence, we might think that the complex political victim is acting as a rational actor, choosing to support the discourse that constitutes her victimization because she has rationally calculated that the benefits of this discourse outweigh the negative effects of victimization.

This would be a serious misunderstanding of the complex political victim. In fact, the complex political victim cannot be thought of as a rational actor maximizing her happiness because she does not have a fixed, unified identity, a stable vantage point from which to make "rational" calculations. True, the complex political victim is a unified subject. But her identity cannot be reduced simply to that of victim, nor does she rank order the various aspects of her identity (victim, mother, worker, etc.). She does not have a *fixed* identity. All of the partial identities within the complex political victim are constantly in flux, moving about within the space of the subject. With such continual internal movement, such juggling of subjectivations, the complex political victim never has a singular point, a singular identity, from which to decide what maximizes her happiness. Hence, the complex political victim cannot be understood as a rational actor; rational decision making requires not just a unified identity, but a fixed one—a characteristic not to be found in the complex political victim.

The Complex Political Victim in Sum

The complex political victim can be understood as a victim who knowingly and purposefully supports certain discourses that contribute to the space of her political victimization. This is neither because she wants to be victimized, nor because she has "given up hope" and resorted to supporting these discourses because of a lack of better options, nor because she has made a "rational choice" to support this discourse. Rather, the complex political victim supports these propitious discourses because they construct her identity in other ways beyond the identity of a victim. Furthermore, these are identities that she values, and she does not want to be undone by the deconstruction of these propitious discourses.

THE COMPLEX POLITICAL VICTIM: STILL A VICTIM?

Given the above discussion, which suggests that victims may at times support the very discourse(s) that create the space for their political victimization, we may rightly ask: Is such a person still a victim? What is meant by invoking the term "victim" in regards to the complex political victim? What theoretical or practical justifications exist for retaining the label of "victim" for such a subject?

In answer to the first question it is useful to conceive of the term "victim" as referring to a position in a particular relation. I am careful to say "position in a particular relation" as opposed to discursive position, as it was just shown that any one individual may occupy multiple positions within a discourse. It is not, then, that Bosnian Muslims are victims in regards to a discourse of ethnic nationalism, rather that they are victims in their relations with the Serbs in the context of a particular period (late 1980s–1990s) of ethnic nationalist politics. Clearly, there are meaningful points at which we can suggest that a subject occupies a position of victimization. The complex political victim is not completely subsumed by this position as a victimized subject; she is not reducible to "victim," as other components of her identity remain. Invoking the term "victim" in regards to the complex political victim signals a context- and relation-specific position, a partial identity that may be one of several identities created by a particular discourse.

Poststructuralism and the Signifier "Victim"

Skeptics (particularly poststructuralists) at this point may rightly wonder, in the midst of recognizing nuance and complexity in identity, why continue to make use of a label like "victim"? Arguably, there are two reasons that the "victim" label merits continued use. First, it is important to separate how a term has been used in the past from the possibilities for its future use. A term such as "victim" may have had an essentialist past, but that does not relegate it to an essentialist future. As Chantal Mouffe argues, the recognition of nonessential identities and the use of nonessential methodologies do not preclude continued use of categorical terms.

> To deny the existence of an a priori, necessary link between subject positions does not mean that there are not constant efforts to establish between them historical, contingent, and variable links. This type of link, which establishes between various positions a contingent, unpredetermined relation is what we designate an "articulation." Even though there is no necessary link between different subject positions, in the field of politics there are always discourses that try to provide an articulation from different standpoints. For that reason every subject position is constituted within an

essentially unstable discursive structure since it is submitted to a variety of articulatory practices that constantly subvert and transform it. This is why there is no subject position whose links with others are definitively assured and, therefore, no social identity that would be fully and permanently acquired. This does not mean, however, that we cannot retain notions like "working class," "men," "women," and "blacks," or other signifiers referring to collective subjects. (Mouffe 1992, 373)

Mouffe continues on to suggest that we can retain these collective signifiers understood as partially fixed identities, discursively and temporally contingent. To use the term "victim" in the context of a discursive theory means that the position of victim is always contingent on a discourse that recognizes a relation of victimization. Turning again to Mouffe, she articulates precisely how these contingent and partial identities, such as victim, can be constructed.

The central issues become: how is "woman" constructed as a category within different discourses? How is sexual difference made a pertinent distinction in social relations? And how are relations of subordination constructed through such a distinction? The whole false dilemma of equality versus difference is exploded since we no longer have a homogenous identity "woman" facing another homogenous entity "man," but a multiplicity of social relations in which sexual difference is always constructed in very diverse ways and where the struggle against subordination has to be visualized in specific and differential forms. (Mouffe 1992, 373)

Mouffe has made the above argument to counter a strong tendency in the poststructural tradition which suggests that categorical signifiers and labels must by abandoned in order to achieve a discursive understanding of identity. Speaking of the complex political victim is not to reference an always-there, universal identity; it is to refer to a meaningful concept—a concept which suggests that when an individual or group is engaged in relations in which they are subjugated, and further in relations constituted by a discourse(s), it is useful to see this individual or group as victimized.

Second, the "victim" label ought to be retained because of its crucial role in motivating the international community to take action against acts of unwarranted harm. Indeed, this project is critical of the particular image of the victim that motivates the response of the international community (the ideal victim), *not* the fact that victims motivate a response from the international community. Such an argument is an instrumental argument. Historically, images of the victim have motivated recognition and assistance from the international community, and images of the victim will likely continue to do so. Hence, theorizing the complexity of victimization ought not do away with the victim identity altogether. It is firmly and rightly entrenched as a signal to the international community, but should be better theorized to allow for more ethical and effective practices of victim recognition and response.

A Caveat about Overuse

The above arguments defended the continued use of the term "victim," suggesting that even when victims are complex we can and should continue to see them as victims. But if, by introducing the concept of the complex political victim, we are expanding the population that we can recognize as victims, must we be concerned about overusing the term? That is, insofar as the complex political victim remains a victim because of her victimized position in some relation (and not necessarily her innocence), we would be able to see, for example, Eichmann as a victim. This is because of his relation to the "banality of evil," the denial of his independent human faculty even while it is also clear that he is an active participant in the discourse and acts of Nazism. So how do scholars, or the international community, know when to invoke the term "victim"? How can we make meaningful distinctions between who deserves to be recognized as a victim, absent their matching the stereotypical image of the ideal victim?

Unfortunately there is no one simple answer. However, some measure of guidance may be found in making a conscious effort to identify what types of victimization the international community deems most critical. That is to say, rather than trying to use some criteria such as innocence, purity, or lack of responsibility to determine who is a victim (and who deserves assistance), the international community could instead focus on prioritizing the types of victimization that most demand attention (genocide, for instance). In so doing, it would be possible to prioritize our responses to victimization rather than being paralyzed by the sea of victims who could potentially emerge, were the international community to seriously embrace a notion of complex political victimization. Certainly the development of such norms would not be without contest; however, it would afford an opportunity to move away from the unrealistic and ineffective dialectic of innocence and responsibility in recognizing and responding to victims.

Undoubtedly the issue of "capabilities" will continue to help define the international community's response to political victimization as well. All policy options are obviously constrained by the resources and abilities of the international community, and this consideration necessarily interacts with whatever "norms" of victimization discourse exist within the international community. In other words, if the international community decides to prioritize genocidal victimization, this norm emerges in part because the international community envisions itself as having some capabilities to effectively identify and respond to victims of genocide (that is, the legal authority to try the architects of genocide, a UN Convention that supports intervention, a high level of international political will to stop genocide, etc.).

Between the development of international norms prioritizing the recognition and assistance of certain types of political victims and the constraints of the international community's capabilities, there are real barriers to the "overuse" of the term "political victim." Neither of these constraints, however, directly addresses the ethical significance of recognizing so many complex political victims. While this project advances the argument that it is ethically preferable to recognize an expanded set of victims, there will undoubtedly remain those who suggest that such a tactic is nothing more than the watering down of real victimization, the victimization of the pure and the innocent. But as has been articulated throughout this volume, the advancement of a victim identity that hinges on a nearly unreachable standard of innocence and purity seems a deeper ethical transgression than recognizing the complexity and nuance of all people, even as they suffer the injustice of political victimization.

BEGINNING TO CONSIDER THE COMPLEX VICTIM IN THE POLITICAL

After having established how a complex political victim can be understood as a victim and why we can and should still make use of the concept of "victim," it is necessary to consider seriously how the complex political victim will function in the political. Specifically, how will the international community recognize political victims if their identity as victim is one of many identities? What happens when we can no longer look for "women and children" or "innocence" as a stand-in for political victims? What tools and strategies must the international community have in order to recognize complex political victims? This is a serious concern, particularly in this book, which is in part motivated by a desire to expand our ability to recognize victims. If the international community cannot see the complex political victim as a victim, how can we expect the emergence of policies to assist these victims?

In order to see these complex political victims, the international community must adopt a two-part strategy. First, it will be necessary to abandon the reliance on a familiar set of images as the sole means of recognizing victims. The international community simply cannot rely exclusively on images of "women and children" or "innocents" in recognizing political victims; too many legitimate victims will be overlooked, which will be detrimental to both the victims and the prospects for a lasting peace in the aftermath of political victimization. Second, the international community must become more attuned to recognizing relations of victimization—policies of political discrimination, ethnic exclusion, and so on—and recognize and assist those who are harmed by these relations of victimization *regardless of whether that individual fits the familiar image of the victim.* This may mean having to recognize, as a political victim, individuals or groups that do not comfortably fit our familiar images of the innocent and pure victim, but this is a reality of developing an ethical politics of the victim in modern times. The international community will be faced with serious challenges, such as what to do with Bosnian Muslim victims who are deeply supportive of ethnic and religious differentiation, or how we ought to respond to Palestinian victims in light of their election of Hamas. What do we do with propitious discourses given the tangled web they weave, the many identities they construct?

However interesting the complex political victim is theoretically, many of the institutions and practices of the international community are presently incongruous with recognizing and assisting complex political victims. As will be shown in subsequent chapters, institutions and practices ranging from the construction of foreign policy to truth commissions are oftentimes ill-suited in recognizing and assisting the complex political victim. Such an identity is not readily incorporated into foreign policy decisions where there must be a victim and an aggressor, nor does it fit readily into a truth commission where those who have suffered unwarranted harm must assume the totalizing mantle of "victim" in order to participate. These difficulties stem from the fact that the complex political victim is a subject whose victimization is but one component of a diverse self, yet many of the institutions and practices of peacebuilding are premised on the notion of a singular, simplistic subject who is either wholly a victim, or not at all. The challenge of recognizing such a complex identity in the political space of peacebuilding is not underestimated by this project. Though as subsequent chapters show, it is not an insurmountable challenge; there is space within peacebuilding institutions and practices to recognize and incorporate the complex political victim. And the very practice of continuing to articulate political victims as nuanced and complex will further challenge the dominance of the simple image of the victim and perhaps allow for even more strategies to recognize and assist political victims. These challenges to the simple political victim discourse must in and of themselves be understood as critical steps in recognizing and assisting the complex political victim.

CONCLUSION

This chapter has developed a theory of the complex political victim. The complex political victim is a victim who does not want to suffer unwarranted harm. However, the complex political victim may knowingly and freely contribute to her victimization by supporting propitious discourses that construct the space of her political victimization. Such a victim is intrinsically complex and may behave in contradictory political ways. Such a victim may not play the role of the stereotypical ideal victim and certainly may not appear as a "moral beacon." She may not reject every propitious discourse that contributes to her victimization. Yet she remains a victim suffering unwarranted harm, and ought to be recognized and assisted as a victim. Freeing the victim identity from its past simplicity is no doubt a radical departure from earlier victimization discourses that posited the victim as an innocent and uncomplicated subject. The challenges of this task, recognizing complexity yet retaining the victim status, will become apparent in the following chapter when examining the case of the Bosnian Muslims. Through this case it is possible to see just how difficult, yet critical, it is to grant victim status when flooded with images of complexity.

NOTES

1. Moya (2000) continues a further and well-developed summation of poststructural concerns with the concept of identity.

2. Though see Moya (2000) for a discussion of a limited and emerging interest in reclaiming the concept of "identity" as an object of theorization for poststructural theory.

3. Though it should be noted that the inherent normative nature of methodologies is somewhat contested, with Kubalkova, Onuf, and Kowert (1998) emphasizing that poststructuralism is normative primarily in the sense that it deals with norms and rules but is not necessarily inherently a methodology of criticism and emancipation. Jorgenson (2001) also weighs in on this debate noting that poststructural methodologies are inherently interested in change, however there is no inherent predisposition for "progressive" change, or change for the better.

4. Such a characterization could be applied to numerous theoretical perspectives, but as an example one might recognize certain renderings of fascism within peace and conflict studies, or Orthodox Marxism outside peace and conflict studies.

5. At this point, it may appear as if the complex political victim is some sort of a rational agent who chooses to allow her oppression to continue because of some other benefits. This concern is addressed later in the chapter, as refuting this argument requires a discussion of the unification of partial identities—a discussion that follows shortly.

6. It should be noted that Elster discusses how the support of the discourse of exploitation may be both anticipated and desired, yet it is not intended. See Elster (1983, chap. 2) for more.

7. This process can, of course, be occurring simultaneously with the rationalization-and-justification processes characteristic of "sour grapes."

8. For a discussion of some of the other essentialisms of Elster's subjects, see Stephen Cullenberg's *The Falling Rate of Profit* (1994).

9. Arendt wrestles with this idea herself, wondering whether there is any innate independent human faculty that totalitarian discourses obliterate, whether we should view the preferences of people under totalitarian discourses as "adaptive" and in opposition to some innate preference for humanity or not. She ultimately does not resolve this issue, though at times she seems to lean strongly toward rejecting any organic conception of independent human faculty, though it clearly is a guiding normative principle in her work.

6

The Delicate Task of Considering Complex Political Victims

Bosnian Muslims

The previous chapter put forth a theory of the complex political victim, specifically highlighting the multiple ways in which she engages and is constituted by discourses propitious to political victimization. In this chapter, this theory of the victim is used both to analyze and critique the response of the international community to the Bosnian conflict, but also to explore the victimization of Bosnian Muslims in greater depth.

First, I consider what discourse(s) of victimization informed the international community as they responded to the genocide of Bosnian Muslims. Delays in intervention and the ultimate decision to intervene were both premised on a discourse of the ideal victim. For those who departed from depicting Bosnian Muslims as ideal victims, it was often to deny that they were indeed legitimate victims. The theory of the complex political victim is used here to show that though Bosnian Muslim engagement with discourses that led to political victimization were sometimes complex (particularly in regard to the salience of ethnic identity and ideas about the state), they remain legitimate victims nonetheless. A more thorough appreciation of complex political victims would arguably have allowed for a more timely and effective engagement with the conflict. Further, appreciation of the complex political victim is important in considering the healing of the community and the rebuilding of the Bosnian state and the surrounding region. If support of a discourse that constructs identity around ethno-religious affiliations is present both in the Serbian aggressors and the Muslim victims, arguably it is critical to address this issue both in condemning the Serbian aggression and in the healing of Muslims, if a sense of community free from political violence is ever to emerge.

BOSNIA-HERZEGOVINA: BACKGROUND

Nearly all accounts of the Bosnian conflict begin with the unraveling of Yugoslavia and the fall of the Tito regime. Historical tensions between the different ethnic and religious groups within the region can be traced back hundreds of years (including tensions during the Ottoman Empire and World War II); however, the fall of communism clearly pushed the question of Yugoslav identity to the forefront of politics in the late 1980s and early 1990s. Ethnic relations in diverse Bosnia became particularly strained.[1]

> The sense of Bosnianess began to unravel in the latter half of the 1980s, and by 1989 the deterioration of interethnic relations in Bosnia became sufficiently visible to be mentioned in the local press. (Ramet 1996, 243)

As early as the autumn of 1991, Serb military and political leaders were calculating the risks of a military campaign to pursue a "Greater Serbia" through taking Bosnian Muslim and Croat territories and making them "Serbian" (Ramet 1996). Before the end of 1991, Bosnian President Izetbegovic was already asking for international assistance, though his requests were largely ignored, and ultimately the only international "assistance" was an arms embargo against all sides. In early 1992, Bosnia-Herzegovina held an independence referendum, and despite a Serb boycott, independence was declared. The international community recognized the independent state of Bosnia-Herzegovina (Ramet 1996). Almost immediately following the independence referendum, Serb armies moved to occupy Muslim and Croat sections of Bosnia-Herzegovina, and full-scale war began.[2] Reports of atrocities were abundant by the spring of 1992 (although they were slow to reach and be recognized by the West, a fact considered shortly). Serb militias were torturing, killing, and raping Bosnian Muslims, and much of the Bosnian Muslim population that was not immediately killed was forced into concentration camps (Ramet 1996). Reluctantly, the international community became involved; UN troops were sent to protect humanitarian relief, economic sanctions were placed against Serbia, and in October 1992 the Vance-Owen Plan was developed in an attempt to end the fighting and reconstruct the map of Bosnia to decrease ethnic conflict and bring about peace. These international efforts were ultimately ineffective in ending the conflict, and reports of violence, including human rights atrocities, continued into the mid-1990s (Salzman 2000, Ramet 1996, Gutman 1993).

The United States and Europe continued to be intermittently involved in the conflict: pushing for the establishment of a war crimes tribunal as early as 1992, devising multiple peace plans, and eventually engaging militarily against the Serbs (primarily through targeted air strikes carried out by NATO forces). However, by the end of 1994, total deaths continued to rise, with estimates ranging from two hundred thousand to four hundred thousand. Further, another 2.7 million people were refugees (Ramet 1996, 267). The majority of deaths and refugees were among the Bosnian Muslim population, as they were the target of a clearly defined policy of genocide against non-Serbs. The majority of these deaths were civilian deaths (Ramet 1996).

Not until 1995, after forty-three months of civil war, was a tentative peace in Bosnia-Herzegovina reached through the acceptance and implementation of the Dayton Accords. Both the international community and Bosnians recognized the particularly delicate nature of this peace agreement, and the UN "stabilization force" continues to play a large role in maintaining the peace. In 1999, the International Crisis Group reported the following:

> Today Bosnia and Herzegovina has three de facto mono-ethnic entities, three separate armies, three separate police forces, and a national government that exists mostly on paper and operates at the mercy of the entities. Indicted war criminals remain at large and political power is concentrated largely in the hands of hard-line nationalists determined to obstruct international efforts to advance the peace process. In many areas, local political leaders have joined forces with police and local extremists to prevent refugees from returning to their pre-war homes. The effect has been to cement war-time ethnic cleansing and maintain ethnic cleansers in power within mono-ethnic political frameworks. The few successes of Dayton— the Central Bank, a common currency, common license plates, state symbols and customs reforms—are superficial and were imposed by the international community. Indeed the only unqualified success has been the four-year absence of armed conflict. (International Crisis Group 1999, 1)

Up until 2002 the international community was responsible for the design and management of elections, and instrumental in many other government decisions. In 2003 Bosnians held, for the first time since the end of the war, their own elections (though still in the presence of the UN Stabilization Force). And while peace has been maintained in Bosnia for the time being, the results of these elections indicate much ethnic and religious baggage; the only nonnationalist party, the Alliance for Change, has collapsed, and nationalist parties consistently win local, regional, and national elections (Freedom House, 2003). Further, the Office of the High Representative has had to put forth 473 pieces of legislation designed to help build a stable multiethnic democracy, because elected representatives have been unwilling to do so themselves (Freedom House, 2004).

MUSLIM RESPONSIBILITY, CIVIL WAR, AND THE UNCONSTITUTED VICTIM

Much of the Western reluctance to participate meaningfully and effectively in the conflict can be traced to a narrative of the conflict as a "civil war."[3] For many, the conflict was seen as one where all parties are seen as responsible, including the Bosnian Muslims, the victims of genocide. Then-President George H. W. Bush routinely described the conflict as "complex" and "convoluted," resulting from all sides acting upon "age-old animosities" (Gutman 1993, xxxi). The administration crafted a picture of the conflict in which it was a "civil war in which all sides were to blame and all sides were crazy" (Gutman 1993, xxxi). Further, Gutman argues that many Western governments actually borrowed from the Serbian analysis the idea that there was a "moral equivalency between the aggressor and the victim" (Gutman 1993, xxx). One American official characterized the conflict as one in which all sides were "morally equivalent"; the conflict was not of "moral significance" but rather an "acrimonious political divorce" (Cigar 1995, 117). Finally, Cigar notes that

> the role of foreign observers in evaluating the situation in Bosnia-Herzegovina has also been important in influencing policy responses. At times their reactions were not only outright denial that the Muslims were being victimized but even, on occasion, implicit justification for that policy. (Cigar 1995, 113)

At times senior U.S. officials took pains to highlight the "all sides" nature of the conflict. Particularly from the perspective of the Bush administration during the early part of the conflict, there were no easy markers to tell the good from the bad. Indeed even when U.S. State Department spokesman Richard Bucher received reports of Serb-run "detention centers" (which he admitted also engaged in torture and killing), he was quick to note that "we have reports that the Bosnians and Croatians also maintain detention centers" (Power 2002, 272). Here we might consider Canadian General Mackenzie's suggestion that at times the Muslims actually attacked their own people and buildings, and blamed Serbs in an attempt to win international sympathy (Cigar 1995, 94).

It should be noted as well that these tendencies to believe rumor are not only found among Serbs. General Mackenzie's suggestion that Muslims were bombing their own people also can be traced to Serbian propaganda, and indeed was ultimately shown by the UN to be completely unfounded (Cigar 1995, Salzman 2000, Ramet 1996, though see a further discussion below about the controversy of this finding).

The media as well contributed to this early narration of the conflict as a "messy" conflict where all sides were motivated by ancient hatreds and a desire to seek revenge for past atrocities, with authors such as Robert Kaplan popularizing the notion of a bloody and confused conflict where all sides bore responsibility.[4] Some argue that this tendency toward seeing a civil war, where all sides are guilty, dominated the Western intellectual tradition as well.

> [M]any Western intellectuals—despite their curdled indignation at the
> reported atrocities and genocide in Bosnia—have taken some variant of the
> ambivalent position that all sides are equally guilty (specifically the Croats,
> Bosnian Muslims, and Serbs). . . . [I]n contrast to an earlier age when intel-
> lectuals were inclined to choose sides and fight for a cause, the dominant
> disposition of the contemporary intellectual is to be ambivalent in relation
> to the dramatic conflicts that are emerging in the "new world disorder.". . .
> Balance is a necessary quality of intellectual life, except when it comes, as it
> has in the case of much analysis of events in the former Yugoslavia, at the
> cost of confusing victims with aggressors, and the failure to recognize those
> who are the perpetrators of genocide and crimes against humanity. (Cush-
> man and Mestrovic 1996, 5)

Cushman and Mestrovic are indicting the moral relativism of Western
intellectuals and the manner in which it encouraged a discourse of civil war.
Certainly it was not moral relativism but a deep sense of righteousness that
motivated Serbian attempts to "spread responsibility," and indeed this righteousness and desire to spread blame can be seen in the words of Serbian General Mirko Babic. He suggests that particularly in the case of rape, Muslim
women actually "wanted" to be sexually assaulted by Serbian soldiers. He
told a story of Muslim women "enticing" Serbian soldiers to engage in sexually activity, an "enticement" they almost always resisted. Babic describes
Muslim women who continually laundered their "intimate apparel" in full
view of the Serbian soldiers, and frequently discussed "how long it had been
since they had been with a man" (Babic 1993, 43). This attempt to spread
responsibility to the Muslim women can, of course, be dismissed as simply
untrue. I mention this attempt at "spreading responsibility" not because it has
any validity, but rather to be comprehensive in articulating the multitude of ways
in which people (in this case, the Serbs) have tried to put blame elsewhere.

This rhetoric included rumors of the rape of Serbian children ages five to
seven years, the castration of all Serbian men and boys, stories of lions in the
Sarajevo Zoo being fed Serbs, the numerous alleged "lists" full of the names
of Serbs who were to be executed, and finally, references often made to past
instances of Serb victimization, such as during the Tito administration (Stiglmayer
1994, Allen 1996, Cigar 1995, Salzman 2000, Ramet 1996). Indeed, in
numerous interviews with Serb soldiers, leaders, and civilians, the "why" of the
aggression toward Muslims often produces a strikingly scripted answer:
"Muslims want to annihilate Serbs" or "Muslims are raping and killing our
children" (Stiglmayer 1994, Cigar 1995, Salzman 2000). In one particularly
striking example, Stiglmayer interviews a Serbian soldier as to the reasons
behind his participation in rape and murder. He is, in the words of Stiglmayer,
a "very confused man" whose story changes frequently, an individual who
seems quite disconnected from reality. In the telling of his story, the reason

behind his participation remains stable: first, because he was ordered to do so, and second, as sort of a moral justification, he references Muslim atrocities.

> "I had been told that in Sarajevo terrible things are going on. That they have prisons and whorehouses. That they rape little girls from five to seven. That they throw babies and women to the lions in the Sarajevo Zoo." (Cigar 1995, 151)

What is particularly noteworthy about this answer is the vagueness of the source of this information: "I have been told." Further, these same references to rumored Muslim atrocities appear repeatedly in interviews with Serb soldiers and citizens, yet it is impossible to verify these claims. Their origins lay in publicized speeches and documents prepared by Serb leaders in the early 1990s (Salzman 2000, Cigar 1995).

These sorts of attempts at "spreading responsibility" are not conceptually compatible with the complex political victim. Indeed, in spreading responsibility, these narratives were specifically trying to negate the Muslim-as-victim identity. Suggesting a sexually provocative image of Muslim women is an attempt to portray them as manipulative, willing individuals, not as victims. The Serbian rhetoric about atrocities committed against Serbs was, by nearly all accounts, designed to raise Serbian consciousness about their own victimization, and spur retaliation against the perpetrators of Serbian victimization, the Muslims. "Spreading responsibility" through a discourse of civil war was also, in many instances, attempting to negate the dramatic and disturbing image of the Bosnian Muslim as the victim of genocide (see Cigar 1995 for more).

A variation on the spreading-responsibility theme can be seen in those analyses that manipulate the starting date and/or reason for the conflict, such that Muslims are to blame for the triggering event. Some, such as Momcilo Krajisnik, speaker of the Bosnian Parliament, reference ancient thefts of Serbian lands (often reaching back to a time before the Ottoman Empire), and couch the recent Serbian aggression as a justified attempt to grasp the "ethnic space" that has been stolen for generations (Cigar 1995, 63). Others, particularly Western nations, point toward the Bosnian independence vote in 1991 as the "triggering event" and the "original sin." Lord Owen, representing the EU, noted that

> the problem was setting up a dominant Muslim government, since that would cause a civil war. Everyone warned against that. The cause of this war was the disregarding of the wishes of large minorities, the Serbs and the Croatians. Many expected this war, but insisted on recognizing Bosnia-Herzegovina. (Cigar 1995, 39)

Undoubtedly, this sort of attitude influenced decisions such as the arms embargo that denied arms trade with the Serbs, Muslims, and Croats, despite knowledge that the Serbs had vastly greater arms supplies. In shifting the triggering event to 1991, the West largely ignored the vast anti-Muslim rhetoric of the 1980s, and instead treated this conflict as one in which the Muslims could not be seen as victims, but rather should be seen as a foolish nation whose decisions led to a war in which they were not necessarily victims, but rather active and responsible participants.

General Charles Boyd, former deputy commander in chief, U.S. European Command (November 1992–July 1995), wrote a piece for *Foreign Affairs* in which he was quite critical of those who sought to portray Bosnian Muslims as victims. In rebutting this image of the Bosnian Muslims he emphasizes that they too ought to be held responsible for having the goal of being a majority within their state.

> All factions in the former Yugoslavia have pursued the same objective—avoiding minority status in Yugoslavia or any successor state—and all have used the tools most readily available to achieve that end.... [T]heir approach [Bosnian independence vote] was tactically sound and, as a practical matter, the only course available to Bosnia's well-educated but under-armed Muslim plurality if it was to preserve its newly proclaimed independence. (Boyd 1995, 24)

By articulating that all sides had the same aims, Boyd is spreading responsibility across the conflict parties. Even as we may condemn the Serbs for their most horrific atrocities, their "different tactics," all sides are responsible for wanting to be a majority in their state, and this naked goal makes it hard to reconcile any of these parties as pure and legitimate victims.

I discuss these attempts to spread responsibility to highlight the fact that they were not attempts to show that the Muslims were victims who happened to bear some responsibility, but rather to demonstrate that Muslims were not thought of as legitimate victims because they were responsible for the "hatred and cruelty," opportunism, and political ambition that typified the Balkan conflict. This denial of the Muslim as victim can of course be seen most clearly in the Serb propaganda, but is also evidenced by the Western decisions to maintain the arms embargo and delay official recognition of mass atrocities, genocide, prison camps, rape camps, and so forth.

> In order to legitimize nonintervention, we found a face-saving rationale, suitably provided by the stratagem of moral relativism: apportioning blame to all sides became the most convenient device to justify noninvolvement.... [E]verybody was to blame, as a result of "Balkan savagery."... [T]hose Balkan savages are outside the realm of universal human values and perhaps are really inhuman at heart, so peoples in the Balkans do not even deserve the most elementary human rights. Or so the story went. (Conversi 1996, 271)

So long as the narrative was one where Muslims were thought to bear some responsibility, the international community was not morally able (and certainly not compelled) to see them as victims. From the perspective of this book, such a relationship between responsibility and victim identity indicates a reliance on an image of the victim as innocent. As Bosnian Muslims were seen as partially guilty, impure, and certainly not "ideal" (according to widely accepted narratives), it was not possible, nor necessary, to recognize these victims as such.

A VICTIM EMERGES
(BUT NOT A COMPLEX POLITICAL VICTIM)

An element of morality has to be woven into these stories. . . . Life obviously is full of gray areas most of the time. But sometimes in life there are clear examples of black and white. . . . I think during the three-and-a-half-year war in Bosnia, there was a clear aggressor and a clear victim. (Moeller 1999, 261, quoting reporter Samantha Power)

Over time, however, some in the international community did begin to recognize Bosnian Muslims as victims. This recognition of the Muslims as victims was in part due to media accounts that began to show a different picture of the conflict. Starting in August 1992, Roy Gutman began publishing stories in the *Washington Post* and *New York Newsday* that depicted the atrocities occurring in Bosnia. In particular, he awakened international sympathy with his portrayal of widespread and systematic rape (Gutman 1993). One piece, "Like Auschwitz," described the deportation of Muslims in locked train cars, no water or food for days. The language, imagery, and even victim quotes ("we all felt like Jews in the Third Reich") presented a clear picture; Bosnia was the Holocaust of the 1990s, and the Holocaust is "the ultimate metaphor in the dictionary of horrors" (Moeller 1999, 273, quoting Berenbaum). Other media outlets followed suit, and by the fall of 1993, the international community was well informed about the atrocities of the war in Bosnia. For some, particularly the American, European, and Arab public, these images of rape, torture, and murder were sufficient to convince them that the Bosnian Muslims were clearly the "victim" in what had previously been portrayed as a civil war.

The U.S. government also began to change its public discourse of the Balkan conflict, and was increasingly willing to identify the Bosnian Muslims as victims. At a U.S. State Department daily briefing, Nicholas Burns defended actions that many in the international community thought represented "siding with the Muslims," by highlighting the difference between the aggressor and the aggrieved. And though Burns stopped short of invoking the term "victim," he clearly articulates a moral difference between the two parties.

> Let's not forget what the Bosnian Serbs are responsible for. This summer alone the rape of Srebrenica, the fact that if you look at Srebrenica and Zepa combined—when those cities were emptied out by the Bosnian Serbs—over 55,000 people were made homeless and had to seek refuge elsewhere, and many, many thousands of people were killed, and some in very horrifying and brutal ways. These are the people that also produced the marketplace disaster two weeks ago today, and so they now have to bear some responsibility for their actions. That's why NATO and the United Nations have unleashed the bombing against them, and it's very clear what they have to do to end that bombing. They're the responsible ones here, and they can end this very quickly by actions, not just words. (U.S. Department of State Daily Press Briefing, 9/11/95, Nicholas Burns)

The recognition of Bosnian Muslims as victims was also evidenced by the desire of the Clinton administration to lift the arms embargo (a move thought to be beneficial to the severely underarmed Bosnian Muslims). The United States also refused to pressure the Bosnian Muslims to agree to peace settlements that "required the victim to make the bulk of the concessions" (Cigar 1995; see also Ramet 1996).

We should take care in not overstating the case for American recognition of Bosnian Muslims as wholly innocent victims, and though the discourse emerges throughout Clinton's 1992 presidential campaign, and is amplified in response to media coverage of Serb-run concentration camps, some within the administration were not wholly swayed by the "emaciated men behind bars." Secretary of State Warren Christopher argued that Bosnia was "somewhat different than a holocaust. It's been easy to analogize this to the Holocaust, but I never heard of any genocide by the Jews against the Germans" (Christopher testimony before the House Foreign Affairs Committee 5/18/1993). We have already seen Boyd's criticism of the depiction of Bosnian Muslims as innocent victims, and indeed, by 1995 he was deeply opposed to what he identified as the dominant U.S. position of presenting Bosnian Muslims as innocent victims and Serbs as evil, aggressive perpetrators.

> The linchpin of the U.S. approach has been the underinformed notion that this is a war of good versus evil, of aggressor against aggrieved. . . . For some, the war in Bosnia has become a tragedy of proportions that parallel the Holocaust, an example of plain good against stark evil. For these people the Serbs are the forces of darkness, responsible for most if not all of the atrocities, the ethnic cleansing, mass rapes, concentration camps, and indiscriminate killing. . . . [T]he public view of this war has come largely through the eyes of one party, a people, as Rebecca West warned, whose status as victim has been a valuable and jealously protected tool of war. (Boyd 1995, 23–27)

Despite these critics, American foreign policy—particularly public remarks by President Clinton, after 1992–93, and particularly after the massacre at

Srebrenica—suggest at least a greater willingness (if not a full consensus) and desire to see the Bosnian Muslims as victims of genocide, innocent victims, and emaciated and helpless pawns of Serbian aggression.[5]

A willingness to see the Bosnian Muslims as victims was much weaker among European governments.[6] Russia blatantly supported the Serbs, as did Greece (Ramet 1996). Other European countries were less forthcoming in their support of the Serbs, though the heads of state of France and Britain in particular insisted upon seeing the Balkan conflict first as a civil war among "morally equivalent" parties, and only to a much lesser degree an example of genocide. Simms (1996) and Conversi (1996) both argue that the British had a historical preference for the Serbs over the Muslims and had "previously equated victims with perpetrators in the Balkans" (Cushman and Mestrovic 1996, 19). This bias is also evidenced by the contours of the Vance-Owen plan, developed in 1993. This plan was widely recognized as "rewarding the aggressor" (a fact that Canadian General Mackenzie acknowledged without regret), and called for the division of Bosnia-Herzegovina in a manner that would put the Muslims at substantial risk for future victimization (Cigar 1995, Ramet 1996). Nonetheless, Lord Owen himself, speaking on behalf of the EU, strongly encouraged the Muslims to agree to this accord, threatening to cut off humanitarian aid and impose economic sanctions on any party that did not agree. Most strikingly, Owen suggested that any perception of the Muslims as victims would disappear if they refused to agree to this plan. Cigar recounts as follows:

> At the summer 1993 Geneva talks, moreover, Lord Owen threatened President Izetbegovic publicly that if the Muslims continued to fight, they would no longer be recognized as *victims* and the world community would treat them the same way it did the Serbs. (Cigar 1995, 154, emphasis added)[7]

Insofar as the international community began, in a limited sense, to recognize the Bosnian Muslims as victims, it is clear that this identity was contentious.[8] Further, the recognition of Muslims as victims was not due to a conception of the complex political victim. Indeed, those who saw some degree of Muslim responsibility or thought that Bosnian Muslims departed from the "ideal victim" were those most inclined to reject the Muslim claim to the victim identity *because* of this lack of innocence. Rather, for those who did see the Muslims as victims, this was most often due to a visceral exposure to the atrocities of rape, torture, and genocide (via the media)—an exposure so jarring as to negate concerns with responsibility per se, an exposure that was most strongly an impetus to do something, to stop the horror, the genocide, the rape. This is not to suggest that all those who were motivated by the gruesome depiction of genocide in the Balkans avoided any calculation or consideration of responsibility, victim vs. aggressor, and so forth. Rather, these images, this information, led to a decision to override the complex discussions of responsibility and blame that had characterized international response to the Balkans thus far, and rather focus simply on ending the genocide.

As the media began to depict the horrors of the Balkan conflict, as the descriptors "genocide" and "systematic rape" emerged to categorize these events, questions of responsibility were able to fade to the background in part because of the connotations that go along with the victimization scripts of genocide and rape; these images and these scripts supported the notion of the "innocent victim." The case of genocide most frequently referenced in discussions of the Balkan genocide was the Holocaust. President Clinton referenced the Holocaust in discussing the Balkan conflict, and Thatcher drew an explicit parallel between "Milosevic's Serbia" and the "madness of Nazism" (*Wall Street Journal* 5/6/99). Certainly, the genocidal script that emerged out of the Holocaust was one where questions of responsibility were unimportant; the identity of the aggressors (the Nazis) and the victims (Jews) was clear. In drawing on the genocide script, questions of responsibility are answered. Those who are victimized (those whom we see in photos of concentration camps, rape camps, etc.) are assumed to be irresponsible and innocent—ideal victims.

> Comparison of a crisis to the Holocaust is an exercise in moral equivalence. . . . How better to communicate the urgency of a crisis to an audience than to evoke scenes from Auschwitz and Bergen-Belsen? How better to cut through the impenetrable internecine politics of a Bosnia or a Rwanda than by suggesting that the Serbs or the Hutus are the new Nazis and the Bosnian Muslims or the Tutsis are the new Jews? The outlines of a crisis are modeled by such references. (Moeller 1999, 224)

Similar comments can be made about the invocation of the rape script. It is a narrative of victim innocence, and as accounts of systematic rape, often carried out in concentration camps, began to filter into the West, this script helped construct the Bosnian Muslims as innocent victims. As the Bosnian Muslim experience began to be understood (at least by some) as genocide and rape, the identification of victims and aggressors, and the self-evidence of responsibility in this relationship, became apparent.

The Marketplace Bombings: Where Images of the Ideal Victim and Responsibility Get Tangled Again

The dominance of the ideal victim discourse that replaced (for many) the discourse of civil war can be seen through a consideration of the Sarajevo marketplace bombings and the investigations and airstrikes that followed. On February 5, 1994, and again on August 28, 1995, Sarajevo's marketplace was bombed. The February bombing killed sixty-eight, over one hundred were wounded. The August bombing left thirty-three dead, dozens more wounded.

As these attacks targeted Bosnian Muslims, it was of course assumed that the Serbs were responsible. The Serbs had, during the four years of conflict, frequently targeted civilians, and such an attack was fitting with their strategy of aggression toward Muslims. Further, particularly in the case of the United States, the discourse of the conflict in Bosnia was one in which the genocidal acts of the Serbs had clearly delineated the Serbs as the aggressors (and most likely to bomb civilians) and the Bosnian Muslims as vulnerable victims. However, following the February 1994 bombing, and even more significantly following the August 1995 bombing, voices of dissent began to emerge, implicating the Bosnian Muslims in the bombings in an attempt to provoke NATO action against the Serbs. The United States and the UN quickly and strongly dismissed this possibility. UN investigators declared barely one day after the August bombing that the attack was "without a doubt" carried out by the Serbs (Binder 1995). Binder (1995) notes the unusual haste with which this finding was made, particularly in comparison to the investigation that followed the February bombing.

> Similar suspicious were raised following the February 5, 1994, mortar shell explosion that killed sixty-eight Sarajevans in the adjacent Markale marketplace. The origin of that shell was never determined officially. The UN's after-action report in 1994 (also classified) was based on separate examinations of the impact site by eleven artillery specialists over a period of nine days and ran forty-six pages. Gen. Smith's report was based on three hours of on-the-spot investigation and covered only one page. Yet virtually nobody questioned how the blame was assigned this time almost immediately to the Bosnian Serbs. (Binder 1995)

This finding was used to support the next day's action, NATO airstrikes against the Serbs, and the largest show of NATO force in its history.

Despite the quick and decisive UN finding, many other inspectors insisted that there was significant evidence implicating the Bosnians not only in the August attack that led to NATO airstrikes, but in the February attack as well. British, French, Canadian, and Russian artillery inspectors, working under the auspices of the UN noted several technical aspects of the attack that indicated Muslim responsibility. The low level of the mortar trajectory suggested the mortar had been fired from within the Bosnian Muslim area, not from the more distant Serb-controlled areas. The mortar fuse was also unlike those used by the Serbs. Finally, evidence suggested that the Serbs, from their distant position over hilly terrain, would have been unable to see the marketplace or to aim so precisely into the center of the crowd (Binder 1995). Some U.S. inspectors also concurred with these facts implicating Bosnian Muslims, yet the official word from the United States and the UN was a continued commitment to Serbian responsibility.

Weeks after the August marketplace attack and subsequent NATO airstrikes, international headlines suggested that acceptance of Serb responsibility for the attacks was not as widespread or undisputed as the initial UN report had suggested. A sampling of headlines in October and November 1995 include "Bosnian Army Said to Shell Own Territory" (*New York Times*, 11/10/95) and "Serbs Not Guilty of Massacre (*The Sunday Times*, 10/1/95). Each of these pieces quoted several UN inspectors (all unnamed) that stated with certainty that the Bosnian Serbs could not have been responsible for either marketplace bombing. Of course, by this time, NATO had already "bombed the Serbs to the negotiating table," and such calculations of responsibility were largely overshadowed by a push for fruitful negotiations that would result in a stable ceasefire and a move toward peace.

I bring up the specific case of the marketplace bombings to highlight one fact in particular regarding the victim and responsibility. Earlier in the chapter, I sketched how the United States had, by this time, espoused a willingness to identify the Bosnian Muslims as the victims, the Serbs as the aggressors. Such a commitment was less firm from the French and British (and certainly the Russians, though for very different reasons). Once this identification of victim and aggressor had been solidified in the foreign policy discourse of the United States, suggestions of Muslim responsibility, *victim responsibility*, were a threat to the image of the ideal victim and to the moral clarity which by now surrounded the American discourse on the Balkan conflict. The narrative of the evilness of the Serbs and their identification as genocidal aggressors had generated, at least among U.S. foreign policymakers, a need to identify the Bosnian Muslims as innocent victims. Conceiving of possible Bosnian Muslim responsibility for slaughter was incompatible with a discourse of the ideal victim, even when material evidence emerged that suggested the contrary.

There are many indications that the United States had reached a point of exasperation with the Serbs and that the United States was ready to act militarily in accordance with their calculation of Serb aggression and Muslim victimization. Assistant Secretary of State Richard Holbrooke had, just two days prior to the August attack, threatened the Serbs with NATO airstrikes, and interviews with Holbrooke suggest that he had, for some time, been pressing for earlier and more extensive bombing (Binder 1995; *Frontline* interview with Holbrooke 1999). However, the United States had been prevented from acting on this desire in part because of lagging support for such a plan from NATO allies, and also because of Republican congressional reluctance to get involved in a messy, seemingly remote conflict (Holbrooke 1999). When the "tipping point" emerged—the "senseless and horrific" slaughter of civilian marketgoers on the morning of August 28—the United States quickly took action, pushing for, and getting, NATO airstrikes just two days later.

Support for such an attack would undoubtedly have been undermined if there had been serious and immediate suggestions of Bosnian Muslim responsibility. In the words of Sarajevo UN Commander General Mackenzie, "If the Muslims were that conniving, they didn't deserved to be helped" (Conversi 1996, 267). In the confines of a discourse of innocent victimization (the sort of discourse that had, at least from the U.S. perspective, dominated since recognizing genocide three years prior), suggestion of victim responsibility would have undermined the very identity of the Bosnian Muslim victim. As such, it was critical for the United States to silence dissent about the possible Muslim responsibility for the marketplace bombings. To allow such dissent was to allow a possible reframing of the conflict that did not readily suggest a clear victim (Bosnian Muslims) and aggressor (Serbs).

While wrangling over the details of the mortar shells in the marketplace was most immediately about uncovering which side was responsible for the attack, in the broader discourse of the conflict, we can see such disagreements as relating directly to the issue of victim identification. The United States had for three years been concerned that the British and French were unwilling to see the Bosnian Muslims as true victims (recall Lord Owens's qualified use of the term), and the international community was similarly concerned that the United States was too intent on siding with the Bosnian Muslims as the clear victims in the conflict.

In situations like these, the significance of the complex political victim is particularly pronounced. If a discourse of complex political victimization had been available to, and embraced by, the international community, merely highlighting some degree of Bosnian Muslim responsibility would not necessarily have blinded the international community's ability to see them as victims. The United States would perhaps not have felt it necessary to prematurely, and perhaps improperly, find the Serbs guilty of the marketplace bombings, in order to justify NATO airstrikes to punish the aggressors and protect the victims. Similarly, and more importantly, noting that the Bosnian independence vote may have heightened Serbian aggression would not have negated our ability to see Bosnian Muslims as victims; rather we could have seen these victims as complex political victims. Some have even argued (with much controversy) that Bosnian Muslims became determined to maintain the international perception of them as "innocent victims." Former UN Deputy Director of UN Monitors, Carlos Martins Branco, suggested that Bosnian Muslims avoided military resistance even when it would have saved civilians as it would "jeopardize the image of 'victim,' which had been so carefully constructed, and which the Muslims considered vital to maintain" (UN Press Conference, 2005, report on Srebrenica Massacre by Srebrenica Research Group). Even if such a characterization of Bosnian Muslim decision making is only partially true, it demonstrates that it is problematic to have the "ideal victim" be the only image of the victim that persuades and engages the international community insofar as it might encourage conflict parties to actively manipulate their image in the international community in order to receive attention and assistance.

The discussion so far indicates that the international community's reliance on a discourse of the ideal victim initially made it difficult to recognize the Bosnian Muslims as victims, as there was an appreciation (though somewhat false) of the role that the Bosnian Muslims played in the Balkan conflict. Further, a discourse of the ideal made it difficult for the United States and the UN to investigate thoroughly and properly the marketplace bombings. Had the discourse of victimization not relied on a conceptualization of victims as innocent, it is possible that the international community would have recognized the Bosnian Muslims as victims earlier in the conflict and possible that the United States and the UN would have felt less pressure to rush to judgment regarding the marketplace bombings.

Paradoxically, this same conceptualization of the ideal victim ultimately enabled the international community and particularly the United States to see the Bosnian Muslims as victims. When the Bosnian Muslims were seen as victims of genocide and rape, when the Holocaust script was invoked, their status as victims in these narratives compelled many in the international community to dismiss concerns about their responsibility, and about the possibility that this conflict was merely a civil war. The Bosnian Muslim story, much like the Holocaust story, demonstrates that, at times, the ideal victim discourse is critical to either recognizing and assisting victims (in the case of Bosnian Muslims), or rebuilding community (in the case of the Holocaust). However, the Bosnian Muslim story also illustrates how relying on the ideal victim discourse also may lead to an incomplete assessment of the conflict. Further, relying on the ideal victim discourse may lead to political paralysis (for example, by not recognizing a victim, the international community does not feel motivated to act), and such paralysis might very well allow victimization to perpetuate.

RECOGNIZING A COMPLEX POLITICAL VICTIM

Complex political victims engage and are constituted by propitious discourses in multiple, and at times contradictory, ways. In order to articulate a complex political victim in the case of Bosnian Muslims, the following section engages two propitious discourses: the salience of ethno-religious identity and the practice of "othering," and the support for and practice of what Hayden (1996) calls "constitutional nationalism." Both of these discourses are without a doubt propitious in the Balkan conflict and specifically in the genocide of Bosnian Muslims. As such, we could say that Bosnian Muslims were clearly victimized by these discourses. Yet as the following discussion shows, Bosnian Muslims in fact engaged and were constituted by these discourses in multiple ways, and not always as victims. This does not discount the fact that the Bosnian Muslims were victims, but it does support the argument that they were complex political victims.

"Being Muslim the Bosnian Way"

To begin to understand the Bosnian Muslim as a complex political victim, it is critical to consider her engagement with a discourse of ethno-religious identity. In this regard we must recognize that the term "Bosnian Muslim" contains a reference to both a national identity and a religious identity.[9] Bringa (1995) suggests that the best way to conceptualize the "Bosnian Muslim" identity is as an ethno-religious identity—that is, one that is not tied to a particular conception of national identity, but nonetheless is a distinct identity defined by a unique ethnic lineage and specific religious and cultural practices. She examines how the Bosnian term for this ethno-religious identity, *nacija*, is used interchangeably with "faith." But she nonetheless suggests that the term in fact incorporates important ethnic and cultural connotations as well.

> To refer to people of a different ethno-religious background, villagers themselves use interchangeably "someone of a different faith," and "someone of a different *nacija*." . . . [H]owever. . . a religious identity is also a social and cultural identity, and in the Bosnian context has an ethnic aspect, since a person usually "inherits" his or her religious identity from his or her parents, and, above all, from the father who passes on his surname to his children and thus establishes an ethnic identity. (Bringa 1995, 21)

Bringa's analysis suggests that the "Bosnian Muslim" identity is simultaneously about religious beliefs and practices, as well as one's ethnic heritage. However, she is quick to distinguish the Bosnian Muslim reliance on religion to conceptualize their identity: religion over heritage.

> [A] myth of origins was neither part of, nor necessary to, knowing one's origins. This is where the nation-state aspiring, ethnically focused Serbs and Croats differed from the Bosnian Muslims. Among the latter, shared collective identity was not perceived through the idiom of shared blood and a myth of common origins, which is so often invoked in discourses on ethnic or national identity by other European people. (Bringa 1995, 30)

Despite the differing weights of religion and ethnicity, these are both "positive" characteristics; for example, they suggest that one *is* of a particular ethnic lineage, and one *does* hold certain religious beliefs. However, particularly in the context of Bosnia, this identity is also important insofar as it communicates "negatives," that is, what one is not. Bringa argues that these "negatives" of identity, this contrast against what one is not, appear most prominently in the distinction between the daily practices, beliefs, and traditions of the Bosnian Muslims. The following passage articulates the notion of "us and them" in relation to the Catholics, but the pattern of identity and "other" construction holds with the Serbian (Orthodox) community as well.

> In differentiating between themselves and the Catholics, Muslims would emphasize practice or "custom" (*obicaj/adet*). "Custom" ("ours" or "theirs") was a category much invoked in village discourse.... [It is] primarily what people do that defines their membership in a particular *nacija*.... [T]hese practices which defined Muslims as different from non-Muslims were largely religiously and morally based. (Bringa 1995, 81)

Being a "Bosnian Muslim" is, then, both a positive identity and a negative identity; that is, it relies on a differentiation, an "othering" of people of different ethnic origins or religious beliefs.[10] Why, from the perspective of genocidal victimization, might this be important? Kelman (1973) offers some insight into this question as he argues that there are two fundamental, psychosocial steps that must be taken in order for genocide to be committed by "normal people."

> When a group of people is defined entirely in terms of a category to which they belong, and when this category is excluded from the human family, then the moral restraints against killing them are more readily overcome. (Kelman 1973, 49)

The first step is the formation of an "exclusive identity"; next is the process of dehumanizing this identity, and from this widespread killing becomes an acceptable act. The first step is of the greatest interest for this discussion, since it is in the formation of an "exclusive identity" that we might question how, if at all, this exclusive identity built upon existing notions of ethno-religious identity held by Bosnian Muslims (in addition to Serbs and Croats). Arguably, the ethno-religious identity of "Bosnian Muslim" was generally not exclusive, in that Bosnian Muslims did not see themselves as only "Bosnian Muslim," but also frequently cited the difference between being an urban or rural dweller, and at times even referenced their identity as "Yugoslav" (Bringa 1995). However, the primacy of this ethno-religious identity (particularly among rural populations) in influencing major life events (such as marriage, living situations, education, etc.) is apparent (Bringa 1995). That is to say, the ethno-religious identity of "Bosnian Muslim" was rarely their only identity, but it was an identity of primary importance that offered definition and guidance in many life choices. Further, it should be remembered that this identity relied on "othering"—defining *Muslim* choices for spouses, education, and so forth, as opposed to "their choices" (the choices of orthodox Serbs or Catholic Croats).

We must now pose the question: to what extent did this conception of Bosnian Muslim ethno-religious identities contribute to the space for political victimization? The answer to this question is quite complex, as we could never tease out all of the "enabling conditions" for political victimization, much less hope to rank the extent to which they influenced the appearance of genocide. Yet an argument can be made that the Bosnian Muslim identity, insofar as it was maintained as an ethno-religious identity through practices and beliefs of "othering," and insofar as it was an important (though not exclusive) identity, did contribute to the necessary space for political victimization. It provided the fundamentals of a discourse that supported ideas of ethno-religious identity, supported notions of "othering," and supported the importance of these two ideas in major moments of identity definition.

Cognitive Frames of Ethno-Religious Identity and Times of Turmoil

Earlier it was argued how some within the international community held Bosnian Muslims partly responsible for their victimization because of their decision to create a Bosnian state where Serbs were a minority while Bosnians enjoyed a comfortable majority. A more thorough consideration of the Bosnian independence vote is in order, with particular attention to how such a vote, as both a statement of ethno-religious identity and a statement of political identity, might relate to the "othering" that Kelman identifies as critical in the process of political violence and genocide in particular. The early 1990s were a tumultuous time for Yugoslavia. The transition from communism was rife with economic, social, and political upheaval, and the nationalist tendencies long suppressed under Tito began to emerge. Croatia and Slovenia were the first to declare independence from Yugoslavia in 1991. Immediately following these declarations of independence, the Yugoslav army attempted to crush Slovenian independence. Similarly in Croatia, Serbs and Croats began engaging in low-level violence as the Serbs did not support an independent Croatia (particularly because of the significant Serb population within Croat territory). In a preemptive effort to halt the further breakup of Yugoslavia, the Serbs began warning the Bosnian Muslims that should they try to create an independent Bosnian republic (in which Serbs would be a minority), they too would be subject to violence. However, the Bosnian government, bolstered by the United States' and Europe's recognition of Slovenia and Croatia as independent states, opted to hold a referendum on the creation of an independent Bosnian state. The referendum passed with overwhelming support. However, it was boycotted by Bosnian Serbs (meaning that, in essence, an overwhelming number of Bosnian Muslims and Croats supported the creation of an independent state). Shortly thereafter, the bloody three-year Bosnian war began.

The argument that I would like to make here is perhaps rather simple, but important in understanding the process of "othering" and the complexity of victimization in Bosnia. Clearly, the early 1990s were a time of resurging nationalism in the former Yugoslavia. The many skirmishes of secession that followed the breakup of Yugoslavia were conflicts about the identity of a people, and the right of those people to engage in self-determination, creating their own independent polities where their cultural, religious, and ethnic identities could dominate (for a good discussion, see Glenny 1996). There are many explanations as to why this previously ethnically diverse state would suddenly find itself breaking off into nationalist enclaves. Oberschall (2000) summarizes some of the ways in which this Yugoslav fracturing has been explained, including a resurgence of primordial ethnic identities, instrumental manipulation of national and ethnic identities, elite manipulation of the salience and meaning of existing ethnic identities, as well as explanations centered on the "security dilemma" that emerges in anarchic political conditions (Oberschall 2000, 983–84). Oberschall (2000) offers his own assessment of why the Yugoslavia situation erupted in the manner that it did and emphasizes that Yugoslavs had two "cognitive frames" regarding ethnic identity.

> Yugoslavs experience ethnic relations through two frames: a normal frame and a crisis frame. People possessed both frames in their minds: in peaceful times the crisis frame was dormant, and in crisis and war the normal frame was suppressed. *Both frames were anchored in private and family experiences, in culture, and in public life.* (Oberschall 2000, 989, emphasis added)

Oberschall (2000) is arguing that Yugoslavs, inclusive of all ethnic and national groups, collectively and individually maintain two frames for processing ethnic relations. These two frames, differentiating ethnic relations in times of peace as opposed to times of conflict, are compatible with the history of Yugoslavia from multiple ethnic perspectives. That is, the Serbs, Croats, and Muslims all have shared experience with violent ethnicity during periods of crisis (both World Wars, for instance) and nonviolent ethnicity during times of peace (for example, Tito's rule). Though Oberschall is not invested in a project of assigning responsibility for the Bosnian war among different ethnic groups (indeed, he only touches on responsibility as it relates to elites and the media), we can see, in his theory of Yugoslav cognitive frames of ethnicity, a space where we might begin to understand how all Bosnians, including the victimized Bosnian Muslims, were participating in a discourse of ethnic identity that was prone to, and accepting of, "othering" at times of crisis.

A few points need clarification. First, logic suggests that we saw such a high (and violent) level of "othering" coming from the Serbs during this time period as they were feeling particularly threatened; the "crisis" was particularly real for them as their population experienced a decline, they ran the risk of being a minority, and so on. It should be noted, however (as Oberschall 2000 does), that this "othering," a flirting with the crisis mode of processing ethnic relations, can be seen across ethnic groups during the early 1990s with some political parties from each of the ethnic groups leaning toward nationalism, language taking on an increasingly differentiated and ethnic character, and so on. It is critical to point out that this "crisis" cognitive frame allowed for political victimization and genocide in Bosnia, and this crisis frame allows for a violent "othering." The practice of maintaining two cognitive frames for processing ethnic relations clearly was, according to Oberschall (2000), widespread among Yugoslavs, reaching back several generations.

Mainstream analyses of the Bosnian genocide generally did not investigate the possibility that Bosnian Muslim discourse may have contributed to the space for their political victimization.[11] As such, the participation of all ethnic groups in a discourse with two cognitive frames for ethnic relations, and the tendency for one of these frames to lead to "othering," was hidden. Even Oberschall (2000), who articulates well the manner in which the crisis-cognitive frame contributed to the genocide in Bosnia, does not explore seriously the issue of how, and by whom, these cognitive frames are maintained. And what does this have to say about the complexity of victimization? These issues are raised as mere questions now, but are revisited in the discussion of postapartheid South Africa, as they are critical when considering the building and maintenance of postvictimization peace.

Constitutional Nationalism

The above arguments are about the social salience of ethno-religious identity but do not address specifically the *political* discourse of ethno-religious identity. In other words, to what extent and in what ways were ethno-religious identities understood to be politically important, and what was the role of the state in regard to ethno-religious identity? Hayden (1992) argues that for all of the parties in Yugoslavia, the period after the death of Tito was a time of rising nationalism. In particular, he argues that the various Yugoslav republics embraced constitutional nationalism, defined as

> a constitutional and legal structure that privileges the members of one ethnically defined nation over other residents in a particular state.... It is a departure... from currently accepted democratic constitutional norms which view the individual citizen as the basic subject of constitutions. (Hayden 1992, 655)

Constitutional nationalism, in privileging and protecting an ethnically defined nation via the state, can be understood as emphasizing the salience of ethno-religious identity in the political. Hayden (1992) argues that all of the Yugoslav republics, in drafting their new constitutions, incorporated this idea of constitutional nationalism into their state architecture, though in different ways. A passage from Hayden illustrates precisely the changing nature of the Bosnian constitution and state architecture:

> Until late 1992, constitutions in Bosnia-Herzegovina did not reflect consti-
> tutional nationalism. The 1974 constitution stressed the equality of the
> constituent nations of Bosnia-Herzegovina (that is, articles 1, 2, 3). How-
> ever, after 1989 the politics of the republic were driven by the same nation-
> alist forces that dismembered Yugoslavia. Thus the result of the 1990 elec-
> tions read like a census of the republic's national groups, with nationalist
> parties of the three major groups taking 80 percent of the vote in propor-
> tions reflecting their percentages of the population. While the leaders of the
> groups agreed to share power, at the level of each *opstina* the victorious
> party of the majority ethnic group took absolute control over local govern-
> ment, purging all not of their nation. At the republican level, agreement of
> all three major parties would have been necessary to enact a new constitu-
> tion, but this could not be achieved and no constitution could be adopted.
> In October 1991 the Serbian Democratic Party's representatives walked out
> of the Bosnia and Herzegovina parliament in protest over the agreement
> of the Muslim and Croat parties to vote to proclaim the sovereignty of
> the republic. After that walkout Bosnia and Herzegovina was in the
> same constitutional position as the Socialist Federal Republic of Yugo-
> slavia. . . with the same constitutional illegitimacy. (Hayden 1992, 661)

Bosnia, then, suffered from a predilection for constitutional nationalism, and particularly after 1989, leaders in Bosnia were committed to the protec-tion of ethno-religious groups and found it impossible to conduct a politics that transcended these group identities. Indeed, Hayden notes that in 1992, the only constitutional document that did not come from or further entrench a politics based on ethnic nationalism was the "Proposed Constitutional Structure for Bosnia and Herzegovina." Despite the appearance in this docu-ment of nonnationalist recommendations, Hayden notes that it was neither representative of, nor effective for, Bosnian politics.

> [T]his document was not drafted by any of the democratically elected lead-
> ers in Bosnia and Herzegovina but rather by the International Conference
> on the Former Yugoslavia. Further, the "Proposed Constitutional Struc-
> ture". . . the proposed (or perhaps wishfully thought) "state" of Bosnia
> Herzegovina could be paralyzed by the refusal of provincial governments
> to honor central authority. (Hayden 1992, 663)

In short, Bosnian political leaders, including Bosnian Muslim political lead-ers, were engaged in and supportive of a discourse of constitutional national-ism. Further, this political embrace of ethno-nationalist politics was instru-mental in securing their authority at the local level, which is of interest for this book precisely because this same discourse of constitutional nationalism may be thought of as propitious to political violence in the Balkans. As such, we may characterize Bosnian Muslims, as a group, as complexly engaged with the discourse of constitutional nationalism.

Implications and Objections

The sections above suggest that Bosnian Muslims, as a group, participate in and are constituted by discourses of ethno-religious identity, the maintenance of two cognitive frames for processing ethnic relations, and their practices of constitutional nationalism. This implies, given the earlier elucidation of the complex political victim, that Bosnian Muslims, as a group, are victims but not necessarily victims that match the image of the "ideal victim." They may not be wholly innocent, pure, and morally superior. Further, none of these arguments contradict the recognition of Bosnian Muslims as legitimate victims. However, in articulating Bosnian Muslim engagement with ethno-religious identity and constitutional nationalism, I am suggesting a form of responsibility for the ensuing political victimization—an argument that certainly might be identified as objectionable if only because of the horrific suffering of the Bosnian Muslims; as such, it is necessary to consider some of the most obvious objections.

First, even if the above argument is true, participating in a discourse that values ethno-religious identity and "othering," or even supporting constitutional nationalism, is a far cry from committing genocide. This is quite true, and certainly, in a discussion of responsibility, we must recognize these differences. Hayden (1996) does in fact recognize these differences, identifying the process of "othering" and the process of genocide and chooses to strongly delineate between the two in terms of responsibility. That is to say, he recognizes how discourses and practices of genocide rely upon the reimagining and redefining of "othering," yet does not hold those engaging in "othering" as responsible—only those who chose to redefine this "othering" to fit a prescription of genocide.

> Patterns of social life—the use of one script instead of another, rates of intermarriage, or rates of the utilization of lexical items—are observable and may often not be congruent with prescriptive views of what such patterns should be. It is this lack of congruence between the present reality of life as lived and the objectification of life as it suddenly must be lived that produces the mortal horrors of ethnic cleansing. (Hayden 1996, 784)

While Hayden recognizes the connection between a discourse of "othering" and its redefinition into genocide, he does not assign responsibility (practical or moral) among participants in both of these discourses. I am suggesting that we should assign at a minimum a level of practical responsibility given the clear linkage between the two. However, the suggestion is only that certain Bosnian Muslim discourses about ethno-religious identity may have contributed to the space necessary for Kelman's "first step"—that is, the distinction between us and them. This is not akin to arguing that their practices of "othering" are comparable to the process of dehumanizing other groups (as the Serbs did), and quite obviously does not negate the moral treatment of humans. Much as Arendt discusses the way in which the Jewish discourse of "us" vs. "them" contributes to the space for large-scale group violence, she is clearly not equating such discursive practices with the actual acts of genocide that these practices facilitated.

A second objection may be that the analysis is in some ways unfair toward the Bosnian Muslim discourse of identity and politics; that is, it assigns some responsibility to this discourse in creating the space for political victimization, without recognizing the fundamental right of self-determination of a people's identity. If Bosnian Muslims choose to define themselves as a distinct ethno-religious group, wishing to solidify this choice politically based on real and legitimate experiences of their own history, is this not their right? Indeed, some even suggest that these practices of "othering" are unavoidable; identity necessarily requires an "other" (see Waever 1996 for a discussion of this assumption). And if this is their "right," or perhaps even unavoidable in the construction of their own identity, is it really fair to see the exercise of this approach as a marker of responsibility? In French's criteria for ascertaining moral responsibility (French 1998), the presence of alternatives is stipulated. In other words if there are no choices to "othering," individuals cannot be held morally responsible for the consequences of this "othering" even if we recognize that it played a causal role.

Can we—ought we—recognize these Bosnian Muslims as complex political victims, diversely engaged with discourses propitious to political victimization and perhaps bearing some responsibility, moral or practical, for their political victimization? At this point it seems that we can answer the first two propositions in the affirmative. Many Bosnian Muslims were diversely engaged with and constituted by discourses propitious to political victimization. And these engagements, including support for salient ethno-religious identities and constitutional nationalism suggest a certain level of practical responsibility. As such, they are not "ideal victims"; as a group they are not simple, innocent, and pure, but rather nuanced and complex, yet their horrid suffering no doubt lends credence to their identification as legitimate victims. Hayden's (1992) account of constitutional nationalism in particular suggests that Bosnian Muslim leadership ought not be characterized as "moral beacons," though nothing thus far has definitively answered the questions as to whether Bosnian

Muslims bear any degree of moral responsibility for their victimization. This hinges on the issue of options. If we assume that all complex political victims are diversely engaged in and constituted by discourses propitious to political victimization, including active support of such discourses, then we might be inclined to say that complex political victims are morally responsible, at least at some level, for their political victimization. This assumes that complex political victims have options; they could decide, for instance, to disengage from ethno-religious "othering" and support of constitutional nationalism. But that is precisely the paradox of complex political victims: these very same "discourses propitious to political victimization" are also constituting these victims as members of a culture, valued individuals, viable political actors, and the like.

And while we could suggest that there are always other ways in which to ensure a sense of cultural community, self-worth, and political presence, we must also recognize that accessing these other discourses may not be easy without significant individual and community cost. This is not to suggest that complex political victims ought rarely be held morally responsible for not disengaging from discourses propitious to political victimization on account of it being "too hard," but rather a caution against rashly assuming that complex political victims are morally responsible because of their complex engagement with discourses propitious to political victimization. Further, the calculation of the moral responsibility of complex political victims benefits from an appreciation of context. Obviously not all discourses propitious to political victimization are the same (for instance, promoting a strong cultural identity is different from advocating a political system of apartheid). In addition, some actors may have more options to disengage from these discourses as opposed to others (for instance, Bosnian Muslim political leadership in the early 1990s had more choice about whether to engage constitutional nationalism as opposed to a rural peasant woman's option to engage a discourse of ethno-religious identity).

To be sure, we must recognize this connection between engagement with discourses propitious to political victimization and victimization not to deny individuals and groups victim status, but to better understand why events such as conflict and genocide occur. Further, we must recognize this connection so that we "see" victims, even when these victims are partaking in belief systems and practices that are contributing to ethnic and religious hatred, political violence, and so on. Importantly, we must recognize that in the healing process, and in the rebuilding of society, we must be able to address these discourses. We must recognize that, in this case, it was not only the Serbs who engaged in discourses of exclusive ethno-religious identity and constitutional nationalism, though they certainly acted on these discourses in a decidedly more aggressive manner. This list of imperatives is not an easy one to enact.

It is relatively easy for both sides to acknowledge one another's pain. Much more difficult—indeed, usually impossible—is shared acknowledgment of who bears the lions' share of responsibility. For if aggressors have their own defense against truth, so do victims. People who believe themselves to be victims of aggression have an understandable incapacity to believe that they too have committed atrocities. Myths of innocence and victimhood are a powerful obstacle in the way of confronting responsibility. (Ignatieff 1997, 176)

Finally, we must recognize that in the Bosnian Muslim healing process, we can expect disgust at the idea of genocide and political victimization, but engagement with some of the discourses that contribute to political victimization, such as exclusive ethno-religious identities or constitutional nationalism, may not be so uniformly despised.[12] In the words of Arendt, abandoning such discourses may be "burdensome." Despite the fact that they helped create space for political victimization, this discourse of the Bosnian Muslim ethno-religious identity and the discourse of constitutional nationalism constitutes much more in Balkan society. It constitutes a history, a culture, a sense of self-worth and self-knowledge. So we cannot expect, nor *should* we expect, that identifying these discourses as propitious to political violence would lead to a dismantling or breaking down of these discourses; the ramifications for identity and society may be too severe. Rather, it becomes important to bring more nuance to the discussion of ethno-religious identity and the state, to understand the many ways in which it constructs or is constructed by identity, social practices, and so on. We cannot fully tease out the "good" and "bad" effects of a particular discourse; that is, it is not a simple matter of analyzing the discourse and "removing" those aspects of it which contributed to the political space necessary for political victimization.

CONCLUSION

No genocide since the Holocaust has been completely black and white, and policymakers have been able to accentuate the grayness and moral ambiguity of each crisis. . . . In Bosnia the Muslim army carried out abuses, too. "All sides" were said to be guilty. (Power 2002, 307)

In the context of the above quote, the goal of this chapter is simple. "Accentuating the grayness" must not lead straight toward a path of "moral ambiguity"; it must not lead to a blindness towards the victim. Moral clarity, the ability to recognize or assist a victim, cannot be possible solely in conflicts of the Holocaust sort. Even when a "black and white" mapping of an episode of political victimization is impossible, it is still critical to be able to identify victims, respond to victims, and incorporate these complex political victims into peace. Were some conceptualization of the complex political victim to have informed the international community during this episode in history, it is possible that we would not have had to wait for the genocide and Holocaust narratives of victimization to replace the civil war narrative of victimization in order to see the Bosnian Muslims as victims. The narrative of genocide, the invocation of the Holocaust, did allow the international community to recognize victims, but victims of a particular sort, and too late for the many victims who died while the conflict was understood as a "civil war." Indeed, we might recall aid worker Tony Land's frustration at having to wait for the Holocaust images of "men behind barbed wire" in order to really motivate international assistance. Further, such narratives at times encouraged hasty assessment of the conflict, and not without consequence (for example, the marketplace bombings and the subsequent NATO bombings). The ideal victim script shaped heavily what the international community "saw" in the Balkan conflict, and I have argued that, at times, it impeded effective political action.

A discourse of the complex political victim might have shaped the postintervention strategies as well. While assessments of group aggression and responsibility would arguably have still played a large role particularly in immediate matters of territory division and war crimes prosecution, a discourse of the complex political victim would have encouraged additional assessments of responsibility for violence within a society. Perhaps a greater effort (and less shame) would have encouraged a discussion of ethno-religious identity practices among all parties. As Bringa (1995) in particular shows regarding ethno-religious identity, the creation and maintenance of the "other" were complex practices within Balkan society. And according to Kelman (1973), precisely this complex process constructs the space necessary for political victimization and genocide. If we are to fully understand political victimization of this sort, it is imperative to more deeply investigate this complex process, even if it contradicts our desire to see particular groups as innocent victims. Rather than giving up a commitment to seeing a particular group such as the Bosnian Muslims as victims or turning a blind eye to their role in the process of othering, we should instead abandon the chain of equivalence between victim and the states of innocence, purity, and moral superiority. In breaking this chain, we are able to continue to see the Bosnian Muslims as victims and investigate the complexities of political victimization. A more nuanced approach to analyzing the victimization of the Bosnian Muslims would have made space for a true unpacking of ethno-religious discourse, how it functions in times of conflict and peace, in private and public spheres, and in the lives of individuals and communities.

Politics in the Balkans are still largely played out along ethno-religious lines that are rife with tension and mistrust. Nationalist parties still fare well in elections, despite significant efforts by the international community to support more moderate, multiethnic parties. Kosovo emerged as another tragic example that ethnic identities, fear, and claims to victim status and attending claims to justice are likely to degenerate into violence. Though it is unlikely that a discourse of the complex political victim could have single-handedly prevented the continuation of such political practices, such victimization, perhaps a discourse of the complex political victim, would have enabled a more substantive consideration of this issue among all in the Balkan community, and in particular highlighted the more subtle ways in which the maintenance of ethno-religious identities and constitutional nationalism among all communities contribute to the political space necessary for political victimization.

NOTES

1. Ethnic demographics of Bosnia as of April 1991; 43.77 percent ethnic Muslim, 31.46 percent Serbs, 17.43 percent Croat (Ramet 1996, 244).

2. My discussion of victims in this chapter is focused on Bosnian Muslims, as they indeed suffered the greatest numbers of deaths/tortures/rapes, and were the explicit targets of Serb policies of genocide. The story of the Croats is a complex one, as they too were at times victimized for being "non-Serb," though throughout much of the war they also allied with the Serbs and attempted to take pieces of Bosnian territory. It was not until late in the war, and after much U.S. prodding, that Croats began to mend fences with the Bosnian Muslims and actually position themselves against the Serbs. My focus on Bosnian Muslim victims is obviously selective; it is not meant to be an exclusive depiction of victimization during this conflict, but rather demonstrative of the way in which a particular group was victimized.

3. Some (including Gutman 1993) argue that this civil war narrative was simply a cover-up for the fact that the West did not want to get involved in another far-flung conflict that could become a quagmire. This issue is considered shortly.

4. Kaplan is the author of *Balkan Ghosts: A Journey through History*, and also wrote during the early 1990s about the Balkans for news media such as the *New York Times* (see, for instance, his "A Reader's Guide to the Balkans," *New York Times Book Review*, 4/18/1993, p. 71).

5. In *Problem from Hell*, Samantha Power presents a somewhat different analysis of the American perception of Bosnian Muslims in the Balkan conflict. She argues mainly that while Clinton began his tenure as president with a clear willingness to see Bosnian Muslims as innocent victims (and this was strengthened by media coverage during/after his election), ultimately the Clinton administration, and particularly Secretary of State Warren Christopher, withdrew their support of this sort of discourse on Bosnian Muslim victimization, with Christopher even going so far as to publicly refute the Holocaust analogy. So in some ways, Power's argument might seem to contradict my arguments about the American willingness to see Bosnian Muslims as innocent victims. However, much of the substance of Power's argument is that the Clinton administration withdrew from this public discourse of the "innocent victim" because of tactical and political pressures that made the "rescue" of these innocent victims difficult. In other words, her arguments don't necessarily suggest a clear change in the sentiments

of the Clinton administration (and certainly the American public remained inflamed for a time after seeing the gruesome media coverage of Bosnian Muslim victimization), but rather that the Clinton administration changed its public discourse about the Bosnian Muslims because it was unwilling to lead a strong military response.

6. It should be made clear that I am referring to European governments at this time, as indeed, much of the public in Europe, like in the United States, was horrified at the media accounts of Muslim victimization, and were inclined to recognize Muslims as victims of genocide, not participants in a civil war. Further, there was significant discord within the governments of France, Britain, and Germany, with outspoken members of the British Parliament vehemently attempting to persuade their leaders and foreign policy representatives that the Muslims were in fact victims of genocide, and should be aided as such (see, for instance, comments made by Michael Foot, member of the British Labour Party).

7. There is a certain irony to this statement, as by many accounts, Lord Owen specifically, and many European governments, never fully recognized the Muslims as victims at all, repeatedly articulating that this conflict was simply a civil war, denying the existence of genocide, etc.

8. For more on who saw the Bosnian Muslims as victims, and who did not, see Ramet (1996).

9. It should be noted that considering "Bosnian" to be a national identity is quite contested, most obviously by the Serbs and Croats, many of whom argue that most "Bosnians" are in fact either Serbs or Croats, but also by those who prefer to recognize the Yugoslav state as the only "real" nationality in the region.

10. This could, of course, be said of many identity constructs, female as to male, African American as to white American, etc. My point here is not that this "othering" is particularly unique (arguably it is integral to most instances of identity formation), but rather to point out the dimensions on which this "othering" occurs for Bosnian Muslims' ethnicity and culture.

11. Again, there are exceptions here, as we have seen in, for instance, Boyd (1995); the following discussion of Hayden (1996) also investigates this issue more thoroughly.

12. Hayden (2005) has an excellent discussion of the continuing discourse of ethnic politics and constitutional nationalism in the former Yugoslavia, particularly as it is being incorporated under the auspices of democracy.

7

Political Practices of the Complex Political Victim

Up until now, I have articulated and advocated for an understanding of complex political victimization primarily to insist that external actors, such as the international community, ought to be better equipped to recognize and respond to complex political victims. But certainly such victims have an agency of their own: the ability to play a role in challenging their victimization and contributing to peace. This chapter, then, is devoted to articulating this agency and to arguing that the practice of self-care and subjectivation is a particularly apt strategy to resist political victimization and to participate in peacebuilding. It offers the complex political victim critical space to work on herself, to resist imposed subjectivations of violence. But further, a practice of caring for the self can provide the complex political victim with a particular and unique energy and knowledge to directly engage in community peacebuilding.

VICTIM AGENCY

How might we understand political victims as possessing agency? Certainly in the situations of political victimization discussed in this project, victimized people are deeply and egregiously stripped of power. In what ways might these political victims still possess some measure of agency, and how might they act to challenge their victimization and contribute to peace? Recent peacebuilding literature has increasingly highlighted the role that victims can and do play in the peacebuilding process. Victims play a central role in truth commissions, can be critical in trials of war criminals, sometimes are cast in the role of "forgiver" in the process of reconciliation, and sometimes form victims' groups to directly influence the peacebuilding process and outcomes. Certainly, then, political victims do possess important agency in the process of peacebuilding.

Another way we might conceive of victim agency is with regard to the particular discourse of political victimization. Political victims may not always or even usually have the ability to change the material reality of their victimization. While at times political victims have been able to revolt against their physical oppression, the realities of political victimization are often such that the possibility of physical resistance is all but extinguished. The sort of agency presented here suggests, however, that victims *can* be powerful agents in reshaping the understanding of the discourse of their victimization, giving to terms like "relocations," "work camps," and "apartheid" new meanings that expose to the world the tremendous political victimization couched in euphemisms of repression. Further, the sort of victim agency emphasized here is the power that victims have to recraft their own identities in a way that resists political victimization and the pressure to conform to the ideal victim image. Political victims then have agency both in terms of the many roles they can play in the postconflict peacebuilding process but also in terms of their ability to foreground and condemn the discourse(s) legitimizing their oppressions.

Taking this idea a bit further, Laclau and Mouffe suggest that discourse exists as a system that "only exists as a partial limitation of a 'surplus of meaning'" (Laclau and Mouffe 1985, 111). While a hegemonic discourse may partially fix and limit meaning, there always exists this "surplus," reflected in the presence of alternative, competing discourses. Even in situations of domination, victimization, and oppression, these discourses can never entirely fix relations and identities. Another way to consider this surplus of space, this ultimate nonfixity, is through the language of tolerance. In the above depiction of the social space, we could say that even a hegemonic discourse creates a social space that is tolerant—that is, a social space that has room for alternative meanings and identities; "we must think that what exists is far from filling all possible spaces" (Foucault 1989, 208). While Laclau and Mouffe suggest that hegemonic discourses strive to finally suture the social space, they argue that they are incapable of doing so; there is always and necessarily tolerance for "subversion" (Laclau and Mouffe 1985).

And even as a hegemonic discourse strives to fix identities, as it strives to create identities such as "ethnic Muslim" as part of a project of political violence, there exists space to challenge these reductionist and fixed identities. Laclau and Mouffe (building on, among others, Althusser) articulate how identity is always overdetermined. To state that identity is overdetermined is to emphasize that many discourses, relations, and practices construct an individual's identity. Even in the presence of a dominating discourse such as Nazism that strives to reduce all those who practice Judaism (or are "ethnically Jewish") to a simple identity of "Jew," even here we must acknowledge the overdetermination of identity. Other relations, other discourses contribute to the identity of the "Jew." Insofar as identity is overdetermined, there exists space to rearticulate identity in ways rejecting the reductionist and simplifying tendencies of, for instance, Nazism.

From this depiction of social space as necessarily tolerant, as containing the space for subversion, and from the depiction of identities as overdetermined, we can imagine individual political practices that both challenge political victimization and may contribute to peace. Because there is always space in the social, individuals are endowed with the ability to engage in practices of individual and discursive difference. Political victimization and the victim identity is discursively constructed, and even in the presence of a hegemonic discourse that justifies, perpetrates, and encourages victimization, there is space within the social to challenge this. What follows is an articulation of how complex political victims can work on themselves to resist their own subjectivation as a victim and to contribute to peace. By articulating some measure of victim agency, I am not dismissing the physical realities of victimization and the way in which some forms of political victimization, such as concentration camps, torture, and so on, sap individuals of the most basic physical resources necessary for life. I am not suggesting that external actors such as the international community have any reduced practical or ethical obligation toward helping political victims. What I am suggesting is simply that (1) many complex political victims retain individual agency, (2) this agency can be used to challenge their victimization on a personal and political level, and (3) this agency is at its best and most effective when combined with support from external actors.

TECHNOLOGIES OF THE SELF: HOW A COMPLEX POLITICAL VICTIM MIGHT WORK ON HERSELF

In Foucault's later work, he develops an interest in what he calls the technologies of the self.[1] Technologies of the self include both an ethical principle that favors the care of the self as well as the practical behaviors of care: self-writing, reflection, nourishment. As he notes, "Taking care of oneself constitutes not only a principle but also a constant practice." Foucault's studies of the technologies of the self include sustained attention to the way in which such self-care was theorized and practiced in ancient Greece as well as early Christianity. He notes how in ancient Greece, taking care of oneself in this manner was considered the way in which one constructed oneself as a free and ethical individual.[2] In ancient Greece, it was through processes such as self-reflection, contemplation, and bodily care that a "new experience of the self" was possible (Foucault 1994b, 233). For Foucault, technologies of the self

> permit individuals to effect by their own means, or with the help of others,
> a certain number of operations on their own bodies and souls, thoughts,
> conduct, and way of being, so as to transform themselves in order to attain
> a certain state of happiness, purity, wisdom, perfection, or immortality.
> (Foucault 1994b, 225)

Foucault further articulates this concern for the self and practice of the self as
very much a physical practice, not simply, or just, a mental approach to self-
subjectivation.

Concern for self always refers to an active political and erotic state.
Epimeleisthai expresses something much more serious than the simple fact of
paying attention. It involves various things: taking pains with one's holding
and one's health. It is always a real activity and not just an attitude. It is used
in reference to the activity of a farmer tending his fields, his cattle, and his
house, or to the job of the king in taking care of his city and citizens, or to the
worship of ancestors or gods, or as a medical term to signify the fact of caring
(Foucault 1994b, 230).[3]

In taking care of the self in this manner, Foucault is discussing the creation
of the self, of an identity—a process of subjectivation. Connolly draws in
Nietzsche in noting that

> these techniques of the self are designed to foster affirmation of the contin-
> gent, incomplete, relational identity interdependent with differences it con-
> tests rather than to discover a transcendental identity waiting to be released
> or to acknowledge obedience to a commanding/designing god. (Connolly
> 1993, 373)

This process of caring for the self is not merely a personal process of subjectivation though, nor is it only a rejection of the idea of a transcendental
identity. The practice of the care of the self has much political resonance and
importance as well; it is the rejection of the politically ascribed identity, the
rejection, in this case, of the identity enabling victimization and the identity of
the ideal victim. Further, Foucault argues that in certain historical periods,
taking care of oneself in this manner, creating an ethical self through reflection
and self-work, was an explicit political principle.

> In the Hellenistic and imperial periods, the Socratic notion of "the care of
> the self" became a common, universal philosophical theme. . . . This theme
> of the care of the self was not abstract advice but a widespread activity, a
> network of obligations and services to the soul. . . . It was an extremely
> widespread activity, and brought about competition between the rhetoriti-
> cians and those who turned toward themselves, particularly over the ques-
> tions of the role of the master. (Foucault 1994b, 240)

Foucault even notes how many in the Hellenistic period suggested that such
an ethical and practical commitment to the self would lead to the creation of

the ideal state. However, here I would like to consider the technologies of the self first, as a process of subjectivation, and second, as a contribution to peace. In regards to political victimization, this means considering the technologies of the self as a way in which victims can begin to subjectify themselves as something other than the reductionist identity that enables their victimization as well as something other than the ideal victim. It further means understanding the rejection of these ascribed political identities as an act of political resistance that contributes to peace. By insisting upon practices of self-subjectivation, by refusing to accept transcendental identities that emerge from a narrow political space, victims are challenging the very legitimacy upon which their victimization is premised and articulating an alternate and nuanced role for their own participation in the peacebuilding process. As such, technologies of the self are understood as political activities because they engage the creation of the self in the context of discourse and power, and second, because they can be theorized as a mode of resistance within a discourse of political victimization.

In Foucault's own writing, he alludes to the manner in which technologies of the self can be seen as a process of subjectivation; indeed, the phrase "to work on oneself" aptly captures the idea that caring for oneself engenders change in oneself (Foucault 1994b, 225). Caring for oneself can even motivate the conscious pursuit of a different self, a self that is more "happy" or "wise" (Foucault 1994b, 225), and he draws a parallel to the way in which discursive modes of domination (for example, his work on sexuality or madness) create "subjectivations" or identities, and the way in which technologies of the self can also be thought of as "technologies of domination. . . the mode of action that an individual exercises upon himself by means of the technologies of the self" (Foucault 1994b, 225). So in the first instance, we can understand technologies of the self as a highly personalized process of subjectivation, an internal and practiced creation of the self. Working on the self is one of the ways in which individual identity is overdetermined.

And yet for Foucault, such practices of subjectivation, individual "technologies of domination," have the potential to be acts of political resistance as well.[4] The internal changes enacted upon the self, the subjectivation of the self through mechanisms of individual domination, can be in resistance to the outward discourses that have, at certain periods of history, dominated processes of subjectivation. As an example, one might consider Foucault's reflections on homosexuality in the modern era. In an interview with *Gai Pied*, he emphasizes the importance of "working on oneself" in order to invent a "manner of being that is still improbable" (Foucault 1994b, 137). When working on oneself, the act of creating a subjectivation that is different than the dominant subjectivation (which in the case of the homosexual was that of a perverse deviant) can be seen as the beginnings of resistance, as the beginning of a sub-version of that which is dominant (and victimizing). Indeed, reflecting upon Campbell's work on Bosnian practices of differences (which were not so much practices of the self but group practices of difference), a similar theme emerges. The conscious effort to work on oneself, to engage in practices of the self that engender a unique subjectivation, can function as a form of resistance. It challenges the "naturalness" of a dominant discourse through individual subjectivations of difference and refutation. Technologies of the self are practices of the self but in the context of other subjectivations (such as that of "Muslim" or "ideal victim") engendered by a dominant discourse, they can be understood as resistance as well.

Subjectivation and Political Resistance

Such a discussion emphasizes subjectivation as an individual, yet highly political practice. It is an inward-looking practice of the self that as a consequence can begin to resist and refute dominant modes of subjectivation. Despite its inward nature as concern with and care of the self, it is still a process that is performed in the social. Subjects do not leave the discursive environment to "work on themselves," but rather their ability to "work on themselves" is contingent upon the discourse in which they are situated.

> ... the subject constitutes itself in an active fashion through practices of the self, these practices are nevertheless not something invented by the individual himself. They are models that he finds in his culture and are proposed, suggested, imposed upon him by his culture, his society, his social group. (Foucault 1994b, 291)

Foucault illustrates how subjects are always contained within a discourse, and even as they try to struggle against it, subjectifying themselves anew and in defiance of the dominant discourse, they nonetheless remain forever engaged. One of the many places where Foucault suggests the impossibility of leaving the "situation" is in his discussion of the politics of the homosexual.[5]

> For instance, being homosexuals, we are in a struggle with the government, and the government is in a struggle with us. When we deal with the government, the struggle, of course is not symmetrical, the power situation is not the same; but we are in the struggle, and the continuation of this struggle can influence the behavior and nonbehavior of the other. ... We are always in this kind of situation. It means that we always have possibilities of changing the situation. *We cannot jump outside the situation.* (Foucault 1994c, 167)

Particularly when subjectivation is engendering a resistance to a dominant discourse of oppression (as it would be in the case of political victims), the very act of resistance, challenging the "asymmetrical relations of power," provides critical space and possibility for such work on the self. In many ways, this conception of resistance, of working on the self, is an incredibly empowering strategy, for on the one hand "asymmetrical relations of power," rather than precluding resistance, actually engender resistance, to the point where Foucault argues that "resistance comes first... power relations must change with the resistance" (Foucault 1994c, 167). Resistance becomes much more than simply saying no, and rather implies the positive construction of a different self with different relations (Foucault 1994c).[6]

This sort of process of subjectivation, as developed by Foucault, has potential as an efficacious strategy for complex political victims to subjectify themselves as something other than political victims, and indeed even something other than the narrow image of the ideal victim. Two characteristics of the practice of these technologies of the self are particularly noteworthy. Both of these issues are mentioned briefly here, but considered in more depth in the context of the South African TRC in the next chapter. First, it is a largely unscripted practice; it does not require, for instance, victims to adopt the subjectivation that emerges from a discourse of the innocent and pure victim in order to escape a subjectivation of victimization. This process of subjectivation rejects a transcendental identity such as "Jew" or "black"—the identity that makes the space for political victimization. But it also suggests rejecting a reductionist form of the "victim" identity insofar as this too is constraining on the development of a nuanced and rich self. Put simply, it allows for resistance against political victimization without having to embrace the identity of the ideal victim. Second, to work on oneself in this manner is a highly personal process; it does not require that one be recognized as an "official" or "legitimate" victim in order to begin these practices of the self and this contribution to peace. And given the difficulty that complex political victims have in being recognized as "legitimate" victims, this characteristic of the care of the self cannot be underestimated. Barring a tremendous change in the dominant discourse of the political victim, it is critical that complex political victims are able to engage in practices to challenge their victimization that is not entirely dependent on the international community granting them "official victim status."

Creating Antagonisms: Politically Informed Spaces of Self-Subjectivation

Despite just stating that one of the benefits of Foucault's understanding of self-care and subjectivation is that it does not require social recognition of a group or individual as victimized, more does need to be said about the victims' understanding of her own victimization. If individuals (victims or otherwise) are to engage in processes of subjectivation that reject social forces of domination and subjectivation, and particularly if they are to understand these practices as *in resistance* to a particular subjectivation, it is reasonable to assume that they must recognize these subjectivations as victimization. In essence, victims must recognize that harm is being done to them and that it is unjust in order for this care of the self, this process of subjectivation, to be understood as challenging victimization and contributing to peace.

In *Hegemony and Socialist Strategy*, Laclau and Mouffe make a distinction between three sorts of unequal power relations. They discuss relations of subordination, relations of oppression, and relations of domination. All are similar in that they refer to relations of power where "one agent is subjected to the decisions of another," where one agent is capable of exercising power over another (Laclau and Mouffe 1985, 151). Yet not all are seen as victimizing, that is, creating an agent who is *conscious of the unwarranted harm she is suffering*. This naming and recognizing of unwarranted harm, the experience of injustice and victimization, does not occur until the relation of subordination becomes a relation of oppression.[7] A relation of oppression, in the words of Laclau and Mouffe, develops when another discourse collides with the first so as to make the relation of subordination be seen and understood as a victimizing and unjust one.

> It is only to the extent that the positive differential character of the subordinated subject position is subverted that the antagonism can emerge. 'Serf', 'slave', and so on do not designate in themselves antagonistic positions; it is only in the terms of a different discursive formation, such as 'the rights inherent to every human being,' that the differential positivity of these categories can be subverted and the subordination constructed as oppression. (Laclau and Mouffe 1985, 154)

Laclau and Mouffe are highlighting the distinction between asymmetrical relations of power (relations of subordination) and their insertion in a discourse that makes these relations of power unjust (relations of oppression). This is a critical distinction, as certainly we would not want to understand all unequal relations of power and the subjectivations that come from them as victimizing. The teacher/student relationship, parent/child relationship, and others are clearly examples of relations of subordination and subjectivation that we do not see as victimizing because our current discourse about education and child-rearing, respectively, legitimize such asymmetrical relations of power and subjectivations and very rarely see such inequalities as victimizing.[8] Laclau and Mouffe articulate clearly that part of the process of seeing the victim is not just recognizing "moments of power asymmetry" but rather recognizing "moments of oppression." And in order to see this victimization, we need to have a discourse that defines the power asymmetries and resultant subjectivations as unjust and infringing upon the rights of individuals.

What must occur to change a "moment of power asymmetry" into a "moment of oppression"? One way of answering this question is by invoking Laclau and Mouffe's concept of an antagonism. An antagonism may be thought of as "the negation of a given order, quite simply, the limit of that order" (Laclau and Mouffe 1985, 126). If a "given order" defines unequal power relations and resultant subjectivations as merely a power asymmetry and not a relation of oppression, an antagonism can serve to challenge this understanding of unequal power. In concrete terms, the discourse of apartheid recognized the asymmetry in power between Afrikaners and black South Africans. It did not deny that blacks had separate and even inferior rights, but this was articulated by apartheid supporters as merely an asymmetry (and one that could be justified) and not as oppressive. The subjectivations of "Afrikan" and "black" while admittedly distinct were not seen as subjectivations of victim and perpetrator *from within the discourse of apartheid*. In order to challenge political victimization under apartheid, it is necessary to introduce an antagonism—to negate the "given order" of apartheid. Laclau and Mouffe argue that the articulation of an antagonism "shows" that for which there was no language in the hegemonic discourse. It shows that apartheid is unjust and that it creates subjectivations of oppressed and oppressor.

The antagonism creates the discursive space necessary to see a victim where previously only an unequal power relation existed, and from this place we can consider the important issue of the motivation to stop victimization. This is a fundamentally different issue than the issue of *ability* to end victimization, though presumably the issue of motivation is at least as important (if not more so) because without the inclination to do so, it really does not matter whether one is capable of ending victimization or not.

Returning to the concept of relations of subordination, it should be remembered that Laclau and Mouffe articulate this relation of power as asymmetrical but not necessarily experiencing it as victimizing. For example, the student who realizes her teacher has a greater ability to exercise power over her than the reverse, but nonetheless feels no unfairness in this situation, does not see herself as a victim. It is reasonable to assume that if she does not feel she is experiencing unwarranted harm, if she does not recognize in herself the identity of a victim, it would be difficult to convince her to engage in any strategy to change the nature of this relation, regardless of its availability. Indeed her first question might logically be, end what victimization? It is interesting to consider that this is precisely the situation in which advocates against sexual violence found themselves, starting a few decades ago. Many women did not feel that, for instance, marital rape was a process of victimization—an asymmetrical relation of power, to be sure, but not a victimizing one. This issue also arises in South Africa as we see in the next chapter. Much of the radical

Africanist movements of the 1970s can be understood as attempts to move from "relation of subordination" (no victim) to a "relation of oppression" (victim).

It is necessary to introduce a limit, to contour and articulate the first relation of power, to create an antagonism that defines a relation of oppression. This creation of an antagonism is necessary in some cases simply to motivate a will to care for the self in a manner that encourages self-subjectivation, and also to understand this process of self-subjectivation as an act of resistance against victimization. The creation of an antagonism allows for the appreciation of injustice, as well as for the contouring of unwarranted harm in the previously indeterminate space of unequal relations. This is not to suggest that the recognition of victimization alone is sufficient to inspire and situate a struggle against it, but rather to highlight the importance of this antagonism in understanding the practice of the care of the self as a practice of resistance.[9]

THE POTENTIAL OF SUBJECTIVATION: THE SELF AND SOCIETY

The practice of caring for oneself, of self-subjectivation, while deeply impacting the individual political victim, contributes primarily to incremental change within the broader social context. Many individuals, over time, can reject ascribed political identities that lead to their victimization as well as the ascribed identity of the "ideal victim." They can work on themselves to create new identities that challenge this double victimization. But could such practices of self-subjectivations do more? Might they form the basis for more direct and obvious—and perhaps more crudely—faster political change and movement toward peace? At the risk of stating the obvious, many of the political victimizations discussed in this project are of the most urgent and horrific sort, the true apex of human suffering. The care of the self is a political process that challenges victimization, but here we are poised, even compelled, to ask in what other ways can the complex political victim, through this care of herself, engage in peacebuilding?

Though the subjectivation of the self occurs within a discursive space, and even depends upon the dominant discourse for practices of resistance and subversion, they are nonetheless retractive in nature; that is, they represent a pulling in, an internalization. These technologies of the self include much reflection, writing, private thinking, and development. Being situated within the social discourse allows for the practice of these technologies of the self, and engagement with forces of social subjectivation creates space in which to work. The very practices are often drawn from the social environment. Yet the actual practice of working on oneself is often conceived of as a more private, inward-looking practice—drawing on and existing in the social, but focused primarily on individual practices and reflection.

Within the work of Foucault, there is evidence of the inward nature of the practice of the technologies of the self. He speaks of "escaping" from the propositions of society, of moving far away from this space and creating anew (Foucault 1994b, 160). Paul Rabinow characterizes Foucault's concern with an ethics of the self as an attempt "not so much to resist but to evade" the dichotomies and fixed identities present in the social (Rabinow 1994, xix). Foucault articulates the historical basis for understanding the care of the self in this inward manner:

> Seneca, Plutarch, and Epictetus urge people to accomplish. . . a kind of turning in place: it has no other end or outcome than to settle into oneself, to "take up residence in oneself" and remain there. The final objective of the conversion is to establish a certain number of relations with oneself. . . to be sovereign over oneself, to exert a perfect mastery over oneself, to be completely "self-possess." (Foucault 1994b, 96)

Deleuze expands upon this notion of subjectivation as a pulling away from dominating power relations, suggesting that for Foucault, this process of working on oneself was in fact about getting out of the trap of power relations.[10]

> What Foucault felt more and more, after the first volume of *The History of Sexuality*, was that he was getting locked in power relations. . . . Foucault wonders how he can cross the line, go beyond the play of forces in its turn. Or are we condemned to conversing with Power, irrespective of whether we're wielding it or being subjected to it? (Deleuze 1990, 98).

It would be incorrect to suggest that the technologies of the self, these processes of self-subjectivation, have been solely conceptualized as an inward-looking, contractionary process. Certainly, it has always been suggested as situated in, and often generated by, a particular moment in the social, perhaps in reaction to ascribed identities. Further, it is doubtful that even Foucault envisions these processes as solely a process of pulling away from dominant discourses and the power relations and subjectivations they engender. Nonetheless, the care of the self, in as much as it is a specifically reflective process, often manifests as a profoundly personal and political moment of construction of the self in the milieu of the social, but not for the social.

We can think of this process of self-care and reflection as a contraction, and indeed there is a great benefit to this sort of contraction. For as much as a contraction is a pulling back, it is also a thickening of that which is contracting. An individual may begin reflecting and writing to remake oneself apart from the dominant discourse and its subjectivations and in doing so is able to develop a more robust, thicker knowledge and identity. And certain interpretations of this thickening of the self through the care of the self explicitly reference how such a process of subjectivation will also thicken and strengthen the broader community. Foucault traces the thought of Alcibiades as recognizing that one "must take care of himself if he meant to attend to others" (and it was also referenced earlier the manner in which the care of the self was at times understood as an explicit principle from which to build an ethical political community). As such, there are two dynamics of motion here: a blooming within the individual and a contraction away from the external subjectivations. Certainly, such themes have a place within peacebuilding activities.

Who Resubjectifies?

Before considering the implications of this "contractionary" characterization of the technologies of the self and how it relates to peacebuilding, it is necessary to take a brief detour to answer the following question: who, or what, is "working on the self"? What entity exactly is retracting from the dominant discourse and its subjectivations in order to remake an identity, to create an ethical self?

The Subject

To begin with, most of the arguments in this chapter have been made via Foucault, a thinker famous for arguing in support of "the death of the subject." Though this is a widely used and misused piece of Foucault's work, it is necessary to lay out clearly that even from the terrain of poststructuralism, there are still beings, selves, capable of engaging in political activities such as self-subjectivation. Though many have argued that Foucault aggressively destroyed the subject as an agent in history, in fact Foucault allows for much individual agency and resistance.[11]

In Robert Strozier's book *Foucault, Subjectivity, and Identity*, Strozier articulates how Foucault recognizes and encourages political resistance at the individual level, all the while refuting the existence of a subject "outside" discourse, positioned uniquely to see and challenge the structures of oppression.

> Foucault reiterates his thesis often: there is no "outside" of power-knowledge; there are no subjects, or rather no useful analysis which focuses on power in subjects, on a Subject prior to discourse, or on "a binary structure with 'dominators' on one side and 'dominated' on the other.". . . Foucault makes a double point: there is no Subject but there are *subjects*. (Strozier 2001, 58–59, emphasis mine)

Applying this concept of subjects to the complex political victim, it is important to understand the complex political victim is a subject in this second sense; not an agent located outside of discourse but rather an agent operating within the constraints of discourse (for example, subjugated) but still capable of acts of resistance. Hence, we can begin to answer the question of "who subjectifies" even further. The "who" is the victim, a subject within discourse who, though inside the discourse, *still has significant abilities to engage in resistance against the victimizing discourse*. This point is mentioned here in order to address specifically the concerns of a contingent of poststructuralists who are troubled by individual resistance owing to their strong commitment to the notion that "everyone" is always within discourse (and hence cannot resist it). I have intended to show here (via Strozier, though similar arguments can be found in Laclau and Mouffe) that even when "everyone" is within discourse we can still conceive of individual agency at the level of the subject. Complex political victims can engage in resistance politics not because they are outside of discourse but rather because they are constituted as subjects *within* discourse.

The Lined Individual and Subjectivation

The composition of the complex political victim has already been discussed in chapter 5, though the discussion here moves toward another aspect of composition—not offered to supplant the previous discussion but rather to further articulate the nature of the complex political victim.

Deleuze's Lined Individual

At numerous points in his work, Deleuze (sometimes in partnership with Guttari) develops the notion of the lined individual.[12] The lined individual suggests that each person comprises different sorts of lines. It is these lines, the way in which they define, contour, and cordon off the self, which constitute the individual. According to Deleuze there are many lines, which, taken together, constitute the individual.

> As individuals and groups we are made of lines, lines that are very diverse in nature. The first type of line (there are many of this type) that forms us is segmentary, or rigidly segmented: family/profession; work/vacation; family/then school/then army/then factory/then retirement. . . . At the same time there are segmented lines that are much more supple, that are somehow molecular. . . . [T]hey trace out small modifications, cause detours, suggest highs or periods of depression, yet they are just as well defined, even govern many irreversible processes. . . . Many things happen along this second type of line, becoming, microbecomings, that don't have the same rhythm as our "history." (Deleuze and Parnet 1983, 69–70)

This passage is an articulation of the two main sorts of lines. The first type of line, the rigid, segmented line, is the sort of demarcating force that has often worked to designate "victim." We see this in many contexts that invoke binaries such as Europeans/barbarians, Afrikaners/blacks, indeed even the evil perpetrator/ideal victim binary.

Poststructuralism, particularly in its use of subjectivation, is much more focused on the second type of line. Deleuze comments particularly on how the making of the individual relates to this second sort of molecular line. He articulates how this line can be folded back upon itself, to make a new individual, an individual who has made and mastered herself.

> [T]his folding of the line is precisely what Foucault eventually comes to call the "process of subjectification" when he begins to examine it directly. . . . [I]t's not enough for force to be exerted on other forces or to suffer the effects of other forces, it has to be exerted upon itself too. . . . That's what subjectification is about: bringing a curve into the line, making it turn back on itself, or making force impinge on itself. (Deleuze 1990, 113)

The concept of the lined individual and the process of subjectivation has been married and explored, most explicitly by Deleuze. However, it seems that there may well be an alternate reading of this marriage, another way to understand the transposition of the process of subjectivation onto the lined individual. In fact, by looking at other places in Deleuze, we can begin to see how subjectivation could be alternately understood.

Subjectivation and the Line of Flight

Turning back to the discussion of line types, one can consider in particular the way in which Deleuze introduces the line of flight. The line of flight is a molecular line, in that it resists binary segmentation. It is a line of possibility, a way to create something new. It is neither derivative from nor directly opposed to any dominant structure. Deleuze and Parnet describe it in the following way,

> [T]here is a third type of line, even stranger still, as if something were carrying us away, through our segments but also across our thresholds, towards an unknown destination, neither foreseeable nor pre-existent. This line, though simple and abstract, is the most complicated and tortuous of all. (Deleuze and Parnet 1983, 70–71)

and later

> . . . of a third [line] which always comes from elsewhere and disrupts the binary nature of the two, no more inscribing itself in their opposition than in their complimentary. It's not a matter of adding a new segment on the line to preceding segments (a third sex, a third class, a third age) but of tracing another line in the middle of the segmentary line, in the middle of its segments, a line that carries them away according to variable speeds in a movement of flight or flow. (Deleuze and Parnet 1983, 82–83)

These depictions of the line of flight, like most throughout Deleuze's work, are rich with images of movement and force. These are not lines that are imposed upon individuals. They are lines that individuals must trace, make, and follow in their departures from the ordinary structures. At other points in his discussion of these lines of flight, Deleuze refers to them as "ruptures," forceful disruptions, breaks, movements and at times the beginning of resistance.[13]

This spirit of movement and force can be captured in a new understanding of subjectivation. If we can understand subjectivation as a folding back of a line, the folding back of power onto power, as Deleuze suggests, then what happens when the object of subjectivation is this line of flight? This certainly is not the simple acceptance of an ascribed identity (that is, as a ruthless perpetrator) nor the simple contestation of this ascribed identity through the adoption of an alternate ascribed identity (that is, as a persecuted victim). What happens when an individual folds back the nonbinary possibilities of her life and remakes her very identity? Doubtless the thickening and contraction occur; it is a fold with all of a fold's attached properties. But consider what is being folded; a trajectory, a force, a flight. And when one folds back a fleeing line there is, captured in the fold, a tremendous tension. Like a loaded spring, the line of flight is folded back, thickening at the fold but also poised to shoot back out, *to reconfront the space beyond the individual*. In this understanding of subjectivation, we can begin to see its additional power as a political strategy in the context of peacebuilding.

Assaults on the Discourse of Victimization and the Outside

For Deleuze, the line of flight, though transversing and at times constituting an individual, also belongs partially to the outside, to the discourse that frames and constitutes or is constituted by the victim.[14] When this line of flight is folded back in, part of the outside, part of the discourse, is also brought in. Drawing heavily on Foucault, he suggests the following:

> If the inside is constituted by the folding of the outside, between them there is a topological relation: the relation to oneself is homologous to the relation with the outside and the two are in contact, through the intermediary of the strata which are relatively external environments (and therefore relatively internal). On the limit of the strata, the whole of the inside finds itself actively present on the outside. (Deleuze 1990, 336)

So this folding of the line of flight, this process of subjectivation, has a special relationship to the outside. Rather than creating a thicker, nonvictim identity that is foreign and removed from the exterior discourse of victimization, this resubjectified individual has intimate attachments to the outside of victimization. The reconstitution of the identity into something other than that which was previously enabling victimization does not preclude a close, knowing relationship with the exterior of victimization. Hence, when considering whether this trapped tension of subjectivation can be effectively used to challenge victimizing discourse, it is important to realize that this subjectified individual is still well placed and well known to victimization. No matter how much one subjectifies and remakes an identity apart from the discourse of victimization, the effects, knowledge, and proximity to this victimization are still near. Rather than being a cause for despair (for example, we haven't lost ethnic violence yet), this proximity and intimacy can be embraced as the perfect release point for the tension and force possessed by the subjectified individual as she emerges as an agent in peacebuilding.

RECONSIDERING SUBJECTIVATION AND THE COMPLEX POLITICAL VICTIM

Why is such an understanding of subjectivation so particularly useful to complex political victims?[15] In particular, this strategy of subjectivation helps aid in our continued ability to "see" these nuanced identities. Subjectivation along the line of flight engages the individual in constructing an identity, even multiple identities. The line of flight and its folding are endeavored to rupture the imposition of binary identities, make space for the development of something "other" than the binary identities that enable political victimization and encourage us to understand it as a process of good vs. evil. This process is one that encourages the experience of many identities and interests, and through the experience of the construction of such identities there is reason to believe that identity will be able to be understood and appreciated in a more nuanced way; we will be more able to *see* the complex political victim.

This is an important benefit of engaging in subjectivation, as it must be remembered that part of the great challenge of the complex political victim, particularly in the context of peacebuilding, is the very act of seeing such an individual as a victim. A process of subjectivation and agency that allows an increased familiarity with such complex identities is critical in aiding complex political victims. By constructing the self in nonbinary ways, it is possible to begin to see others in nonbinary ways. Such processes of subjectivation has the potential to contribute to nuance in political space—a nuance that can stand in resistance to the reductionism that underlies much political violence and, indeed, peacebuilding.

The importance of this process of subjectivation, of this affirmation of nuanced identities, is not lost on Deleuze. Indeed, he articulates clearly that it is not the "end result" of subjectivation that is most sought after; rather it is the process of identity construction in this manner that is so critical. Ideally, subjectivation functions as a model that is ceaselessly set up and that collapses, of a process that cease-lessly extends itself, breaks off, and starts again. . . We invoke one dualism only in order to challenge another. We employ a dualism of models only to arrive at a process which would challenge every model. (Deleuze and Gut-tari 1983, 46–47)

Ending victimization through self-subjectivation is not about the final abol-ishment of victimization and the insertion of a nonvictimizing monism. Rather, it is the process of continual challenge, reflection, and construction, the refutation of monism both as a force of injustice and a force of justice. As shown in the next chapter, it is not the insertion of a simple and absolute rule of law or democracy that will move South Africa away from victimization (though such goals have their place), but most importantly it is the ongoing opportunities for critical reflection, self-care, and practices of difference that have the power to contribute to long-term healing and refutation of South African victimization.

CONCLUSION

This chapter articulated possible practices of the complex political victim. It focused on the care of the self and practices of self-subjectivation as critical opportunities for political victims to both exert agency over their own identity as "victim" and also to use these practices of self-subjectivations as a platform from which to engage in peacebuilding. By rejecting a priori political identi-ties, practices of self-subjectivation contribute to subverting the naturalness and legitimacy of the discourse that supports these identities. But care of the self, when understood as capturing the dynamism and tension of unscripted acts of difference, can also imbue the victim with an energy and direction for sustained and effective engagement during peacebuilding. The resubjectified self also becomes the poised, capable agent, ready to partake in peacebuilding.

While this chapter has provided a sketch of what practices might suit the complex political victim in the process of peacebuilding, it has not endeavored to show the practicalities of subjectivation and self-care. How do victims "work on themselves"? Are certain political or social spaces necessary in order for victims to resubjectify? Which, if any, of our common postconflict tools—from courts to truth commissions to projects of multicultural national-ism—provide space and support for these sorts of political practices? This task is taken up in the following chapter by considering the South African TRC, with particular attention to how it both fostered and limited the use of subjectivation to end victimization and support progress toward peace.

NOTES

1. Nietzsche also is known for his work on the care of the self, and his studies in this area influenced Foucault's discussion of care of the self as well. See Nietzsche's 1968 *Will to Power*.

2. Though see Hadot (1992) in T. Armstrong, *Michel Foucault: Philosopher*, for a different perspective on the care of the self in ancient Greece.

3. *Epimeleisthai* translates to "care of the self."

4. This is not to suggest that Foucault characterized these practices in the context of ancient Greece or early Christianity as acts of resistance. Rather, the idea that I am developing is that technologies of the self, internal subjectivation, can be seen in the context of Foucault's work as an avenue of resistance.

5. Here, the "situation" is the discourse surrounding sexuality.

6. See, in particular, *Social Triumph of the Sexual Will*. (Foucault 1994b)

7. Laclau and Mouffe do not discuss victims, per se. However, their discussion of oppression seems to clearly invoke a notion of the victim—someone who is in a disadvantaged relation of power and who, according to the predominant discourse relating to that power relation (sexual violence, for instance) is recognized as being denied something of which they are deserving (control over their body, for instance). Hence, I take the liberty here of referring to those over whom control is exerted in relations of oppression as victims, as understood in my narrative thus far.

8. The exception, of course, would be when the teacher or parent exercises their power in domains where dominant discourses do suggest that students or children have personal control, such as over their bodies. However, the mere imbalance of power in these relations of subordination is not responsible for creating victims. Victims are created when the exercise of this power extends beyond its discursively defined boundaries.

9. Though throughout this section I have drawn on examples that demonstrate how political victimization must, in some cases, be contoured as victimization (as opposed to, for instance, mere separation of races), this same line of argument applies to articulating the "ideal victim" discourse as itself victimization. If complex political victims are to resist against this double victimization that results from stereotypes of the ideal victim, this too must be articulated as unjust and wrong.

10. Deleuze's comments seemingly refer both to Foucault wanting to get out of the trap of power relations as a point of analytical departure as well as a comment about the actual practice of resubjectivation being about moving away from power relations. It should also be clarified that these comments about "getting away from power relations" are referring only to external power relations—between, for instance, the self and others, for of course the process of subjectivation, as understood both by Foucault and Deleuze, is still importantly about power, the relation of the self to the self, and power over oneself.

11. For arguments suggesting the death of the subject in Foucault (particularly as a sight of resistance), see, for instance, Bove (1986).

12. The clearest discussion of this concept appears in the second half of *On the Line* (a piece he wrote with Claire Parnet) though as with most things Deleuzian, this concept manifests itself repeatedly particularly in his discussion of *becomings* (see Deleuze and Guttari's *A Thousand Plateaus: Capitalism and Schizophrenia*) and in his discussion of *societies of control* (see Deleuze's *Negotiations 1972–1990*).

13. See in particular the discussion of F. Scott Fitzgerald's work in Deleuze and Parnet's chapter in *On the Line*.

14. I am not referring to the Outside, as in beyond discourse, in the way that Laclau and Mouffe do in *Socialist Strategy and Hegemony*. Here, I use the term "outside" to denote (as Deleuze does) what is part of the discourse but separate from the subject (victim) as presently constituted. In other words, a discourse such as capitalism inhabits the outside, the social space in which individuals are constituted, and once constituted as subjects, the mechanisms of this constitution—capitalism, for instance—become this outside. Note that this is not to imply that these discourses are truly Outside anything, but rather that once individual subjects are constituted, these structures appear as the outside, the sight of exploitation. Note that Deleuze also discusses the concept of Outside, in the Laclau and Mouffe sense of beyond discourse, and similarly disagrees with its existence.

15. By focusing on the usefulness of subjectivation for the complex political victim, I in no way am commenting on its lack of usefulness for anyone else.

8

The South African Truth and Reconciliation Commission

Confronting a Victimized People, Victimized Nation

Following decades of apartheid in South Africa, the Truth and Reconciliation Commission (TRC) was created to help the victims of apartheid as well as the nation of South Africa through a process of uncovering truth as a means to reconciliation both individually and nationally. The design and practices of the TRC represent many influences: the political context of negotiated government change, "best practices" from other truth commissions, and the input of political and religious leaders.

This chapter begins by considering the way in which truth commissions, in general, are known for their victim-centered approach. Next, the chapter explores the way in which conceptualizations about the "victim" identity shaped the design and practices of the TRC specifically. Which assumptions were made about the victims of apartheid and their needs in the postapartheid period? Were some victims more readily able to access and benefit from the TRC? Were certain victims excluded because their self-knowledge of their own victimization differed from the image of victimization offered by the TRC? In particular, the case of the TRC demonstrates the political implications of the linkage between victim discourse and institutions of postconflict peacebuilding. It is precisely because the TRC tried so strongly to engage the victim in peacebuilding that it is a rich site to investigate the linkage between victim discourse and the postconflict peacebuilding process.

TRUTH COMMISSIONS AND THE VICTIM

Hayner (2001) defines truth commissions as temporary bodies that focus on past events, investigate a pattern of abuses over a period of time rather than a specific event, conclude their activities with the production of a final report, and finally, are officially sanctioned, authorized, or empowered by the state (Hayner 2001, 14). Truth commissions are also recognized as being victim-centered.

> A fundamental difference between truth commissions and trials is the nature and extent of their attention to victims. . . . [M]ost truth commissions. . . are designed to focus primarily on victims. Although commissions may focus on the involvement of individual perpetrators in abuses, and may receive critical information from reaching out to accused perpetrators and others from within the system of repression, much of their time and attention is focused on victims. They usually take testimony from a broad array of witnesses, victims, and survivors, and consider all of these accounts in analyzing and describing the greater pattern of events. By listening to victims' stories, perhaps holding public hearings, and publishing a report that describes a broad array of experiences of suffering, commissions effectively give victims a public voice and bring their suffering to the awareness of the broader public. (Hayner 2001, 28)

In addition to giving victims a public voice, truth commissions commonly provide victim services. The extent and type of services offered are often dependent on limited funds and the specific needs of victims, but may include reparations (financial or otherwise), formal apologies from perpetrators, the chance to locate and/or bury missing loved ones, and in some instances, access to counseling, medical help, education, and job training.

Further, truth commissions are often thought to contribute to the victim healing process. Participating in a truth commission "allows the victim to unburden herself of the hatred and anger that she has carried for years, freeing her to start the process of forgiveness and healing. . . . [T[he victim is also 'rehumanized'" (Marshall 2000, 22). Hayner notes that "one of the cornerstones of modern-day psychology is the belief that expressing one's feelings, and especially talking out traumatic experiences, is necessary for recovery and psychological health" (Hayner 2001, 134). However, Hayner also notes that what is helpful in healing from general (nonpolitical) trauma is not necessarily true in healing from political trauma. Those who suggest that talking leads to healing are usually making assumptions that do not hold true for truth commissions—namely, that long-term counseling and opportunities to share one's story of victimization are considerably more helpful than the singular instance of storytelling provided by the truth commissions (see also Byrne 2004). The patchwork of literature available on psychological healing and truth commissions suggests, at the very least, that allowing victims to tell their story in a truth commission may only sometimes contribute to healing, and other times it may be ineffective, or worse, lead to retraumatization.[1] Indeed, despite the growing body of literature on truth commissions, there is a disappointingly small amount of work focused specifically on the victim experience (which is particularly interesting given the "victim-centered" conceptual orientation of truth commissions).

> Victim perspectives on truth commissions are sorely lacking in a literature that to date has been relatively uncritical of these proceedings. There is still much for us to learn from and about the experiences of survivors who courageously step forward to participate in such processes. (Byrne 2004, 254).[2]

Despite some controversy over what precisely truth commissions can do for victims (and a lack of significant research to assist in sorting out this controversy) it is critical to recognize that the preexisting "victim-centered" nature of truth commissions makes them an ideal site both to explore the impact of victim discourse on policy, but also, to consider how changes to victim discourse, the introduction of a discourse of the complex political victim, could directly influence policy and postvictimization community peace and reconciliation.

THE SOUTH AFRICAN TRC: BACKGROUND

The South African TRC was formally legislated in July 1995, following an intense and controversial drafting period in 1994. The drafting of the document was a product of both domestic and international political forces. Minow (1998) notes that the South African TRC was unique both in the amount of public debate that was involved in its design and the fact that it was legislated through democratic means. Elites played a role as well; important domestic advocates for the TRC included "key legal thinkers within the ANC... as well as a group of politically influential liberal intellectuals and churchpeople concentrated in the Western Cape" (Lodge 2002, 176). Though these were strong domestic voices, many of these actors themselves were influenced by international thinking on truth commissions, with inspiration coming from the Latin American experience with truth commissions as well as participation in international conferences such as the pivotal IDASA (Institute for a Democratic Alternative for South Africa) conference, which brought experts from around the world (particularly Latin America and Eastern Europe) to South Africa to discuss the route to a stable democracy, and the role of a truth commission in such a journey (Lodge 2002, 177).

The TRC had lofty ambitions. Its four stated goals included:

1) the discovery of the causes, nature, and scope of "gross violations" of human rights between 1960 and 1994
2) the extension of amnesty to those who fully disclosed their involvement in politically motivated violations of human rights

3) the identification and location of victims of violations and the design of reparations for them

4) the compilation of a report, which should contain recommendations for measures to prevent any future violations of human rights (Lodge 2002, 177)

In addition, the creators of the South African TRC had an explicit commitment to healing, to restoring what had been lost under the oppression of apartheid both individually and nationally. The following words were included in the interim constitution: "There is a need for understanding but not for vengeance, a need for reparation but not for retaliation, a need for *ubuntu* but not for victimization" (interim constitution 1993). Humphrey (2003) expands on this by noting that truth commissions aim to "morally reconnect victims," a connection that suggests the need to reaffirm victims as moral beings, and reconnect them into a civil and inclusive society.

The TRC was believed to be an integral step in achieving these aims; indeed, the very development of the truth commission was representative of what Lodge refers to as "the causal connection between truth and reconciliation," a belief that "reconciliation and forgiveness must be based on truth" (Lodge 2002, 178; see also Ignatieff 1998). The TRC was designed to facilitate both of these aims: the uncovering of the truth and the promotion of reconciliation.

The structure of the TRC included three distinct bodies: the Human Rights Violation Committee, the Amnesty Committee, and the Reparations Committee. The Human Rights Violations Committee was given the task of collecting victim narratives, and began its work first in April 1996, with the Amnesty and Reparations Committees beginning somewhat later following the work of the research department in response to the testimony-taking activities of the Human Rights Violations Committee (Lodge 2002, 180). In all, the Human Rights Violations Committee collected 22,000 statements about 38,000 incidents, including 10,000 killings. Seventy-six testimonies were carried publicly on nightly television and radio programs. The Amnesty Committee processed 7,127 applications for amnesty (Lodge 2002). By any standard, the TRC was remarkably swift and far reaching in its activities in a very short time period.

CONCEPTUALIZING AND RECOGNIZING A VICTIM

The victim is not a universal category but one determined by the mandates establishing different truth commissions. (Humphrey 2003, 176)

What sort of victim was in the minds of those who designed the TRC, and how did this in turn shape who was officially recognized as a victim? The TRC invoked multiple parameters in conceptualizing a victim, including the type of victimization suffered (in particular, whether the victimization was political) and the form of victimization (gross violations of human rights or otherwise). The TRC also tackled the issue of race and political affiliation: should whites and/or those affiliated with the National Party and apartheid government be recognized as victims in certain instances? While it is important to consider briefly the controversy surrounding how "gross violations of human rights" was defined, as well as the time period that the commission chose to consider, the more critical discussion for this project engages how race and political affiliation were contested parameters in defining victims. As such, particularly in defining the victim, attention is paid to the issues of race and political affiliation, as it is here that conceptualizing a complex political victim is most helpful, yet in the context of the TRC, significantly underdeveloped.

Gross Violations of Human Rights and Political Motivation

The TRC also defined the victim according to international principles of human rights as well as context-specific parameters of victimization. The TRC was committed to recognizing all victims of gross violations of human rights under apartheid; however, it is also important to clarify some of the additional parameters that emerged (with great controversy) to define who could, and could not, testify in front of the TRC. First, the commissioners decided only to hear testimony from those who had suffered "gross violations of human rights." This approach was used because it was recognized that it would be impossible to hear the stories of all those victimized under apartheid (this could arguably include the whole of South Africa); hence a cutoff point had to be made, and that point was "gross violations of human rights."[3] This decision mirrors the scope of the investigation of many earlier truth commissions (indeed, some truth commissions were even more limiting, such as the truth commission in Chile that only investigated disappearances). Further, the time period of 1960–1994 was chosen; certainly other time periods could have been selected, but this time period was chosen because it coincided with the National Party's seizure of power and the beginning of the extensive, nationally coordinated apartheid policies. Finally, the TRC stipulated that victims must be victims of political violence. Those who experienced theft, domestic violence, and so on that could be closely linked to the pressures of apartheid did not qualify as victims who could testify before the TRC because they were not political victims in the formal sense.[4]

Clearly, these three parameters limited in number those who were formally recognized as victims and could testify before the TRC and potentially receive reparations. These parameters were highly controversial, but do not merit in-depth consideration here for one reason; by excluding victims who were victims of something less than a gross violation of human rights, or victims who were victimized prior to 1960, or victims of something not clearly recognizable as "political violence," the commissioners were not stipulating that these people were not victims; rather they were recognizing the financial, procedural, and political constraints of the TRC and in doing so could only focus on a certain set of victims.[5] The TRC chose to look at "only the extremes of apartheid and not its normality" (Meredith 1999, 20), which can be best explained by understanding the resources of the TRC, not its intent to deny widespread victimization.

Black Victims/White Victims

Race also became an important factor in defining victims. Quite obviously, apartheid policies most directly victimized black South Africans. Black South Africans suffered years of structural discrimination; government policies that denied them standing as citizens, as well as educational and economic opportunities; extreme poverty; and torture and disappearances at the hands of a brutal police force. However, as leaders in the postapartheid era also pointed out (including Archbishop Desmond Tutu), white South Africans also suffered, some certainly were directly harmed by members of the African National Congress (ANC), Pan-African Congress (PAC), and other smaller antiapartheid movements. Many more were thought to be victims because of the way in which they were forced to live in a society ruled by norms of hatred, violence, and discrimination; "[P]erpetrators too are often victims either of systems of ideology and deceit that led them to believe they acted on principle or, later, of simplistic blame that alleviates everyone else of responsibility or even self-scrutiny" (Minow 1998, 121).[6]

When the TRC began conceptualizing victimization and including both whites and blacks, many black South Africans saw this as akin to the "sentimental equalization of all victims of war" and were not comfortable with this conception of who was victimized by apartheid.[7] Many in the ANC still maintained that their acts (including burning people alive by throwing a lighted, gasoline-soaked tire around their neck, popularly referred to as "necklacing") were acts against an oppressive, illegitimate state regime and were morally different from the state-sanctioned plan of apartheid and the atrocities that it generated. A passage from the ANC submissions to the TRC shows quite well the way in which the ANC understood their motives, and actions, to be of an entirely different moral and practical sort than the apartheid government.

> Counterpoised to what we have been discussing [apartheid government] is, of course, the movement for national liberation—the other antagonist in the conflict to which the forces of white minority rule responded in the manner described above. National liberation movements are about the

emancipation of people. They are formed to fight against oppression, for freedom. Where the oppressor must necessarily fight for the state control of the individual, the liberator struggles for the restoration of the democratic rights of the individual and the sovereignty of the nation. These movements necessarily depend on the voluntary support of the population; they have no capacity to offer material rewards to their activists. They must therefore depend on the *moral superiority* of their cause, relying on this as the principal motive force which enables the movement to withstand all attempts at its suppression. Respect for human life and the pursuit of happiness and liberty are fundamental to the philosophy and practice of any genuine national liberation movement. Any objective study would show that the ANC has evidenced all the characteristics mentioned above, whatever the circumstances of the struggle. . . . *When weighed in the scales of history, the ANC and the South African apartheid regime occupy opposite ends of the spectrum both in terms of policy and practical conduct.* . . . Moreover, unlike the racist state, the ANC took special care after being compelled to take up arms in the 1960s to ensure that its conduct was in compliance with international conventions in situations of armed conflict. It argued, and this was widely accepted internationally, that the struggle against apartheid and white minority rule was comparable to other international struggles against tyranny, for example, the American War of Independence, the war against Nazism, and the numerous anti-colonial struggles in the 20th century. International precedents support the notion that no equivalence can be made between the defensive violence of the disenfranchised majority and the institutional and overt or covert violence perpetrated in the name of apartheid; in everyday parlance, *the violence of a victim fighting back cannot be equated with the malevolent aggression of the rapist.* (TRC transcripts, ANC submissions, sections 5 and 6, emphasis mine)

The legitimacy of the ANC actions, their status as unquestioned and exclusive victims, is reinforced through references to Nazism, colonialism, and rape victims. By this point in the project, we can recognize these references as attempts to reinforce the innocence and moral superiority of the ANC movement, to reinforce the space between perpetrator and victims, and to reaffirm their status as victims, despite some participation in violence.

To be sure, it was white South Africans who were most inclined to suggest that "atrocities were committed on both sides, so let us just forgive and forget," lending credence to the belief that the question of who was a victim under apartheid was tightly linked with one's race and past political experiences, and destined to never be a "neutral" question of "objective suffering" (Meredith 1999). However, the following quote by current South African President Mbkei indicates that black political leaders also recognized the manner in which apartheid victimized all South Africans, regardless of race.

In the larger sense, we were all victims of the system of apartheid, both black and white. Some among us suffered because of oppression, exploitation, repression and exclusion. Others among us suffered because we were imprisoned behind prison walls of fear, paralysed by inhuman beliefs in our racial superiority, and called upon to despise and abuse other human beings. Those who do such things cannot but diminish their own humanity. (Statement by President Mbeki to the National House of Parliament and the Nation, 4/15/2003)

The TRC, while understandably more narrowly focused on only those who had suffered gross violations of human rights, was similarly firm in their commitment to recognizing both black and white South Africans as victims of apartheid. The TRC clearly identified white victimization, noting for instance that the ANC was responsible for thirteen hundred of fourteen thousand killings during the period of 1960–1994 (Lodge 2002).[8] In the words of Archbishop Tutu, "A gross violation is a gross violation, whoever commits it and for whatever reason. There is thus legal equivalence between all perpetrators. Their political affiliation is irrelevant" (Tutu, as quoted by Meredith 1999, 211).

Though the TRC agreed that according to principles of a "just war," the liberation movements had a higher moral ground, this did not excuse their participation in gross violations of human rights; they too faced limits on to what was acceptable use of violence.

> Justice of war evaluates the justifiability of the decision to go to war. The two basic criteria guiding this evaluation are: first, the justness of the cause (the underlying principles for which a group is fighting), and second, whether the decision to take up arms was a matter of last resort. . . . The doctrine of justice in war states that there are limits to how much force may be used in a particular context and places restrictions on who or what may be targeted. (*TRC Final Report* vol. 1, chap. 4, para. 66–67)

However, the TRC did further delineate between the apartheid government and those working to overturn it by noting that the government should be held to a "higher standard of moral and political conduct than are voluntary associations" and further that "those with the most power to abuse must carry the heaviest responsibility) (*TRC Final Report* vol. 1, chap. 4, para. 80). Though this was the position of the TRC, it should be noted that many scholars and activists alike still contend that adhering to the "just war" argument should imply that the acts of torture and killing committed by those fighting for a "just" cause deserve a more mitigated consideration (Cronin 1999; Bhargava 1998).[9] This suggests at least implicitly a desire to see black victims as more closely approximating the ideal victim on account of their moral superiority stemming from the just cause for which they were fighting. Further, Wilson (2001) argues that the TRC may very well have been adopting an inclusive definition of victim not to make a statement about moral superiority of certain victims or to engage the "just war" argument, but rather as part of the process of constructing a "new political identity" for South Africans, an identity of a "national victim;" an identity that equated being South African with having experienced sacrifice, suffering, and loss.

From this, it is first imperative to recognize that victims were identified as such by the TRC regardless of their race; apartheid was conceived of as leading to gross violations of human rights for both black and white South Africans, though certainly the disproportionate numbers of these violations were committed against blacks. How might we relate this observation to our theory of the complex political victim? Certainly, it is critical to point out that in recognizing white South Africans who had suffered gross violations of human rights as victims, the TRC was recognizing, *as a victim*, someone who had a complex engagement with the discourse of apartheid that constructed the political space of their victimization. By recognizing white victims of apartheid as victims, the TRC did in fact recognize a complex political victim.[10] The TRC was comfortable with the language of "collective responsibility" for the atrocities of apartheid (that is to say, all whites were seen as in part responsible for apartheid), yet also was able to recognize that some of those who were "collectively responsible" for this discourse were victims too.[11] Minimally, at the level of the collective, the TRC was willing to recognize that whites bore responsibility for apartheid and its oppressions and that some white individuals were nonetheless victimized by the politics of apartheid.

We might be tempted to say that the TRC also recognized some black South Africans as complex political victims, but here we must be careful. Though many observers of South African apartheid maintained a strict separation of innocent victim and evil perpetrator (as Borer 2003 argues), some were capable of identifying that at times these identities overlapped, and frequently these identities were blurry and complex.

> Victims, perpetrators, and bystanders stand in different relationships to the underlying events and to the prospect of healing, and tracing the effects of participation in or knowledge of the truth commission's work for each group would be insuperable. Further complicating matters, particular individuals may be viewed as victims, perpetrators, and bystanders. . . . How and when can such people confess to others what they have done while also telling of their own trauma? How can they forgive themselves and work through horror? (Minow 1998, 63)

Further, the TRC, in its final report, was quite clear in assigning responsibility to the ANC, and to an even greater extent the Pan African Congress (PAC)/Azanian People's Liberation Army (APLA), for their contributions to a "spiral of violence," suggesting a recognition of the fact that categories of victim and perpetrator, at least at the group level, sometimes overlapped. Further, this suggests at least implicit recognition that at the group level, "victims" are not always ideal.

> The ANC was held morally and politically accountable for creating a cli-
> mate during the armed struggle that allowed its supporters inside the coun-
> try to regard violence against opponents as a legitimate part of a people's
> war. (Meredith 1999, 299)

In regards to the PAC, the TRC "rejected the [PAC's] explanation that its
killing of white farmers constituted acts of war" and instead held the PAC
"morally and politically responsible and accountable" (Meredith 1999,
301–2). Certainly, then, responsibility is understood to be shared for the violence of the apartheid period. The TRC did not shy away from understanding
the multiple responsible parties who contributed to the thousands of gross
violations of human rights. This is a significant and noteworthy position as it
suggests a willingness to depart from the stereotype of the ideal victim.

In other words, the notion of "complex engagement with apartheid" was
handled well in terms of being able to simultaneously recognize some practical
responsibility of victims, some appreciation that not all victims are "ideal" in
terms of practical innocence—but they are victims nonetheless. However, as
we have seen, there is more to the complex political victim than some level of
practical responsibility; complex political victims are variously engaged with
discourses propitious to political violence. In the case of Bosnia, these discourses included ethno-religious identity and support for constitutional
nationalism. In the case of South Africa, a deeper exploration of the discourses of race and political tolerance are in order. What emerges is evidence
that black South Africans were and are complexly engaged with and constituted by discourses of racial identity and political intolerance. In short, as a
group, they are complex political victims.[12]

Africanist and Race-Based Liberation Movements: Considering the PAC and Black Consciousness

African nationalism can be traced back to the early nineteenth century, and
was influenced by the teachings of the Christian church as well as limited exposure among elites to an international discourse opposed to colonial oppressions. By the end of the century, more organized African national movements
emerged in South Africa. These organizations included the Union of Africans
(1882), the Natal Indian Congress (1894), and the African People's Organization (1902) (Philip 1986, 89). Philip notes that even during this time period,
there was an emerging and important distinction between those who supported working with the white population and those who believed that such a
tactic would undermine black Africans' political and social progress.

> Before the turn of the century, the lines were already being drawn, based
> on a difference in strategy, between Africans prepared to work with whites

for a new political dispensation as expressed in the slogan 'equal rights for every civilized man south of the Zambezi' (a strategy represented by the Jabavu); and Africanists (represented by the Ethiopians) who challenged white power through African unity. (Philip 1986, 90)

During the early part of the twentieth century, the South African Native Convention attempted to influence the drafting of a new constitution for South Africa but was unable to secure the equal property and political rights they demanded. By 1923, the African National Congress (ANC) was formed. The ANC was committed to enhancing the property and political rights of Africans in South Africa and drafted a Bill of Rights in 1923 that demanded, among other issues, the right to own land and the right to participate fully in national politics (see Philip 1986 for an expanded discussion).

Throughout the 1920s and 1930s, the ANC was somewhat overshadowed by the more militant Marxist All-African Congress, but by the 1940s, the ANC experienced a resurgence in power. Dr. Xuma was appointed president and reenergized the movement with a series of speeches and the production of "African Claims," a document that spelled out the ANC's demands for full citizenship and equal opportunity (Philip 1986, 93). However, racial segregation and discrimination against Africans was only increasing during this time period, as the foreshadowed National Party victory continued and increased policies of oppression.

The ANC, in addition to battling the rise of the National Party, was experiencing internal strife as well. Some within the ANC became disillusioned with the nonviolent, "cooperative" tactics of the ANC, especially in light of the ANC's limited success. As such, the ANC experienced a split within its ranks, with some of its more militant members forming the ANC Youth League. Their leader was Anton Lembede, and he spoke critically of the ANC's "collaboration with the oppressors" and articulated an Africanist solution to end the oppression of blacks in South Africa (Lembede, quoted in Philip 1986, 93).

It is useful to consider the substance of this "Africanist" approach that emerged in the ANC Youth League (which subsequently broke away to form the PAC), because it is a path to ending victimization that in fact engages and supports a discourse of exclusive, racialized political identities and some measure of political intolerance.[13] Lembede identified the "cardinal principles" of Africanism as follows:

a) Africa is a black man's country
b) Africans are one
c) The leader of the Africans will come out of their own loins
d) Cooperation between Africans and other non-Europeans on common problems and issues may be highly desirable; but this must be between the African bloc and the non-European groups as unities. 'Non-European unity is a fantastic dream which has no foundation in reality'

e) The divine destiny of the African people is national freedom

f) After national freedom comes socialism. 'Our immediate task, however, is not socialism, but national liberation; our motto: freedom in our life-time.' (Lembede, cited in Philip 1986, 94)

Lembede was remarkably influential. By 1949, the Programme of Action put forth by the ANC included explicit support for black self-determination, did not refer to a policy or preference for interracial cooperation, and rejected any notion of white trusteeship (which had previously been considered by the ANC) (Philip 1986, 96). However, tensions remained between the Africanist position and the nonracial position, and when the ANC drafted a charter in 1956 and began it with the statement that "South Africa belongs to all who live in it, black and white," many Africanists took offense. By 1959, the Pan African Congress (PAC) had separated from the ANC and adopted an explic-itly Africanist position that also rejected the nonviolence of the ANC.

The PAC split with the ANC in 1959 precisely because of its commitment to a multiracial struggle; the PAC believed in the abolishment of "white set-tlers" and the rule of Africa by "Africans" (blacks) (Meredith 1999). This split indicates two distinct discourses on the social and political role of racial identity as well as different views on political tolerance. The PAC openly espoused a belief that all whites were targets, and the APLA denied the exis-tence of "hard" (political and military) targets versus "soft" (civilian) targets, stating that all "settlers" were targets.

> The enemy of the liberation movement of South Africa and of its people was always the settler Colonial regime of South Africa. Reduced to its sim-plest form, the apartheid regime meant, white domination not leadership, but control and supremacy. This was the desire of the white man to con-tinue to protect himself from the "swart gevaar," the "black danger." The pillars of apartheid, protecting white South Africa from the black danger were the military and the process of arming of the entire white South African society. This militarization, therefore, of necessity made *every white citizen a member of the security establishment.* Whilst uniformed men and women engaged in border and cross-border operations, non-uni-formed men and women became the pillar of the so-called rear-area protec-tion. It would therefore be a fallacy in the context of white South Africa to talk about innocent civilians. *Military trained and armed civilians defy the definition of civilians.* To us an attack on a trained and armed individual was a military operation. It is in this context therefore that the Azanian People's Liberation Army did not have the burden or problem of the so-called "soft or hard target." *In all honesty, the terms "soft or hard" targets did not exist in our vocabulary.* All that mattered was the political and psy-chological benefit that the organisation would derive from such military operations. (Excerpt from the PAC submission to the TRC, emphasis added)

This group popularized the slogan "One Settler, One Bullet" and was responsible for many murders and tortures, including the killing of American Fulbright scholar Amy Biehl (Meredith 1999). At several points in the PAC's submission to the TRC, they assert their hardline stance against white South Africans and refuse to apologize for the violence or hatred espoused by the PAC, indicating deep support for strongly racialized identities and a low level of political tolerance (see PAC submission to TRC). Indeed, the ANC criticized such a perspective as nothing more than a black version of Afrikaner ideology. And as Gibson and Gouws (2003) argue, it is partly the salience of racial identities combined with high levels of political intolerance that constructs the social space for political violence and victimization. By now, we should recognize that such a discourse is critical in creating the political space for racial and ethnic victimization.

The Black Consciousness Movement (BCM) emerged in South Africa in the 1960s. While it was somewhat influenced by the black consciousness movement in the United States, the BCM of South Africa had notable differences, most relating to the fact that they were a majority population in a state whose constitution was not premised on equality as the American constitution was (Philip 1986). The philosophy of the BCM focused on the importance of black solidarity in light of the already-existing structures of racism and exploitation.

> In black consciousness thinking, the history of South Africa can be interpreted according to a dialectical process. From the thesis of white racism and the antithesis of black solidarity a synthesis will emerge: true humanity without regard to race or color. . . . [B]lack consciousness held that in order to play a positive role in the liberation struggle, blacks had to develop a sense of solidarity through the concept of group power. . . . [T]he black person needed to 'come to himself,' and be reminded of his 'complicity in the crime of allowing himself to be misused' by others (usually white) for their own purposes. Black consciousness advocates an awareness of and a pride in blackness—and thus the rejection of the white stereotype. (Philip 1986, 107–8)

The philosophy of the BCM in South Africa was one that relied explicitly on an exclusive racial identity to end victimization and exploitation. Philip (1986) notes how BCM leaders emphasized that the liberation struggle required the full energies of the black identity (socially, politically, culturally), and the participation of the entire black community. However, the BCM does seem to frame the importance of this "black identity" as somewhat transitory: necessary in ending victimization in a racist and exploitative society, but perhaps ultimately unnecessary once the structures of racism and exploitation were destroyed. In this sense, it differs from the Africanist perspective discussed above, where the "African" identity remains personally and politically salient even after victimization ends.

Like the PAC, the BCM had, at times, connections to the ANC. During the 1960s, the BCM was distinct from the more widespread activities of the ANC: however, in the mid-1970s, the two groups began cooperating to the benefit of both.

> [I]n this period, when the [ANC] movement was facing many difficulties in rooting its underground within the country, resisting the temptation to spread such structures and armed actions in an opportunistic fashion was a difficult challenge. One instance of this was when contact was made with members of the Black Consciousness Movement (BCM), when a delegation of BCM leaders met with the ANC in the mid-1970s. They had come to appreciate the futility of student protest on its own as a means to liberate the country, and were seeking assistance to undertake armed actions. Their submission was that they needed military training, and should then be allowed to operate independently within the country, with their own command structures. Given the difficulties the ANC experienced at this time, this was like a godsend. (TRC transcripts, ANC submissions, section 6)

The ANC maintained that a condition of their cooperation with the BCM was a joint commitment to nonracial politics. In their submission to the TRC, the ANC asserts that

> the movement [ANC] asserted its political position: that the politics of non-racialism and national liberation should guide whatever armed actions were undertaken, and that the politics of the ANC should guide whoever carried out operations on the basis of its training and supplies. (TRC transcripts, ANC submissions, section 6)

It is difficult to ascertain to what extent the "nonracialism" of the ANC actually influenced those in the BCM. As was mentioned, within the philosophy of the BCM there was an eventual appreciation of nonracial politics, but this was only after victimization and exploitation had ended—after the structures of racism and victimization had been destroyed. The two groups did become more tightly connected, and by the late 1970s, several senior members of the BCM became full-fledged members of the ANC while maintaining their ties to the BCM. During this time period, there was something of an internal struggle over identity discourses among black South Africans. Whether "black consciousness" or "Africanism" or "nonracialism" should lead the struggle against apartheid was a contested issue; there was disagreement about what roles racial identity should play in politics more broadly.

In assessing black engagement with discourses of race and political intolerance, context is critical. The presence of racialized identities and low levels of political tolerance must be understood in the context of a brutal history of colonialism and apartheid; indeed, this point cannot be overemphasized. Appreciating this context is perhaps most important in thinking about moral responsibility which, to recall, ought only be assigned if community standards are transgressed and there are other choices available to the individual. It is at best debatable whether relying on racial identities to advance a political cause, or even employing violence to achieve these goals, really violated community norms in South Africa during the apartheid period, given the overall climate of South African politics, though these norms certainly have undergone changes in the last fifteen years. Further, some would argue that disengaging from "racial identities" is all but impossible in a society so traumatized by colonialism (though the ANC might prove a strong counter to this claim). While moral responsibility is a critical and always controversial issue, what is perhaps most relevant for continued analysis of victims and the postconflict peacebuilding process in South Africa is the following: both Africanism and the BCM recognized and affirmed the role that race-based identity discourses could play in *positively* constructing identity, and further indicated support for relatively high levels of political intolerance. While the salience of the BCM, and to a lesser extent the PAC, decreased during the 1980s (particularly with the creation of the United Democratic Front, a broad umbrella of antiapartheid groups that supported nonracial discourses of liberation), these race-based discourses of identity and their relation to political intolerance cannot be ignored for the role they played in defining and challenging apartheid victimization.

Certainly, the presence of such groups in South Africa would lend support to the idea that some of the victims of apartheid, though wholly opposed to apartheid, *also* embraced and supported discourses of racialized identities, and at times political intolerance—discourses propitious to political violence. Not all blacks in South Africa wanted to decrease the salience of racial identity, and not all blacks were comfortable with a widely tolerant political climate, even while it could be said with confidence that all blacks wanted apartheid to end. So here we see the emergence of a complex political victim: a victim who supports, participates in, and is constituted by discourses of exclusive, racialized political identities and limited political tolerance, yet wants to see the victimizing practice of apartheid abolished. If we were relying on an image of the ideal victim we might not see these individuals as victims because we could not reconcile their support of racialism and political intolerance with their victimization under apartheid. Deconstructing the discourses of race and political intolerance in order to dismantle apartheid would likely have more complex effects on such complex political victims, effects that extend beyond simply ending the "victim" identity—a phenomenon fleshed out shortly.

By not exploring these tensions in any notable depth, the TRC did not fully recognize the complexity of some victims, or the way in which some blacks, in addition to white South Africans, had identities that were strongly invested in a particular, and divisive, discourse of race, identity, and tolerance. Giliomee

(2003) highlights how difficult it was for white South Africans, particularly Afrikaners, to recraft their identities in postapartheid South Africa, as so many of their cultural markers—their identity as a surviving and resilient group—were tied up in the apartheid experience. We might ask the same question of black South Africans. The TRC, in working from the assumption that blacks were opposed to the discourse of apartheid, did not explore in any great depth the ways in which some black South Africans supported discourses, for instance, about the primacy of racial identity and the ways in which this may have contributed to general racial tensions and intolerance (apart, of course, from the recognition of certain African extremist groups). They too, though in different ways, had an identity that was bound up with the discourses of race and exclusion in many ways, not just as victim and oppressor, but in the construct of other dimensions of identity as well.

Humphrey (2003) notes this lack of exploration into a deeper understanding of responsibility and victimization, which he attributes to the "juridical positivist framework" of the TRC:

> The juridical-positivist framework behind the investigation of human rights abuse has also limited the extent to which political origins and causes were explored. (Humphrey 2003, 178)

Despite the fact that the TRC was not a formal judicial trial, it maintained a certain rigidity—an adherence to juridical-positivist procedures (discussed in more depth shortly) that prevented any deep investigation into the complexity of apartheid and victimization. The TRC was not designed to investigate the broader discourses that constituted the political space necessary for apartheid and related victimization, and as such, was unlikely to fully acknowledge or consider the complex political victims.[14]

In addition, at this point it is clear that norms of victimization, norms of the victim identity, would discourage attempts to engage the complexity of the black South African experience with racialized identities and political intolerance. It was easier, and more urgent, to deal with the victim/oppressor dyad that operated under apartheid and leave out more complex issues of identity that could both detract from the righting of apartheid's wrongs and possibly lead to demonizing and blaming the victim. In short, it was easier to reach out and support the ideal victims—the moral beacons who could lead South Africa out of the horrors of apartheid.

> The framework for passing judgment on the past was essentially moral: the aim was to identify the perpetrators of morally reprehensible actions and the victims whom they had harmed. . . . [T]he task was. . . to produce an account of the past sufficient to portray the moral fact of gross human rights violations. The 'truth' would be told in terms of simple moral binaries of 'victim' and 'perpetrator,' associated with unambiguous judgments

of right and wrong. There was no place here to explore moral ambiguities born of the politics of complicity or collaboration under apartheid; nor to explore the complexities of social causation, where individuals are caught up in structural processes that both motivate and constrain their actions, in ways that may not be intelligible to the actors themselves. (Posel and Sampson 2002, drawing on arguments made by Bonner and Nieftagodien 2002)

A more nuanced exploration of the process of victimization and the victim identity would move beyond the simplistic victim/oppressor dyad of apartheid. It might consider, for instance, the way in which race and identity are discursively intertwined more broadly and not just under the mantle of apartheid, or perhaps explore perceptions about the value of broad political tolerance.[15] Throughout South African apartheid, it was certainly recognized that some black South Africans did in fact support discourses of racialized identities and political intolerance, despite their oppression. However, few of these "complexities of social causation" were considered in regards to the political victimization of black South Africans. The implications of ignoring this complex political victimization are numerous, though two of the most important are biases within the TRC in recognizing only ideal victims, and problems with the future of peace and stability in South Africa.

The final words in this section are reserved for Buur (2002), as he captures well one of the underlying assumptions of those embroiled in the controversy to define apartheid victims—namely, that there was never any doubt that a victim could and should be defined, nor was there a concern that this victim "group" would not have, once properly defined, an "irreducible identity," an innate "victim" core. Arguably these assumptions, coupled with the sensitive political climate surrounding investigating more "complex" stories of victimization, prevented the full conceptualization or recognition of complex political victims.

> Even though the TRC and ANC are in conflict over the status of the victims objectified by the TRC, they share the same grammar for allocation and representation. Neither the TRC nor ANC questions that the right knowledge about who the victims really are can be obtained. It is only a question of "getting it right," counting the numbers differently or rethinking the victim criteria. Thus for both parties there is a trust in practice of representation on the imbued stability and irreducibility of identity and the "group-ness" it supposedly reflects. What is problematic, in this sense, is the grammar, but not the surface product. (Buur 2002)

Reliance on the Victim

It would be remiss in a discussion of conceptualizing and recognizing victims to ignore one of the most basic characteristics of the TRC's engagement with

the victim—namely, that it was so heavily based on experiences of victimization and the victim, despite the fact that some who had been harmed by
apartheid did not see themselves as victims at all. In the words of Andre Du
Toit, involved in the TRC both as an academic and activist:

> The survivors [who do not identify as victims] do not relate to this situa-
> tion. They respond by saying, 'we have had these experiences but we do
> not want to present ourselves as victims in need of healing. We do not nec-
> essarily agree with the message of forgiveness. What political purpose does
> the story serve when it is framed in this way?' (Du Toit, quoted in Minow,
> 1998).

Clearly, some were not comfortable with the label of victimization, which
begs the question: why?[16] Is it because of a stigma against requiring psychological help for healing, moving beyond victimization? For some, this seems to
be the case. Agger and Jensen (1990) document several cases where political
victims were unwilling to admit to psychological victimization, instead characterizing their ailments as simply "medical" (being unable to sleep at night,
for instance).

For others, not identifying as victims may be attributable to the way in
which the TRC linked the victim identity with the role of "forgiver." For those
who did not believe in forgiveness, for the "many long time anti-apartheid
activists [who] cannot accept the Archbishop's call for forgiveness and reconciliation," they may have been reticent to identify as victims because they
were uncomfortable with the entailments of forgiveness that accompanied this
identity (Minow 1998).

Still others preferred to emphasize the heroic nature of their role in South
African society; rather than being remembered as victims of apartheid, they
wished to be remembered as the freedom fighters of oppression. In the words
of Mbkei, "Our fighters were liberation heroes. Do not demean them by call-
ing them victims" (Statement on the Report of the TRC Joint Sitting of the
Houses of Parliament).

Another potential explanation relates to the complex political victim; is it
possible that some of those harmed by apartheid were unable to identify as
victims because the image of the victim presented was ideal—as having an
"innate core" that they did not possess? In not identifying with this particular
image of the victim, perhaps they could not comfortably identify as a victim at
all. This remains an open question; getting people to say that they did not
identify as a victim because they did not conceptualize themselves as matching
this innate core is much harder than drawing out the bitterness of some victims and hearing how they do not believe in forgiveness and hence do not
want to identify with the TRC victim who is expected to forgive. There is,
however, evidence to support this logic. Research on sexual assault victims has

indicated that for some victims, their belief that they are not wholly innocent prevents them from identifying as a victim publicly or in self-reflection (Krahe 1992, Arata 1999). That is, it can be difficult for individuals to identify themselves as victims if they perceive a degree of personal responsibility and sense their failure to possess the innate core presumed common to all victims.[17] In sum, the TRC is characterized by parallel commitments both to the centrality of the victimization experience and victim identity, but also to the narrow, and at times simple conceptualization of this experience and identity. The tensions inherent in these parallel commitments can be further articulated through a consideration of the specific practices of the TRC.

SPECIFIC PRACTICES OF THE SOUTH AFRICAN TRC

The work of the TRC involved several procedures: collecting testimony from victims, accepting applications from amnesty seekers, researching and deciding upon amnesty applications, and deciding upon, and providing, reparations to victims. Further, the TRC had the responsibility of producing a final report, a comprehensive narrative of the "truth" about what happened during the apartheid years. The section considers to what extent these procedures, both individually and collectively, aid in both the recognition of the complex political victim and her opportunity to work on herself.

Collecting Victim Testimony

The project of collecting victim testimony was immense. The commissioners traveled throughout South Africa, transversing a "landscape of suffering," and hundreds of "statement takers" were employed to collect the stories of the victims (Lodge 2002, 180). The vast majority of statements were not publicly delivered, though the TRC did make sure that some statements were publicly shown on television and radio. Nonetheless, the victims' statements were for many the centerpiece of the South African TRC, the outpouring of thousands of repressed stories to a society grappling for the first time publicly with the tremendous horror of years of violence and assaults on human and social dignity.

"The Protocol"

The initial process for taking statements was quite straightforward. A victim came to the hall or public meeting place where the statement takers had set up and were politely welcomed and invited to tell their stories. The statement itself was initially quite open ended.

> Statement takers initially recorded victims' narratives more or less verba-
> tim, as listening to victims' stories was viewed as a vital therapeutic func-
> tion which the TRC should undertake, a process of validation of individual
> subjective experiences of all people who previously had been silenced.
> (Lodge 2002, 180)

From the perspective of the complex political victim, this seems an ideal
intervention, with no scripts assuring the victim that there is one proper way
to understand their victimization, no prompts as to how events unfolded.
Numerous interviews with TRC statement makers indicate that they greatly
appreciated the simple opportunity to be heard (Minow 1998; Lodge 2002).
Indeed, it represents the harnessing of the validation of one's identity as a
victim, and the "therapeutic function" of talking with another human being
about a terrible occurrence in one's life.

However, this process changed in the months after the initial statements
were made, and gradually became a much more scripted interaction. This
switch to a more scripted, truncated statement-taking experience can be
explained first by the sheer number of victims wishing to make statements
(Lodge 2002). What had begun as an open-ended statement-taking procedure
had been reduced to, on average, a twenty- to thirty-minute encounter (Buur
2002). Hayner (2001) also notes the influence of a "legal mindset" that often
attends the architects of truth commissions (despite lack of their status as
formal juridical organizations).

> Those shaping the methodological questions approached their task with a
> legal mind-set, which defined a set of questions on the basis of document-
> ing specific acts of human rights violations. (Hayner 2001, 82)

Hayner (2001) also identifies a tendency to allow the design and limits of a
database to influence the overall process of information and statement gathering, with detailed narratives being much more difficult to capture in information management systems. Fullard (2004), drawing on Buur (2002), characterizes this form of statement taking as quite limiting for the statement maker,
constraining the narrative such as to align and manufacture a victim narrative
that "fit" the victim narrative of the TRC.

> The form directed deponents to address killings, severe ill-treatment, tor-
> ture or abductions only and requested the 'political context' to be specified.
> It provided a 'cognitive landscape' [citing Buur 2002] in which deponents
> had to locate themselves. Most HRV statement forms, moreover, were
> filled in by TRC statement takers who made decisions regarding inclusion
> or exclusion, and the location and shape of the statement. These TRC
> processes therefore delineated the paths down which deponents were
> expected to travel in their narrative account. Testimonies and statements
> were not 'biographies' in which deponents could situate the TRC's cate-
> gories of gross human rights violations within a lifetime of racially shaped

> abuse. Instead, victims were to pluck out the 'incident' of killing, severe ill-treatment, torture or abduction for isolated presentation. . . . Human Rights Violations public hearings tended to be brusque with deponents who wished to speak about matters that did not directly relate to the gross human rights violation, such as their wider experiences under apartheid. (Fullard 2004)

This switch in statement-taking procedures was not without effect on victims; many victims who made statements to the TRC "expressed concern regarding the statement-taking process and procedures and the impact of that on the ability to make their case" (Byrne 2004, 252).

The South African TRC had additional pressures that contributed to the increased scripting of the statement-taking process, notably the need to research individual amnesty applications. Statement takers had the dual task of taking victim statements and mining these statements for corroboration of amnesty applicant stories, to ascertain whether amnesty applicants were telling the "whole truth." Further, as the Reparations Committee began its work in earnest, it also became necessary to corroborate the stories of those applying for financial reparations, in essence to "fact check" victim narratives against one another. Out of respect for the victims, the statement takers did not cross-examine the victims to mine the necessary information, yet nonetheless the statement takers were instructed to find "corroboration" for each statement in order to pass this information on to the Reparations and/or Amnesty Commission (Lodge 2002; see also Buur 2002). The extent of the change to the statement-taking process was notable:

> This concern with collecting what the Commission called 'narrative truth' became less pronounced. . . . [T]he 'protocols' or forms that were used by the statement-takers were revised five times and each revision left less scope for subjective perceptions as victims' experience was categorized through a 'controlled vocabulary' to facilitate its 'capture' in a computerized database. (Lodge 2002, 180, drawing on Wilson 2001)

In the period of a few short months, the open-ended narrative style of statement taking had morphed into the need to "corroborate" and "categorize data" while making use of a "controlled vocabulary." This concerns the complex political victim in two ways; first the scripting of the interaction, the adoption of a "protocol" of this nature, arguably makes the nuance of the complex political victim experience hard to capture. In not telling the "whole" story, complex political victims may have a greater difficulty processing their experience, getting validation for their experience and healing.

> [T]o be effectively therapeutic, the act of narrating experience with oppression should move beyond a plain statement of facts to include also the survivor's emotional and bodily responses and reactions of others important to her. . . . [S]imilarly for healing to occur, the testimony should include

> attention to how the individual has tried to understand what happened,
> and how these understandings can be reintegrated with the individual's
> values and hopes. Ensuring these elements is likely to exceed the time,
> attention, and expertise of a truth commission. Yet unless the commission-
> ers and staff of a truth commission attend to these dimensions of an inte-
> grated personal narrative of meaning, emotion, and memory, the therapeu-
> tic effects for testifying victims will be limited. (Minow 1998, 70).

The above statement refers to all victims who provide testimony before
truth commissions, though arguably complex political victims would be particularly sensitive to these issues. We may understand this transition as in part a
reflection of the increasing pressure for victim statements to part of the nation-
building discourse, rather than merely their own reflections and thoughts. In
the words of Hamber and Wilson (2002), the "nation-building discourses of
truth commissions homogenize disparate individual memories to create an
official version" (Hamber and Wilson 2002, 36; see also Buur 2002).

Equally troublesome though is the reason for the capture of the victim narrative. If a victim knows that what they say, who they implicate, how they
describe their own involvement in violent acts is going to affect both who can
get amnesty and what sort of financial reparations they are likely to get, it is
quite conceivable that this "linking of the narrative" will encourage the adoption of a more traditional victim script—that is, a victim who is innocent and
without moral responsibility, an ideal victim. If a victim knows that by telling
a statement taker of her own participation in supporting, for instance, intolerance of whites, she is less likely to be approved for financial reparations, she
may make the decision not to speak about this dynamic of her victimization
(this will be looked at more closely shortly). It is conceivable that victims were
simply able to take a rather detached, materialistic stance to the "telling of the
right story" and that the psychological trauma of adopting such an identity
was not terribly intense. However, victim comments after they made their
statements indicate that the process of statement taking was anything but
"detached," and in fact was a profound experience with deep psychological
consequences (Minow 1999 and Hayner 2001). Hence, the potential scripting
of this experience to achieve a particular amnesty or reparations decision
should be cause for concern; it may induce further difficulty in identity reconciliation and healing.

One final element of the statement-taking process that merits consideration
is the opportunity to make a public statement. As was mentioned, the vast majority of statements were not publicly broadcast, though a few specially screened
and selected victims did have their testimony recorded and nationally broadcast (on radio and television) (Lodge 2002, 180). Further, nearly all newspapers carried at least some of the victims' testimony, with some local African

newspapers printing daily nearly all victim testimony. The public nature of the victim statements arguably served many functions; Lodge emphasizes the role they played in a national move toward reconciliation.

> The public hearings were not so much concerned with establishing facts, for those who had testified before had already given their statements. Public victim hearings had an important ritual function: they were essential ingredients in what the commissioners understood to be a process of communal reconciliation. (Lodge 2002, 181)

The final TRC report also detailed how the public statements were critical in a larger project of South African education (TRC Final Report). Further, we can understand these public hearings as a literal attempt to construct a social narrative of apartheid. In selecting the victims to testify publicly, the commissioners followed a "chronology prepared by the research department," (Lodge 2002) aimed for a diverse story of how different groups were participants in, and victims of, apartheid. However, the commissioners were also mindful of attempting to present a moving, comprehensive, profound narrative of apartheid.

> When we select people to come to a public hearing what we try to do is select cases which give us some idea of the nature of the conflict. . . . We do not choose people because we think their stories are more important or because they are more important. We also try, we also try to cover the period that the Commission has to look at which is 1960 to 1994. We also try to give as balanced a view of the conflict as possible because we know that the conflict was many sided. (Humphrey 2003, 177, quoting the TRC proceedings in Dudza)

A focus on the victim suggests a more critical consideration of what purpose these public hearings served for the victim, in particular, the complex political victim. There is no one answer to this question, as arguably each victim got something different out of the experience, though it is important to consider the range of reactions to the process of publicly testifying. Perhaps the most commonly cited reactions are relief and progress toward healing.

> Coming to know that one's suffering is not solely a private experience, best forgotten, but instead an indictment of a social cataclysm, can permit individuals to move beyond trauma, hopelessness, numbness, and preoccupation with loss and injury. The clandestine nature of torture and abuses by repressive governments doubles the pain of those experiences with the disbelief of the community and even jeopardy to the victim's own memory and sanity. Holding in the account of what happened exacerbates the trauma. In contrast, speaking in a setting where the experience is acknowledged can be restorative. (Minow 1998, 67)

While public hearings may provide many benefits to the victim, it has also been recognized that further trauma is possible. This may be true either because the media participation makes the victim feel exploited; their expectations of their telling may be high, but their experience may not live up to their expectations; or it may simply be because the "retelling" process triggers a reliving of the trauma. Rather than moving forward toward healing, the victim moves back to the victimization (Minow 1998; David and Yukping 2005; and Hayner 2001).

An additional concern in regards to victims and public hearings involves the pressure to conform to a particular victim identity. As already discussed, the victim may feel some pressure to conform to a particular image of the victim at many points throughout the truth commission process—perhaps in their personal identification as a victim, perhaps if the statement-taking process involves a script that prompts and narrates what victimization "should" be like, and again here, when the entire nation is watching the victim enact her identity. Public statements by victims may be understood as the articulation of the "innate core" of the victim identity. The pressure to assume a particular sort of victim identity, specifically the pressure to not display a complex identity for fear of harsh judgments or perhaps even losing social recognition of one's status as a victim, may very well be enhanced through participation in public hearings.[18]

It is worth noting, though, that the TRC recognized the potential for trauma as a result of participating in public hearings. For this reason, victims were always given the option of private testimony, and this is certainly commendable. It reduces tremendously the pressure to conform to any particular image of the victim, though it is worth noting that some victims may have felt the need to conform simply because they were in the presence of an "official" statement taker (Lodge 2002) and because they had been continually exposed to the public statements of victims before them.

Gregory Edmund Beck

At this point, I address the testimony of one individual who told his story of victimization to the TRC commissioners and the public. This narrative is included to highlight some of the points just made, in particular the pressure to appear as an ideal victim, the possible influence of reparations as a result of one's story of victimization, and the difficulty in allowing a truly complex story of victimization to emerge. It is obviously quite difficult to generalize about all of the victim stories presented to the TRC, as thousands told their stories; in selecting one, the intent is not to capture the breadth of victimization narratives that emerged. However, the story of Beck is representative in many ways and particularly speaks to the challenges to the complex political victim, as Beck can clearly be described as supportive of discourses propitious to political victimization and as a victim.[19]

On April 29, 1996, Gregory Edmund Beck testified before the TRC, telling his story of victimization to the Human Rights Commissioners. Beck, a white South African, had been a police detective for nearly two decades under the apartheid government. In 1988, he was working in Soweto, an area of extreme unrest and violence. On a routine nightly patrol, he and three other police officers were ambushed. Their vehicle suffered heavy machine-gun fire and Beck was hit repeatedly. His injuries were severe.

> I was hospitalized for about approximately a year. I had to be retrained to walk in that time. My legs were—I had several bone grafts and skin grafts. My leg was tied in a brace in order to keep the bones in order to grow back. My right leg is still shorter than my left leg now. I still suffer severely. I have severe pains and my leg is disfigured and flesh from my left thigh was cut to the skin graft on my right leg, so with the result that when I am with people at the beach or when it's a hot day I cannot expose my legs because they are both disfigured. And if you don't mind I have photographs to show to you what the extent of the injuries were. I have it with me right now.

Though no hard evidence as to the individual identity of the attackers was available, it was widely accepted that the attacks had been carried out by anti-apartheid political activists who were operating in the area.

Beck takes pains to portray himself as an innocent victim, despite the fact that he was working for, supported, and had prospered under the increasingly violent apartheid government. This can be seen in his initial description of his patrol as "routine." Such a description connotes nothing provocative, nothing more than a policeman doing his job. Perhaps more telling is the portion of his testimony where he clearly separates his activities as a policeman from the violence and aggressiveness of the security forces and other special security personnel of the apartheid state.

> *DR ALLY:* Mr Beck I don't want you to take the question that I am going to ask as any indication of any insensitivity to what you have experienced. I am sure that everybody here round the table is moved by what actually happened to you and sympathizes. But I would like to know what your opinions are on the—it is well-known that during the period that you are speaking about the police and the army and all other such structures were seen as an extension of the apartheid state which was oppressing people, and therefore as legitimate targets. How do you feel about that position and in the context of what actually happened to you?
>
> *MR BECK:* Okay. Before 1990 I can say that we as ordinary policeman didn't know much about these covert operations. We didn't know anything about it. It was mostly the specialist policemen, the Security Police, Murder and Robbery and all those kind of guys who knew about these type of operations, and as we are now in the transparent and new South Africa more of these incidents are now revealed. . . . As I said earlier I don't know

of any specific atrocities or any specific policeman that partook in any of these activities, because those atrocities were done mainly by the security branch and the security branch had full reign of anything that they wanted to do. And you know they excluded the rest of the police force out of what they have done. They were like a law unto themselves. (TRC, Beck statement)

Beck clearly distinguishes between the "guilty" (the special forces, etc.) and the innocent. He is just a policeman, wholly innocent, indeed even ignorant, of any of the grave wrongdoings of the apartheid government. It is difficult to believe that Beck, with his many years of police service and his prolonged involvement in Soweto (a highly volatile area), was truly unaware of and uninvolved in carrying out the repressive tactics of the apartheid government. While possible, it is more likely that he had some knowledge, some involvement in the repressive security actions of the apartheid regime. Yet he maintains his innocence, his moral separation from the wrongs of apartheid. He asserts and showcases it repeatedly throughout his testimony. It seems likely that he had knowledge about the norms of the victim identity, a knowledge that suggests victims should be innocent, not guilty; moral beacons committed to the rule of law, not angry bigots; that telling of past knowledge or participation in abuse against the blacks in Soweto would not be compatible with his presentation of himself as a victim; that asking for reparations, as he does in the end of his testimony, might not be strengthened by a lengthy discussion of how his participation in a racist government, his participation in the apartheid security apparatus, might have provoked his victimization. Though by all accounts he is a complex political victim, no complexity emerges in his story. The argument here is that it is a combination of factors—including being in the presence of an official statement taker, the norms of victims emanating from the TRC, and the linking of victim statements to possible future access to reparations—that helps contour Mr. Beck's story to read as the "simple moral binary" of truth commissions.

Reparations

The issue of reparations is deserving of more attention, as it is argued that the implicit or explicit linking of victim statements to reparations is particularly constraining on the emergence of complex stories of victimization. The TRC had a committee devoted to reparations activities, the Reparation and Rehabilitation Committee. Though this committee did not have the formal authority to design and grant reparations (this was reserved for the president and Parliament), the committee was integral to the reparations process. Their activities included collecting information about what sorts of reparations victims wanted, making their own recommendations about appropriate reparations, recommending who was to get individual reparations, as well as recommending provisions of societal-level reparations such as the building of schools, clinics, and so on. Reparations are supported by most advocates of restorative justice (Karmen 1990; Minow 1998), and also are supported by the South African principal of *ubuntu*, so their appearance in the TRC process is not surprising. Wendy Orr, a South African physician and member of the TRC, captured a widely held view that "reparations delayed is healing retarded" (Orr 2000).

In determining what sorts of reparations were most helpful, the TRC solicited requests from individuals and communities asking what they wanted (Minow 1998). The requests were, on the whole, quite modest, and included small financial awards, assistance in proper burial, information about the dead, and from some communities, help in rebuilding churches and schools that had been destroyed (Orr 2000, 242). The TRC, in turn, developed a list of recommended reparations, which included "monetary payments, medical treatment, counseling, information about murdered relatives, and the naming of parks and schools" (Minow 1998, 93).

Given these contours of reparations in South Africa, it is useful to ask how they relate specifically to the discourse of the victim. Most basically, the Reparations and Rehabilitation Committee connected TRC recognition as a victim with access to reparations. The only people who were eligible for reparations were those who "made statements to the Commission or were referred to in someone else's statement" (summary proposal submitted by Reparations and Rehabilitation Committee, TRC report). Further,

> Reparation will be given only to those formally declared victims by the Commission. The Commission will decide if someone is a victim by looking at all the information they have on the gross human rights violation suffered by that person. It may be possible, in certain circumstances, that the relatives and dependents of victims will also qualify for reparation. (TRC Final Report)

Clearly, the way in which the commission defines "victim" both formally and in regards to implicit assumptions is critical, as this definition and its application directly affect who is eligible for reparations. Also important is the idea, introduced above, that victims became aware that their testimony was being used to determine eligibility for reparations; they became aware that the commission must "see" them as a victim (here we might reflect upon the testimony of Gary Beck). Their story was not simply a storytelling exercise, and as such they may have been influenced to adopt a particular victim script and identity in order to access much-needed reparations.

Here, we may comparatively reflect upon the UN recommendations on victim compensation programs.

> In general, victims must be innocent of criminal activity and "contributory misconduct," report the crime promptly to the police, cooperate with the criminal justice system and submit documentation of loss to the compensation program. (*UN Handbook on Justice for Victims*, 52)

These recommendations are most directly geared toward "normal" victims of crime (in other words, not exclusively state-sponsored crime), though the norms and recommendations put forth in the UN *Handbook* were developed with the idea of shaping international norms and policies to respond to a wide array of victimization experiences, including political victimization *(UN Handbook)*. This supports the idea that the norms informing reparations were not conducive to allowing complex experiences of victimization to emerge.

The Amnesty Clause

Without a doubt, the most controversial inclusion in the TRC was the amnesty clause. The TRC had the power to grant amnesty to those individuals who applied for it and whose crimes and behaviors met a certain set of criteria.

> To be granted amnesty, applicants had to prove that their actions were politically motivated and that the violations were gross and within the mandated period. They had to disclose all relevant information, including the chain of command responsible for the action, and they had to demonstrate that the violation was a 'proportionate' response to the circumstances (although this last condition was seldom given any serious consideration). Applicants did not have to offer any expression of remorse. (Lodge 2002 182)

Arguably, white South Africans would not have agreed to the TRC at all or even the negotiated settlement to end minority rule in South Africa without some promise of amnesty. Exiting President F. W. de Klerk "insisted that a guarantee of amnesty be written into the new constitution" (Meredith 1999, 20). Conversely, many black South Africans were strongly opposed to the amnesty clause, feeling that granting amnesty limited their right to pursue prosecution and justice, downplayed their victimization, and did little to advance the notion that South Africa, postapartheid, was truly a state committed to human rights, democracy, and the rule of law. The most symbolic action demonstrating disapproval of the amnesty clause came from the relatives of Steven Biko, a young antiapartheid activist who had been tortured and killed in 1976. His family filed several lawsuits against the new government, stating that the amnesty laws were unconstitutional, denying them an opportunity to seek justice, though ultimately none of these lawsuits were successful (Krog 1998). Even certain segments of the white population opposed amnesty, seeing it as an example of elites and politicians escaping the legal and moral judgment that "ordinary citizens" must live with every day (Meredith 1999, 23).

We may now ask what, if anything, the amnesty clause has to say about images of the victim, and in particular, whether it was drawing on a conception of the complex political victim. On the one hand, the amnesty clause could be interpreted as saying very little about any particular image of the victim, and rather interpreting the clause as evidence of the need to appease white South Africans in order to smooth the transition to a democratic state.

> During the final stages of negotiations that ended white rule, de Klerk insisted that a guarantee of amnesty be written into the new constitution; Mandela was obliged to concede. Without amnesty, the white establishment might not have agreed to give up power. Amnesty, therefore, became the price for peace. (Meredith 1999, 20)

South Africa's Justice Minister Dullah Omar also echoed this understanding of the "why" of the amnesty clause, noting that "the commitment to afford amnesty was the price for allowing a relatively peaceful transition to democracy." In short, the amnesty clause was the result of a power struggle between transitioning governments: a political bargain, not a moral statement. If anything, it might be characterized as dismissive of the victim.

Another possible explanation is that the amnesty clause represents a strong acceptance of the complex political victim; that is, white South Africans were seen as victims too, despite their outward support of apartheid policies, and hence were deserving of forgiveness. There is reason to believe this influenced the creation of the amnesty clause, particularly in light of the spirit of reconciliation and forgiveness that came from what has been described as the "Christian foundation" of the TRC.

Important developers of the TRC were churchpeople, and certainly two of the most influential commissioners, Archbishop Desmond Tutu and Alex Boraine, explicitly referenced the Christian teachings of forgiveness during their participation in the TRC hearings. Indeed, work by Meredith (1999), Lodge (2002), and Krog (1998), as well as the autobiographies of Mandela and Archbishop Tutu, all acknowledge the extent to which Christian beliefs about forgiveness guided the TRC generally and the amnesty clause specifically. Whether the Christian emphasis on forgiveness really draws on a recognition of the complex political victim is not clear, for indeed much of the support for forgiveness is based upon the belief that it is the morally superior option (as opposed to vengeance, for instance), not necessarily on the belief that perpetrators of a crime may be victims of some form as well. According to Bhargava (1998), in order to be forgiven, a victimizer must acknowledge full responsibility for the victimization, lending significant doubt as to whether Christian support of forgiveness relies on any conception of complex victimization at all. Rather, such an understanding of amnesty is premised on the evil perpetrator/ideal victim dyad. Further, some people advocated forgiveness and amnesty not because of any particular image of the perpetrators as complex political victims, but simply because it is necessary for victims to let go of their own hatred to heal (see, for instance, Kushner 1996 and Gobodo-Madikizela 2004).

Hence, reading the amnesty clause in relation to the complex political victim does not produce a single answer. Certainly, the amnesty clause could be interpreted, and undoubtedly was interpreted by some, as a recognition of a complex political victim, a victim who deserves forgiveness despite a complex and often beneficial relationship with the discourse and practices of apartheid. In this sense, the recognition of a complex political victim *may* be the motivation for forgiveness and/or amnesty. But even in those who espouse forgiveness, we should not automatically assume that the perpetrators are being seen as some sort of complex political victim, and that this motivates their forgiveness; rather this forgiveness may simply be a part of one's religious or moral beliefs, or a tool to aid in their own healing. And finally, for many, the amnesty clause was simply a product of the political power struggles that invariably accompany a negotiated government transition. This interpretation does not indicate any recognition of the amnesty applicants as complex political victims at all and, as was mentioned earlier, may be understood as quite dismissive of victims altogether. As such, it does not implore a more nuanced look at the discourses of race and identity that created the space for such horrible victimization.

The Final Report

As much as the TRC relied on a certain discourse of victimization in recognizing and assisting victims and allowed for the emergence of individual narratives of victimization, it also actively created a discourse of South African victimization. Here again, we see a mixed ability to engage a discourse of complex victimization. While some antiapartheid activists remain frustrated with the final and official story of apartheid because it was not an entirely simple story of white atrocity and black innocence, the official narrative of apartheid does in fact retain and reify a simple script of victimization. The TRC's Final Report, in the end, does not significantly engage a notion of complex victimization, and rather serves as an instrumentally important "reimagination" of the apartheid era. At times, this reliance on a simple story of victimization serves as a critical platform for the initial steps toward community rebuilding; it serves the role of narrating and condemning the experience of oppression that had for decades been denied. But in the long run it may not have done enough to contribute to a deeply democratic and stable postapartheid society.

A Unified Narrative?

The South African TRC culminated in the drafting and publication of a Final Report. The Final Report was a much-anticipated, highly controversial, tremendously lengthy document; for our purposes here, it is useful to consider both the production of such a narrative and its content. Some (notably the ANC) actually attempted to prevent the publication of the Final Report because they believed its narrative portrayed an overly complex picture of victimization. Antiapartheid activists believed that in explicitly naming the ANC, and others as perpetrators during the apartheid period, the commissioners were failing to recognize the "straightforward and obvious" dynamics of apartheid—dynamics that presumably cast blacks in the victim role and the apartheid state in the role of perpetrator.

Others, such as Teitel (2000), emphasize not the precise objectivity of such reports but rather that such reports put forth a "democratizing truth." A democratizing truth is participatory (victims and perpetrators contributed to the narratives that underlie it), and encourages a broad social engagement with a particular narrative—a legitimate narrative, in stark contrast to the former false or absent stories of victimization that were produced during the period of victimization. As the name suggests, such a "truth" serves, much as Humphrey (2003) argues, as a moral platform from which to build a democratic and inclusive postvictimization state (see also Posel and Sampson 2002). Hamber and Wilson (2002) qualify this platform slightly differently, as shared memory, but give it the same critical task as the base from which to rebuild society.

> A countrywide process of revealing and confirming past wrongs is said to facilitate a common and shared memory, and in so doing create a sense of unity and reconciliation. By having this shared memory of the past, and a common identity as a traumatized people, the country can, at least ideally, move on to a future in which the same mistakes will not be repeated. (Hamber and Wilson, 2002, 35)

The previous chapter highlighted the necessity of creating an antagonism, a suture, to spur a recognition of and challenge to victimization. This is arguably a useful (though not exclusive) way of understanding the production of a final report; it is a production of a social narrative condemning the wrong. The Final Report functioned as a societal-level, broadly legitimate condemnation of apartheid as victimizing. It "allowed," from the perspective of the state, the recognition of apartheid victims as victims; it sutured the social space of South African discourse on race and governance to state clearly that what had happened during apartheid was victimizing. In the language of Hayner (2001), the Final Report moved beyond mere *knowledge* of apartheid to *acknowledging* the tremendous injustice of apartheid. Why was this so important in South Africa? Because for so long, for so many years, the state had denied victimization, casting doubt and blame on those victims who did surface, and in so doing, deepened the feeling of victimization and injustice. The following look at the Trust Feed Massacre highlights why this broadly legitimate condemnation of apartheid was necessary, why victims needed to be "reclaimed," given their status as victims again, and why this official creation of an antagonism was of such political importance for the future of South Africa.

Trust Feed Massacre

Early in the morning of October 16, 1988, eleven civilians, including young women and children, were massacred in the rural village of Trust Feed. These civilians had been gathered at the home of a relative who had passed away and were participating in an all-night wake to mourn his death. The massacre generated much public outcry, with the ANC attributing the violence to the apartheid security forces (referred to by many as the "third force"), while the police were noncommittal in their efforts to solve the crime, suggesting that it was just another incidence of "black-on-black violence." Indeed, the apartheid government aggressively contested narratives of violence against Africans that implicated any such "third force," and remained strong in their commitment to a story of violent infighting between the ANC and the Inkatha Freedom Party (IFP). The (contested) narrative of the Trust Feed Massacre became symbolic of a broader narrative of violence and repression in South Africa, a narrative where the true perpetrators were concealed and the victims were cast as deserving of blame. As Deputy President Zuma noted in an address at the Trust Feed sod-turning ceremony fifteen years after the event:

> The allegations about the existence of a Third Force, which was fuelling violence in this province and Gauteng had been denied by the apartheid government. The Trust Feed Massacre became a concrete example of this. (Zuma address, 10/3/2003)

The apartheid government held this event up as evidence of the "unruliness" of the black population, as an example of how "unfit" black South Africans were at civil behavior and self-governance. However, public outrage (both within South Africa and within the international community) made it difficult for the apartheid government to continue to hide its involvement, and a little more than three years later, in May 1992, a white police commissioner, Brian Mitchell, and four black police officers were found guilty on charges relating to the Trust Feed Massacre. Mitchell was found guilty on eleven counts of murder and sentenced to death for each one, though his sentence was commuted to thirty years in prison. Each of the black police officers received fifteen years for their role in the massacre (Ottoway, *Washington Post*, 5/1/1992). The trial, which dragged on for more than six months, supported the Trust Feed narrative that the ANC had been adhering to since the beginning; there was a "third force" connected with the apartheid government, and this force was being used to contribute to black-on-black violence.

> The trial revealed that the massacre was planned by members of the South African police and local leaders of Inkatha, the Zulu-led faction of Chief Mangosuthu Buthelezi, which has been engaged in a deadly struggle with ANC supporters since 1984, particularly in Natal Province where these killings took place. The guilty verdicts for the white police officer, who commanded a rural police station in Natal Province, and four black assistants lend credence to the contention of the ANC that the political violence largely has been the result of attempts by the South African security forces in conjunction with Inkatha to weaken or destroy the ANC. (Ottoway, *Washington Post*, 5/1/1992)

The significance of the trial extended beyond the Trust Feed Massacre itself. The story that emerged, the story that publicly confirmed that apartheid police were deeply and personally involved in orchestrating violence against antiapartheid activists and were involved in stoking black-on-black violence, signaled the emergence and validation of a new narrative of apartheid victimization. In this new narrative, the perpetrators were clearly and publicly identified, and the insidious nature of their acts was revealed. This narrative demonstrated that the apartheid government had intentionally victimized black South Africans and had attempted to muddy the contours of this victimization by making it look like black-on-black violence rather than the result of a racist, violent government. To be sure, the Trust Feed trial was not the first time such a narrative emerged in South Africa. Antiapartheid activists both within and outside of South Africa had put forth such a narrative of victimization for some time, but the Trust Feed massacre marks the first public, juridical endorsement of this narrative in South Africa (Ottoway, *Washington Post*, 5/1/1992).

When this "new" narrative of the Trust Feed massacre was encapsulated and expanded upon in the TRC's Final Report, the TRC was, in no uncertain terms, legitimating the victims as victims—innocents uninvolved in the insurgent activity. In the words of Michael Ignatieff, such truth commission reports at a minimum "reduce the number of lies that can be told" (Ignatieff 1996, 113). Through stories such as the Trust Feed massacre, the TRC was able to publicly, socially, and legitimately put forth a discourse of apartheid that did not blame victims, a discourse that allowed for individual victims to be acknowledged by the government, a critical first step for many on the path to self-subjectivation (to be discussed shortly).

The Final Report: Fair, Necessary, but Lacking Depth?

Perhaps the best way to characterize the final report, in light of these different interpretations of the narrative it contained, is to suggest that the commissioners attempted to produce a report that was fair in reporting victimization (recognizing atrocities on both sides), but not necessarily deep in probing the complex process of victimization (see also Fullard 2004). Further, it served an important purpose in condemning apartheid and its denial of victimization, a critical step for peace in South Africa.

But what about the lack of a rigorous, in-depth discussion of victimization during the apartheid era? President Mbeki, in a speech to the National House of Parliament, recognized the limitations of the report, choosing to see it as a roadmap with signs pointing to areas of need and further understanding rather than an exhaustive effort that could stand alone in cementing South Africa's transition towards nonracial democracy.

> Our assessment of the TRC's success cannot therefore be based on whether it has brought contrition and forgiveness, or whether at the end of its work, it handed us a united and reconciled society. For this was not its mandate. *What the TRC set out to do, and has undoubtedly achieved, is to offer us the signposts in the long march to these ideals.* What it was required to do and has accomplished, was to *flag the dangers that can beset a state not premised on popular legitimacy* and the confidence of its citizens, and the ills that would befall any society founded on prejudice and a belief in a "master race." (Mbeki speech, 4/15/03, emphasis added)

So while the final report was able to function as a socially accepted platform from which to move forward (though, of course, some were never satisfied with its account), it did not serve as a narrative for a better understanding of how and why, in South Africa, a political space emerged that was capable of supporting such horrific victimization. Bonner and Nieftagodien (2002) argue that the Final Report has a "fatal flaw":

> The relationships between different categories [of violations] of 'incident' are thus rendered opaque. Where 'window' episodes [selected victim testimonies] are selected, only immediate and triggering factors are taken into account as 'causes.' The possibility of an alternative explanation of the apartheid years and the immediate aftermath vanishes from view. Motivation becomes truncated, accountability leaches away. Historical process is utterly obscured, and explanations are reduced to a single political realm. (Bonner and Nieftagodien 2002, 177)

If we conceptualize the purpose of a final report only as broad documentation of wrongs and a platform for moving toward a more just society, such a report may function adequately. However, final reports are arguably much more than this. In the postvictimization period, these reports are often the most widely read item in the nation (as was the case in Chile; see Humphrey 2003), and they contribute greatly to the processing and understanding of the events surrounding the victimization. Such reports may contribute to the "reimagining" or "re-remembering" of the victimization (O'Donnell 1986). Reimagining is a process by which the victimized reconstruct a narrative of victimizing events—a narrative that often sharpens the distinction between the innocent and the guilty, and straightens the wavering line of responsibility. Humphrey (2003) argues that this process of reimagining is a particularly likely occurrence in postvictimization societies where trials are the main form of justice, though the juridical-positivist nature of truth commissions and their reports may also contribute to the appearance of this process.[20]

The production of a final report that does not substantively engage the complexities of victimization may encourage this sort of reimagining. Humphrey (2003) argues that the reimagining of the victimization experience, the sharpening of the line between innocent and guilty, and the unwillingness to consider the complexity of victimization, "can undermine the need for people to draw lessons from events in which they were morally implicated but now forget" (Humphrey 2003, 181). Such a perspective suggests that while the final report served as an effective platform of "democratizing truth," it may be less effective in helping South Africa, and the greater international community, understand decades of victimization.

Arguably, the Final Report could have served as a vehicle for understanding the complexity of victimization. The Final Report could have critically engaged the role of racialized identities more broadly, but it did not. The Final Report could have seriously considered how victims of apartheid who had adopted an "Africanist" or "black" identity to challenge their victimization could begin the difficult path towards the prescribed nonracial South African identity, but it did not. The Final Report could have considered in more depth the possible trauma to victims when these victims are asked to participate in a nonracial South Africa when their own identities were constructed in racial terms (despite their racial victimization), but it did not. It could have deeply investigated norms of political intolerance in South Africa, but it did not. What it did, instead, in creating a "democratizing truth," was construct a narrative of guilt and innocence, right and wrong—a narrative for comfortable personal and social "reimagining" but not a narrative of deep understanding.

AND NOW WE ASK, TO WHAT EFFECT?

It is impossible to assess comprehensively the effectiveness of the TRC. This is due first to the fact that "effectiveness" can be measured in so many areas, only a few of which were to be explicitly captured in the ambitious goals of the TRC. Here, the focus is on its effectiveness for victims and in contributing to a peaceful and stable postconflict society.

Effectiveness for Victims

In the preceding sections I have articulated how in some cases, the parameters and practices of the TRC may make it difficult for some individuals to self-identify as victims, preventing them from seeking assistance. Others, who do identify as victims, may find the processes and types of assistance offered ill-suited to their personal understanding of their victimizing experience. While this should concern us on the individual level—for example, all those who are victimized should be able to pursue a path of healing—it is also concerning on the social level.

In the case of South Africa, there is evidence of significant victim dissatisfaction with the truth commission process, with "heavily negative" victim reactions noted and suggestions that this "clearly raises the question of whether (or how) the TRC process truly contributed to reconciliations for such survivors" (Byrne 2004, 250). The social implications of this individual dissatisfaction are still emerging, but evidence from earlier truth commissions suggests that when victims feel excluded and dissatisfied from their participation in truth commissions and reconciliation, this has significant social impacts as well. Work by Suarez-Orozco (1991) documents the continued fractures between those in Argentina who felt they were helped and healed in some way by the truth commissions and reparations, and those who were not. Those victims, largely consisting of the relatives of the disappeared, refused to partake in much of the truth commission and reparations process, feeling that such processes were incapable of providing justice and offered healing only at the price of agreeing to "move on." This group of victims, the *Madres* of the *Plaza de Mayo*, are now politically excluded, ostracized by the nation for their unwillingness to participate in the state-sanctioned process of healing and rebuilding, and serve as a continual reminder of the tensions and difficulties associated with Argentina's past.[21] Buur (2002) also notes the emergence of dissatisfied victims' groups in South Africa, who are organizing not just to support one another, but importantly to voice their dissatisfaction with the TRC.

Another widely recognized issue is the benefit of getting into counseling those who were victimized. Hamber (1998, 16–17) notes that in regards to individual counseling, "inadequate follow-up, limited referral and sporadic support of individuals who have testified or made a statement to the TRC has occurred across the board." While this was identified as an issue for the individual (for example, by being unable to recognize oneself as a victim, it is unlikely that one would seek postvictimization counseling), it is a profound social issue as well. Many studies of apartheid victims have noted how these victims have tremendous difficulty participating in healthy relationships, employment, and so on because of unresolved issues related to their victimization (Hamber 1998). As a society, particularly one that is struggling to rebuild itself economically and politically, South Africa can ill afford to have traumatized individuals partaking in abusive parental and spousal relationships, grappling with basic life skills issues, or struggling with employment and education.

Despite significant evidence of victim dissatisfaction with their TRC experience (which, of course, does not even capture those who did not engage with the TRC, perhaps because they could not identify with the "victim" of the TRC), it would be inappropriate to characterize the TRC as wholly uninformed by complex notions of victimization, nor entirely ill prepared to recognize and assist complex political victims. Certain practices of victim recognition and participation may have supported the healing of complex political victims and their ability to engage in processes of self-subjectivation (for example, the early, open-ended statement-taking procedure), whereas others might have made difficult the recognition and healing of the complex political victim (the changes in statement-taking procedures, public testimony, certain reparations practices).

Dealing with Race and Political Intolerance: The Political Future of South Africa

Whatever partial successes exist, however, the fact remains that South Africa as a society is still grappling with challenges numerous and complex. In part in response to these lingering individual and social challenges, President Mbeki launched a plan for an "African Renaissance," an explicitly nonracial program designed to overcome social, political, and economic problems in South Africa and throughout the African continent.[22] Below, Mbeki identifies the following problems as those most pressing for the new South Africa,

- the establishment of democratic political systems to ensure the accomplishment of the goal that "the people shall govern"
- ensuring that these systems take into account African specifics so that, while being truly democratic and protecting human rights, they are nevertheless designed in ways which really ensure that political and, therefore, peaceful means can be used to address the competing interests of different social groups in each country
- establishing the institutions and procedures which would enable the continent collectively to deal with questions of democracy, peace, and stability

- achieving sustainable economic development that results in the continuous improvement of the standards of living and the quality of life of the masses of the people
- qualitatively changing Africa's place in the world economy so that it is free of the yoke of the international debt burden and no longer a supplier of raw materials and an importer of manufactured goods
- ensuring the emancipation of the women of Africa
- successfully confronting the scourge of HIV/AIDS
- the rediscovery of Africa's creative past to recapture the peoples' cultures, encourage artistic creativity, and restore popular involvement in both accessing and advancing science and technology
- strengthening the genuine independence of African countries and continent in their relations with the major powers and enhancing their role in the determination of the global system of governance in all fields, including politics, the economy, security, information and intellectual property, the environment, and science and technology (Mbeki 1999)

The achievement of even some of these goals, much less all of them, arguably requires a healthy, competent, and engaged population. A population that has been able to "work on itself" is poised and ready to reach out and engage in the political and social challenges ahead—a population not left behind by a system of recognition and assistance ill equipped to deal with certain victims, a society that has grappled with the complexity of political victimization, the "complex social causes," and what at times may be an uncomfortable engagement with race and political intolerance.

In addition, many of these goals, while not couched in the language of race by the African Renaissance platform, are still very much racial issues.[23] Estimates suggest that one in nine South Africans are HIV-positive, and the vast majority of those affected are black (World Health Organization, 2005). Emancipating women cannot come without engaging differing racial and cultural conceptions of gender. Rediscovering culture requires a reconsideration of the intersection, both past and present, between race, culture, identity, and power. Establishing a deeply democratic political system requires a high level of political tolerance. South Africa must more closely consider the complex contours of its discourse on race and identity, particularly in the political sphere.

President Mbeki proclaimed that "Yesterday is a foreign country—tomorrow belongs to us!" (speech at the African Renaissance Conference, Johannesburg, 9/28/1998). While this note of hope and optimism is important as South Africa faces an uncertain future, it is important to more deeply consider just what belongs to them and whether sufficient efforts have been made to unpack what has belonged to South Africa in the past, and continues to belong to them today.

Thought must be given to dealing with the remnants of the BCM and the racial politics of certain political groups, because even as the salience of these groups decrease in "nonracial" South Africa, the influence of these groups on identity formation remains. Apartheid South Africa cast black South Africans as inferior, second-class citizens at best. Modern South Africa, while premised on equality, still unfortunately has black South Africans filling the role of the diseased, impoverished, and destitute. That such a people would search for a more positive image of the black South African and remain skeptical and even intolerant of the privileged, much as they did during the 1960s and 1970s, is certainly a possibility.[24] Indeed, Mbeki's notion of an African Renaissance speaks to this need to reconceptualize decades, even centuries, of a victimized identity, a victimized people. In the words of Buur (2002), the narrative produced by the TRC attempted to do this by putting forth the image of "a rainbow nation. . . a defense against a violent and fragmented past," and certainly a desire to build politically on this narrative is evident in Mbeki's African Renaissance platform. However, it remains to be seen whether a nonracial African Renaissance will shepherd South Africans into the future, or whether lingering racialized politics, reinforced by real and lived racial disparities and political intolerance, will dominate the political landscape.

Recent findings by Gibson and Gouws (2003) indicate that nonracialism has a long way to go in South Africa. Rather, "othering" is rampant in South Africa, and it may be particularly well poised to create space for political victimization. Gibson and Gouws (2003) have found that nearly all South Africans accept one of the four following categories as their primary social identity: African, white, colored, or Asian origin. Gibson and Gouws also note a high degree of subcultural pluralism that includes, but is not limited to, racial divides.

> The country is divided, and deeply so, along a variety of racial, ethnic, and linguistic lines. Race is certainly central to South African politics, but intraracial (or ethnic) divisions are terribly significant as well. (Gibson and Gouws 2003, 72)

Further, Gibson and Gouws note, "for South Africans of every race, these identities are indeed important. Roughly three-fourths of each group rated their identity as "very important," the highest on a five-point scale (Gibson and Gouws 2003, 80). Despite the end of apartheid, exclusive group-based identities still matter tremendously to South Africans. And in many instances, these identities matter in a positive way, with two-thirds of respondents saying they derive at least some "psychic benefits" from their identification with a racial or ethnic group (psychic benefits being described as security, self-esteem, or importance). Indeed, more than half of South Africans responded that their race-based social identity provided all three of these psychic benefits. So here we see the contours of a discourse of othering that comes from and may create the space for political victimization, yet also is positively constructing the identity of many South Africans.

Gibson and Gouws's (2003) findings on social identity in South Africa are particularly illuminating when combined with their findings on political intolerance. Gibson and Gouws's research indicates that South Africa is a politically intolerant nation. The conceptual map that links strong social identities to political identities is articulated as follows:

> Strong identities, tinged with authoritarianism, lead to anti-identities. These in turn lead to the perception that outgroups are threatening. Since authoritarianism and closemindedness involve making harsh distinctions between friends and foes, those who are dogmatic are more likely to see the world as comprised of ingroups and outgroups, with a rigid divide between the two. Since the perception of threats from groups is one of the strongest predictors of intolerance, strong identities therefore lead to intolerance. (Gibson and Gouws 2003, 76)

"Political intolerance" does not necessarily mean violence, but it does suggest an unwillingness to accept the presence and participation of disliked groups (of which there are many in South Africa, including not just extremists but also more mainstream parties). For those groups that are most disliked (the Afrikaner Resistance Movement [AWB] and Inkatha Freedom Party [IFP]), only one in five think that these groups should have the right to engage in legal political activities such as organizing, protesting, and running candidates.

In addition, Maloka (2001) notes how Mbeki's enthusiasm for a nonracial African Renaissance is not shared by all, not just because it will be difficult to achieve, but also because it may not be normatively preferable.

> Some warned against the African Renaissance becoming a totalizing idea. Others, especially among the minorities, wondered whether this wasn't the ANC's turn towards narrow Africanism. As for the PAC, an organization that broke away from the ANC over the latter's non-racialism, it is battling to enter the debate on its own terms. (Maloka, 2001, 3)

While there is guarded enthusiasm among many South Africans for a nonracial African Renaissance, there is concern that such a plan has its own problems: first, with "othering" and the creation of exclusive political identities, and second, that its platform of nonracialism insufficiently handles lingering discourses of race and identity among all South Africans—discourses that Gibson and Gouws (2003) have shown matter tremendously among South Africans (see also Maloka 2001). Auvinen and Kavamaki (2001) also note how important the "deconstruction of racially informed social practices" is in tackling the deep transformation of the conflict and injustice in South Africa. While the African Renaissance plan has end goals of racially blind social practices, it does not adopt the task of deconstructing the deep and complex discourse of race that still permeates South African society—in particular, how to deal with the fact that much of the discourse on race in South Africa constructs "psychic benefits" as well as obstacles and injustice. Engaging a discourse of complex victimization in South Africa may prove useful in reforming the African Renaissance to more adequately tackle these issues. On the one hand, it would perhaps alert its supporters to the way in which even "positive" discourses of nationalism, race, and identity can contribute to future spaces of political victimization. It would reinforce the idea that victimization does not just occur because an evil perpetrator introduces an oppressive ideology such as apartheid. Second, a discourse of complex victimization would caution that while a speedy transition to nonracial politics has significant normative appeal, a more careful consideration of the complexity of political and racial victimization is warranted. This is necessary both to deal with the "psychic benefits" aspect of race and identity discourse but also to confront the fact that many "real" problems of race, politics, and identity remain, problems such as disproportional HIV/AIDS rates, employment opportunities, education, and poverty.

Peace, Reconciliation, and Beyond

> One of the challenges a political community faces in seeking to make the transition into a properly functioning democracy is therefore to create conditions that encourage replacing enmity with, if not love or friendship, then at least regard for others as fellow humans. (Gobodo-Madikizela 2004, 127)

The maintenance of postvictimization peace in South Africa demands healthy, competent citizens who can work toward a better future. Some, such as Hayner (2001) put the emphasis on reconciliation as critical in producing citizens capable of working together toward a better future. Hayner (2001) distinguishes between individual and national reconciliation, but in each case suggests that reconciliation "implies building or rebuilding relationships today that are not haunted by the conflicts and hatreds of yesterday" (Hayner 2001, 161).[25] Hayner (2001) notes the difficulty of "seeing" reconciliation; however, the above definition and Hayner's discussion of the matter suggests that relationships based on the present, and not encumbered with the trauma of the past, are signs that "reconciliation" is happening or has happened. Hayner (2001) notes the importance of the following as prerequisites for reconciliation: the cessation of violence, acknowledgment and reparation, binding forces joining previously opposing groups (joint projects, for instance), and attending to basic inequalities and needs.

To this, I would add an additional prerequisite: a rigorous consideration of the complexity of victimization. Equitable, deeply democratic relationships are not possible if lingering discourses of "othering" abound (see Dahl 1989; Horowitz 1985, 1991). David and Yukping (2005) note that political victims in the Czech Republic had a strong tendency to favor an "us and them," dichotomous worldview, an "othering" that threatens democracy in that country.

> [T]he frame of reference of some of our respondents is very rigid. Many hold a dualistic worldview that divides people into two categories: "we" and "they," "mukls [former political prisoners]" and "communists," "good" and "bad," those who adhere to these principles and those who do not. This dualism, paradoxically, mirrors dualistic categories held by their totalitarian oppressors who were determined to liquidate class enemies for a "better future." Such a dualistic mentality runs in direct conflict with democratic mentalities, which emphasize the pluralistic character of the world and which rest on compromises. (David and Yukping 2005, 429)

Further, if relationships are to be "based on the present," it is critical that the present is truly a discourse inhospitable to victimization, not the picture that emerges in Gibson and Gouws's (2003) discussion of a racialized and politically intolerant South Africa. South Africa presents as a nation that still is grappling with strong and salient "othering," and a tendency to view disliked "others" as unwelcome political and social participants. Reconciliation, peace, and democracy in South Africa demand Hayner's prerequisites for reconciliation as well as a serious consideration of the complexity of victimization and discourses of othering. Without them, South Africa runs a very real risk that lingering discourses of racial "othering" and political intolerance will combine with economic, social, and health crises in the black community to produce a space for political violence.

CONCLUSION

The South African TRC was a complex, ambitious project of healing and nation building. As Hamber and Wilson (2002) note, these two processes, though often lumped together in postconflict situations, share few similarities, in timeline, needs, or desires. Perhaps for this reason, an analysis of the complex political victim, and her ability to work on herself and the healing of her community in regards to the TRC, is so full of contradiction. The production of the final report, which can serve as an antagonism and articulate the discourse of apartheid as broadly and unequivocally victimizing, might be tremendously beneficial as a motivation to work on oneself and resist victimization. But it can also prove a hindrance to this deeply personal process of working on oneself because of its tendency to produce scripted narratives of victimization, its reliance on an image of the ideal victim, and its tendency to develop shallow narratives of consensus. The opportunity afforded to "work on memory," to engage in processes of subjectivation that challenge victimization, to potentially reach out again to contribute positively to the changing norms of racial identity and tolerance may be stifled by the lingering discourses that the TRC was never inclined to probe.

Supplanting the discourse of the victim that informed the postapartheid process with a discourse of the complex political victim is unlikely the complete answer. For instance, some of the international moral outrage that contributed to the end of apartheid, and the recognition of victimization might have been stunted, had a nuanced story of apartheid victimization butted against the simpler narratives of victimization prevalent in the international community at that time (though as this book has shown, the very fact that the "simple" narrative has more moral strength than the "complex" narrative is deeply problematic). As such, developing a more complex discourse of political victimization is critical, and it is critical that such a discourse challenge the assumptions that the simple notion of ideal political victims is morally preferable to victim complexities and nuance.

In the immediate South African context, complex political victims do matter tremendously. Our ability to recognize and assist these victims is critical to continued individual and social healing. In part because the TRC did not significantly engage the complex political victim identity, many victims never identified as such and were not included in the process of healing. Further, the few tendencies within the TRC that indicated a partial acceptance and assistance of the complex political victim, such as open-ended statement taking, were at times hindered by national reconstruction goals. Other possible places to recognize complex political victims, such as within the context of amnesty, deteriorated rapidly into weighty political contests, not meaningful discussions of victimization. President Mbeki identifies the shortcomings of the TRC as the fault of society, but this chapter has endeavored to show that some of these shortcomings might have been mitigated by incorporating an understanding of the complex political victim into the architecture and practices of the TRC.

> The extent to which the TRC could identify and pursue priority cases; its ability to bring to its hearings all relevant actors; the attention that it could pay to civil society's role in buttressing an illegitimate and illegal state; and the TRC's investigative capacity to pursue difficult issues with regard to

which the actors had decided to spurn its call for co-operation—*all these weaknesses were those of society and not the TRC as such.* (Mbeki, 4/15/03)

If the TRC had difficulty bringing all relevant actors to the table, it was because of problems within society, not the design of the TRC. If other actors spurned a call for cooperation, it was because of societal problems, not the design of the TRC or the sometimes simplistic narratives of victimization on which it relied. While Mbeki is correct in pointing out that the TRC faced many challenges, many of which it could not control, I have argued here that some of these shortcomings could have been addressed through a more careful consideration of the victimization discourse that informed the TRC.

The importance of this neglect of complex political victim discourse is only beginning to be felt in South Africa. As the TRC winds down, the amnesty hearings close, and plans for reparations are put on hold, there remains a contingent of unrecognized, unassisted victims. Many of these individuals cannot heal and have great difficulty in partaking in the rebuilding of South Africa. South African political leaders, such as President Mbeki, must navigate complex domestic and international issues of continued victimization, both personal and structural, without the benefit of a national dialogue on the complexities of victimization, on the discourses of race, identity, and political tolerance—discourses that may again open up the space for the return of large-scale political unrest and victimization. In his own words, Mbeki recognizes how much there is to be done, how the potential for political violence remains.

> The situation we face demands that none of us should succumb to the false comfort that now we live in a normal society that has overcome the legacy of the past, and which permits us to consider our social tasks as mere business as usual.
>
> Rather, it demands that we continue to be inspired by the determination and vision that enabled us to achieve the transition from apartheid rule to a democratic order in the manner that we did. It demands that we act together as one people to address what are truly national tasks.
>
> We have to ask ourselves and honestly answer simple questions.
>
> Have we succeeded to create a non-racial society? The answer to this question is no!
>
> Have we succeeded to build a non-sexist society? The answer to that question is no!
>
> Have we succeeded to eradicate poverty? Once more the answer to that question is no!
>
> Have we succeeded fully to address the needs of the most vulnerable in our society, the children, the youth, people with disabilities and the elderly? Once again the answer to this question is no!
>
> Without all this, it is impossible for us to claim that we have met our goals of national reconciliation and reconstruction and development. It is

not possible for us to make the assertion that we have secured the well-being of all South African citizens. (Mbeki Statement to the House of Parliament, 4/15/2003)

Answering yes to these questions, no matter what discourse is invoked, will be a challenge for South Africa, yet incorporating a discourse of complex political victimization has the potential to help South Africa on this path.

NOTES

1. Hayner (2001) does an excellent job of discussing this "patchwork" of literature on whether truth commissions help victims heal or not; see particularly chap. 9.

2. Though see Buur (2000, 2001, 2002) as well as the edited volume (Posel and Sampson 2002) *Commissioning the Past: Understanding South Africa's Truth and Reconciliation Commission.*

3. As but one aspect of the controversy, many were strongly opposed to the notion of "gross" violations of human rights, suggesting that human rights violations, by their very nature, were "gross."

4. See Buur (2002) for an excellent discussion of the difficulty this "political motivation" stipulation resulted in, particularly in regards to acts that were racially motivated, but without clear political connections.

5. Humphrey (2003) takes a somewhat different stance on this issue. He argues more strongly that the state, by recognizing only certain victims for the purposes of the Truth Commission, in some ways inhibits the identification/constitution of other victims. See also Posel and Sampson (2002).

6. There are obvious similarities here to the arguments put forth by Arendt, and the response to these statements of white victimization are markedly similar to the response to Arendt's suggestion of understanding the Nazis as victims.

7. Here we see a similar resistance to what was perceived as a definition of the victim that was too "inclusive," much as Morrisey and Smyth (2002) note in the context of Northern Ireland. Some blacks in South Africa, much like Catholics in Northern Ireland, were deeply opposed to recognizing whites, or Protestants respectively as victimized.

8. This is not to suggest that all of the deaths attributed to the ANC were white victims, as many were in fact black South Africans thought to be informants, members of politically opposed parties, etc.

9. Note that this is different than saying that the acts of the apartheid government deserve more rigorous consideration because they were *state* actions, the position of the TRC.

10. We return shortly to this question of the white South African as a complex political victim, and how much the TRC actually recognized such a victim in the practice and proceedings of the TRC.

11. Although it should be noted that by recognizing that in some ways all South Africans were victimized by apartheid, the TRC was not affirming what could be called the "victimized Afrikaner" narrative. Hermann Giliomee's excellent book *The Afrikaners* notes how some Afrikaners (particularly Verwoerd, former South African

president), articulated a narrative of Afrikaner victimization. Main themes of this narrative focused on their treatment under the British, never being a majority in their homeland, and the like. Some within the Afrikaner community clung to a narrative of the white Afrikaner as the always persecuted, always vulnerable (not unlike Holocaust theologians). The TRC in no way recognized or supported this script of Afrikaner identity, but rather recognized how apartheid, in failing to uphold and protect human dignity, could be seen as an affront to all humans living within such a system.

12. I am drawing on Gibson and Gouws's (2003) definition of political intolerance, namely an unwillingness to "put up with" disliked political groups. This includes a willingness to repress or ban legal political activities of such groups (such as the right to organize, demonstrate, etc.).

13. It should be noted that I am not equating Africanism with apartheid. Rather, this discussion is intended to illuminate how both discourses rely on exclusive, racialized political identities. Where they go from there (both theoretically and practically) is of course quite different.

14. More on this topic is discussed shortly in the context of the production of the Final Report.

15. I say "for instance" because arguably there are many other discourses that participate in the creation and maintenance of apartheid policies, such as the discourse of the sovereign state, the discourse of patriarchy, etc.

16. The following discussion of why some did not self-identify as victims should be understood as distinct from the fact that some victims were not recognized "officially" by the TRC because they were out of mandate (for example, their victimization was not defined as gross violations of human rights, was not found to be politically motivated, etc.). Here I am speaking only about victims who in a general (not official) sense were not inclined to self-identify as victims.

17. The social implications of not identifying as a victim are discussed in the final portion of this chapter.

18. There are similarities here to the pressure a victim may feel in making a victim information statement in a courtroom. Also, it should be noted that the TRC's dedication to a "balanced view" of apartheid references the selection of both blacks and whites to present victim testimony and seemingly does not suggest a commitment to a more balanced or nuanced understanding of individual experiences of victimization.

19. The transcripts of this victim testimony (and indeed most victim testimony) are available on the South African Department of Justice online archive.

20. See Rosenberg (1995) and Osiel (1997) for more on instances where reimagining has occurred in response to trials and truth commissions in postvictimization societies.

21. Morrisey and Smyth (2002) note similar issues in Northern Ireland.

22. Mbeki first put forth the idea of an "African Renaissance" in 1996 in his speech "I Am an African." In the past decade it has continued to play a prominent role in South African politics, and when Mbeki became president in 1999, he worked to further incorporate policies of an African Renaissance into domestic affairs as well as South African leadership on the African continent.

23. Mbeki acknowledges this fact. Indeed, Mbeki is generally considered the president more willing to deal with race in politics (though he has also espoused a nonracial platform), in comparison to his predecessor Mandela, whose political position was informed by a strong commitment to a "nonracial" paradigm. See the Center for the

Study of Violence and Reconciliation's ongoing reports in the Race and Citizenship in Transition series.

24. For an interesting look at how South Africans experience poverty and lack of basic material needs, see the Institute for Democracy in South Africa Report Afrobarometer Briefing Number 11, April 2004 "Lived Poverty." Of particular note is the finding that not only are many South Africans quite destitute, but they do not believe this situation is "normal"; they are tremendously dissatisfied with a situation that many South Africans see as worsening. Such a picture of dissatisfaction and perceptions of injustice (some racial, some not) certainly support the possibility that black South Africans will again search for a "positive" identity.

25. See also David and Yukping (2005) for an additional discussion of the individual and social components of this process, in particular their discussion of sociopolitical redress and inner healing.

Epilogue

The Role of Complex Political Victim Discourse

[T]o challenge fixed conceptions of will, identity, responsibility, normality, and punishment is to be cruel to people (and aspects of oneself) attached to established moral codes: it is to open up new uncertainties within established terms of judgment; and sometimes it is to incite punitive reactions among those whose sense of moral self-assurance has been jeopardized. (Connolly 1993, 365)

The motivation for this book was, in part, to show that victimization, particularly political victimization, is rarely a simple process with only discreet, easily recognizable perpetrators and victims. This book has challenged fixed conceptions of the victim identity, and characteristics and roles in the process of victimization. And while care was taken to undertake this task in a manner that was not cruel to people and aspects of oneself, such a project rests with the creation of a somewhat uncertain moral terrain. Yet bringing nuance and complexity to the narratives of victimization is nonetheless critical because these narratives matter so much—because they shape the ability of the international community and other actors to recognize and assist victims and to rebuild postconflict societies. This task could have been accomplished much as Arendt often does, by highlighting the responsibility and interests of the *human* community to partake in a discourse of humanity that shuns othering in order to prevent and stop victimization.

Instead this project focused specifically on victims; to suggest that at times victims may bear some responsibility for creating the space of their victimization; and even further, that victims may or may not be interested in disengaging from the discourses that contribute to the space necessary for their victimization. The same could be said of most all people: our responsibility and interests in most events, victimizing or otherwise, is often quite complex. The question may rightly be asked, as it was in the very beginning: why focus on unpacking victims? The perils of using a simplistic script of victimization have been demonstrated, but what are the benefits of deconstructing victims in particular, especially given the risks?

It seems that one of the strongest arguments for presenting a discourse of the complex political victim is that it allows for more precise, contextually based discussions of how victimization occurred, what spaces may allow it to occur again, and what facets of the victim identity are critical to address both in the process of healing and in the process of rebuilding community. For instance, a discourse of the complex political victim, in the Bosnian case, allowed an exploration of the discourses and practices of ethno-religious identity and constitutional nationalism. Or alternatively, in the case of South Africa, it allows for the consideration of how a simplistic narrative of racial victimization was critical in the challenging and condemning of apartheid, but such a discourse of victimization provides little guidance in how to carry out an "African Renaissance," consolidate democracy, and prevent subcultural pluralism from again giving rise to political violence.

A discourse of the complex political victim would have enabled actors both domestic and international to more effectively engage in situations of political victimization. It is arguably no coincidence that Bosnia and South Africa are still plagued by tremendous discursive practices of othering in social and political life; indeed even modern-day Germany has traditions of delineating between native and foreigner, traditions that have resurfaced strongly in light of increased migration from Turkey and other eastern European countries. A discourse of victimization that highlights the complex interactions between "victims" and "perpetrators" and shows how these interactions create space for political victimization highlights the need for more nuanced dialogues during the process of peacebuilding, reconciliation, and nation building. An appreciation of the complexities of political victimization can provide a strong impetus to construct a social narrative that condemns injustice and to use this platform for a new political order, one based on equality and the protection of basic rights. But it can also encourage the much more difficult, messy dialogues about how victimization occurs, unpacking the nuance of the relations and practices that constitute the space for political victimization.

As indicated in the first chapter, the argument made here is not one that suggests international discourse on victimization where the complex political victim is the only image of the victim available. Other discourses of victimization, particularly ones that are much more simplistic in their accounts of responsibility, are critical in certain situations—for instance, the courtroom prosecution of war criminals. That said, the invocation of a discourse of the complex political victim seems to me particularly useful in the following areas.

First, it can be critical in recognizing victims who are embroiled in complex ethnic and civil conflicts. Such a discourse would prevent international inaction simply because the victims, though disproportionately harmed, seemed to bear some responsibility, as happened in the early years of the Balkans conflict. Second, such a discourse can be useful to include when developing policies of victim assistance. Ideally, victim assistance policies include a plethora of strategies designed to reach out and heal a diverse set of victims. A discourse of the complex political victim would encourage the inclusion of open-ended narration and the provision of space for effective subjectivation and would refrain from the forced casting of innocent victims as moral beacons—especially insofar as it often leads to an exclusion of so many other victims. Further, a discourse of the complex political victim would support the large-scale social projects that articulate the wrongness of victimization (for example, the production of truth commission reports), yet would recognize these steps as the first in opening the space for subjectivation, not as an attempt to bring closure to individual and social victimization. Though many truth commissions, war crime tribunals, and the like are state-centric in their construction, a discourse of the complex political victim would encourage domestic and international actors to understand the role that self-subjectivation of victims can play. These victims, as they work on themselves, are also primed to reach out and effect social change and development. Subjectivation does not simply trap them in their role as victims and force them to serve as a perpetual reminder of why we must never let such victimization occur. In the words of Humphrey (2003), the state often sees the victims as the "fulcrum of pain" around which the old society terrorized and the new society establishes itself. Subjectivation encourages more than this. Victims, through their own identity work, can take on a role more dynamic and personal than merely being the fulcrum of pain.

Last, the discourse of a complex political victim can contribute to the long-term viability of peace in postvictimization societies. The unfolding process, after subjectivation, fosters inclusiveness, creativity, and participation. To be sure, the strength and legitimacy of the state is important in managing this creative participation, but it alone cannot be the genesis of such inclusion. Appreciating the complexities of victimization can serve to remind the new government, and indeed the international community, of discourses propitious to political violence, and the many ways that individuals engage these discourses. And the discourse of the complex political victim can serve as a reminder to all that we must carefully reflect upon our own values and practices, for they constitute many spaces and many identities, and we must be ever mindful of the creation of the space necessary for acts of political victimization.

Bibliography

Abu-Nimer, M., ed. 2001. *Reconciliation, Justice and Coexistence*. Lanham, MD: Lexington.

Agger, I. and Jensen, S. 1990. "Testimony As Ritual and Evidence in Psychotherapy for Political Refugees." *Journal of Traumatic Stress*, 3(1): 115–130.

———. 1996. *Trauma and Healing Under State Terrorism*. London: Zed Books.

Albin, C. 2001. *Justice and Fairness in International Negotiation*. Cambridge: Cambridge University Press.

Allen, B. 1996. *Rape Warfare: The Hidden Genocide in Bosnia-Herzegovina and Croatia*. Minnesota: University of Minnesota Press.

Arata, C. 1999. "Coping With Rape: The Role of Prior Sexual Abuse and Attributions of Blame." *Journal of Interpersonal Violence*, 14: 62–78.

Arendt, H. 1978. *The Jew as Pariah*. ed. Ron Feldman. New York: Grove Press.

———. 2003. *Responsibility and Judgment*. New York: Schocken.

Arendt, H. and Jaspers, K. 1992. *Correspondence, 1926–1969*. ed. L. Kohler and H. Saner. New York: Harcourt Brace and Company.

Arendt, H. and McCarthy, M. 1995. *Between Friends: The Correspondence of Hannah Arendt and Mary McCarthy 1949–75*. ed. Carol Brightman. New York: Harcourt Brace and Company.

Arendt, H. and Scholem, G. 1964. "Eichman in Jerusalem: Exchange of Letters between Gershom Scholem and Hannah Arendt." *Encounter*, 22(1): 51–56.

Armstrong, T. 1992. *Michel Foucault: Philosopher*. New York/London: Routledge.

Auvinen, J. and Kivimaki, T. 2001. "Conflict Transformation in South Africa" *Politikon*, 28(1): 65–79.

Babic, M. 1993. Bilten Prve Majevicke Brigade. Reprinted (trans) in FBIS-EEU-93-105, 1/26: 45.

Baker, P. (2001). "Conflict Resolution vs. Democratic Governance: Divergent Paths to Peace?" in *Turbulent Peace* ed. C. Crocker, F. Hampson, and P. Aall. Washington, D.C.: United States Institute of Peace.

Barstow, A. 2000. *Wars Dirty Secrets: Rape, Prostitution, and Other Crimes Against Women*. New York: Pilgrim.

Bayley J. 1991. "The Concept of Victimhood." In *To Be A Victim: Encounters with Crime and Justice* ed. D. Sank and D. Caplan. New York: Plenum Press.

Berdahl, R. 2002. "Reflections on 9/11" speech given at the University of California, Berkeley, September 11, 2002.

Bernauer, J. 1990. *Michel Foucault's Forces of Flight*. New Jersey and London: Humanities Press International.

Berton, P., Kimura, H., and Zartman, Z., ed. 1999. *International Negotiation: Actors, Structure/Process, and Values.* New York: St. Martin's Press.

Bernstein, R. 1996. *Hannah Arendt and the Jewish Question.* Cambridge: MIT Press.

Bhargava, R. 1998. *Secularism and its Critics.* Delhi: Oxford University Press.

Bhoutrous-Ghali, B. 1992. *An Agenda for Peace.* New York: United Nations.

Biggar, N. 2003. *Burying the Past: Making Peace and Doing Justice After Civil Conflict.* Washington, DC: Georgetown University Press.

Binder, D. 1995. "Bosnia's Bombers." *The Nation.* October 2.

Bonner, P. and Nieftagodien, N. 2002. In *Commissioning the Past: Understanding South Africa's Truth and Reconciliation Commission.* ed. D. Posel and G. Sampson. Johannesburg: Witwatersrand University Press.

Borer, A. 2003. "A Taxonomy of Victims and Perpetrator: Human Rights and Reconciliation in South Africa." *Human Rights Quarterly,* 25(4): 1088–1116.

Borris, E. 2001. "Reconciliation in Post-Conflict Peacebuilding: Lessons Learned from South Africa." in J. Davies and E. Kaufman eds. *Second Track/Citizens' Diplomacy: Concepts and Techniques for Conflict Transformation.* Lanham and Oxford: Rowman and Littlefield.

———. 2003. "The Healing Power of Forgiveness." Occasional Paper #10, *Institute for Multi-track Diplomacy.*

Bove, P. 1986. *Intellectuals in Power: A Genealogy of Critical Humanism.* New York: Columbia University Press.

Boyd, C. 1995. "Making Peace with the Guilty." *Foreign Affairs,* 74(5): 22–38.

Braumann, R. 1993. "When Suffering Makes a Good Story" in *Life, Death and Aid: The Medecins Sans Frontieres Report on World Crisis Intervention.* ed. Francois Jean. London: Routledge.

Bringa, T. 1995. *Being Muslim the Bosnian Way.* Princeton: Princeton University Press.

Brown, M. ed. 1996. *International Dimensions of Internal Conflict.* Cambridge, MA: MIT Press.

Brownmiller, S. 1993. "Making Female Bodies the Battlefield. *Newsweek,* 1/4: 29–43.

Butler, J. 1990. *Gender Trouble.* New York and London: Routledge.

Buur, L. 2000. *Institutionalizing Truth: Victims, Perpetrators, and Professionals in the Everyday Work of the South African Truth and Reconciliation Commission.* Dissertation submitted to the Department of Ethnography and Anthropology, Aarhus University, Denmark.

———. 2001. "In the Name of Victims: The Politics of Compensation in the South African Truth and Reconciliation Commission." *South African Reconciliation Project,* available at http://www.wits.ac.za/csvr.

———. 2002. Monumental historical memory: Managing truth in the everyday work of the South African Truth and Reconciliation Commission. In *Commissioning the Past: Understanding South Africa's Truth and Reconciliation Commission.* D. Posel and G. Sampson, eds. Johannesburg: Witwatersrand University Press.

Byrne, C. 2004. "Benefit or Burden: Victims' Reflections on TRC Participation." *Peace and Conflict: Journal of Peace Psychology,* 10(37): 237–256.

Callari, A. and Ruccio, D. ed. 1996. *Postmodern Materialism and the Future of Marxist Theory: Essays in the Althusserian Tradition.* Hanover and London: Wesleyan University Press.

Campbell, D. 1998. *National Deconstruction: Violence, Identity, and Justice in Bosnia.* Minneapolis: University of Minnesota Press.

Campbell-Ruggard, J. and Van Ryswyk, J. 2001 "Rape on Campus: Numbers Tell Less Than Half the Story." In *Sex Without Consent* ed. M. D. Smith, 283–299. New York and London: New York University Press.

Carpenter, C. 2005. "Women, Children and Other Vulnerable Groups: Gender, Strategic Frames and the Protection of Civilians as a Transnational Issue." *International Studies Quarterly*, 49: 295–334.

Churchill, W. 1941. *Address to the Allied Delegates*, given at St. James's Place, London, June 12, 1941.

Cigar, N. 1995. *Genocide in Bosnia*. College Station: Texas A&M University Press.

Cockburn, R. 1999. "If Slobo, Why Not Bill?" *The Nation*. June 3.

Connolly, W. 1993. "Beyond Good and Evil: The Ethical Sensibility of Michel Foucault." *Political Theory*, 21(3), 365–389.

Conversi, D. 1996. "Moral Relativism & Equidistance in British Attitudes to the War in the Former Yugoslavia." In *This Time We Knew: Western Responses to Genocide in Bosnia*, ed. T. Cushman and S. Mestrovic. New York and London: New York University Press.

Copelon, R. 1994. "Surfacing Gender: Re-Engraving Crimes against Women in Humanitarian Law." *Hastings Women's Law Journal*, 5: 243–265.

Cordero, I. 2001. "From Victims to Actors in Peacebuilding." In *Victims, Perpetrators, or Actors?* C. Moser and P. Clark, ed. London: Zed Books.

Cousens, E. ed. 2001. *Peacebuilding as Politics*. Boulder: Lynne Rienner Publishers.

Crocker, C., Hampson, F., and Aall, P. 2004. *Taming Intractable Conflicts*. Washington, DC: United States Institute of Peace.

Crocker, D. 2003. "Reckoning with Past Wrongs: A Normative Framework." In *Dilemmas of Reconciliation* ed. Prager and Govier. Ontario CA: Wilfrid Laurier University Press.

Cronin, B. 1999. *Community Under Anarchy*. New York: Columbia University Press.

Cuevas, V. E., Rojas, M. L. O., and Baeza, P. R. 2002. *Truth Commissions: An Uncertain Path? Comparative Study of Commissions in Argentina, Chile, El Salvador, Guatemala and South Africa from the Perspectives of Victims, their Relatives, Human Rights Organizations, and Experts*. Santiago de Chile and Geneva: CODEPU and APT.

Cullenberg, S. 1994. *The Falling Rate of Profit*. London: Pluto Press.

Cushman, T. and Mestrovic, S. ed. 1996. *This Time We Knew: Western Responses to Genocide in Bosnia*. New York and London: New York University Press.

Dahl, R. 1989. *Democracy and Its Critics*. New Haven: Yale University Press.

David, R. and Yukping, C. S. 2005. "Victims on Transitional Justice: Lessons from the Reparation of Human Rights Abuses in the Czech Republic." *Human Rights Quarterly*, 27(2): 392–435.

Deleuze, G. 1987. *A Thousand Plateaus: Capitalism and Schizophrenia*. Translation B. Massumi. Minneapolis and London: University of Minnesota Press.

———. 1990, 1995 for translation. *Negotiations 1972–1990*. Translation M. Joughin. New York: Columbia University Press.

——— 1994. "Foldings, or the Inside of Thought (Subjectivation)." In *Critique and Power* ed. M. Kelly, 315–346. Cambridge, MA and London: MIT Press.

Deleuze, G. and Guttari, F. 1983. *On the Line*. Translation J. Johnston. New York: Semiotexte.

Deleuze, G. and Parnet, C. 1983. "Politics." In Deleuze, G. and Guttari, F. 1983. *On the Line*. Translation J. Johnston. New York: Semiotexte.

Dimsdale, J. ed. 1980. *Survivors, Victims, and Perpetrators: Essays on the Nazi Holocaust*. Washington, DC: Hemisphere Publishing Corporation.

Doxtader, E. and Vicencio, C. eds. 2003. *Through Fire With Water: The Roots of Division and the Potential for Reconciliation in Africa*. Trenton, NJ: Africa World Press.

Drakulic, S. 1993. *The Balkan Expression: Fragments of the Other Side of the War*. New York: Harper Perennial.

Dube, P. 2002. "The Story of Thandi Shezi." In *Commissioning the Past: Understanding South Africa's Truth and Reconciliation Commission*, D. Posel and G. Sampson eds. Johannesburg: Witwatersrand University Press.

Eikenberry, K. 1987. "Victims of Crime/Victims of Justice." *Wayne Law Review*, 34: 29–49.

Eisenberg, A. 1975. "The Lost Generation." *Aleph-Tav: Tel Aviv University Review*.

Eisenman, D., Bergner, S. and Cohen, I. 2000. "An Ideal Victim: Idealizing Trauma Victims Causes Traumatic Stress in Human Rights Workers." *Human Rights Review*. July–September: 106–113.

Elias, R. 1986. *The Politics of Victimization*. Oxford: Oxford University Press.

———. 1993. *Victims Still*. Newbury Park: Sage Publications.

Ellis, M. 1990. *Beyond Innocence and Redemption: Confronting the Holocaust and Israeli Power*. San Francisco: Harper and Row.

Elster, J. 1983. *Sour Grapes: Studies in the Subversion of Rationality*. Cambridge: Cambridge University Press.

Enloe, C. 1999. "All Men Are in the Militias, All the Women Are the Victims: The Politics of Masculinity and Femininity in Nationalist Wars." In *The Women and War Reader*, eds. L. Lorentzen and J. Turpin, 50–62. New York: New York University Press.

Everett, T. Speech of the Congressman available at http://wwwc.house.gov/everett/.

Fattah, E. 1966. "Towards a Criminological Classification of Victims." *International Criminal Police Review*, 209: 162–169.

Feldman, A. 2003. "Strange Fruit: The South African Truth Commission and the Demonic Economies of Violence." *Social Analysis*, 46(3): 234–265.

Fisher, R. 2001. "Social Psychological Processes." In *Reconciliation, Justice, and Forgiveness*, ed. M. Abu-Nahmer. Lanham: Lexington Books.

Flynn, T. 1985. "Truth and Subjectivation in the Later Foucault." *Journal of Philosophy*, 82(10): 531–540.

Foucault, M. 1989. "Friendship as a Way of Life." In *Foucault Live*, ed. S. Lotringer. Translation J. Johnston. New York: Semiotexte.

———. 1994a. *Aesthetics, Method and Epistemology*. Volume Two of *Essential Works of Michel Foucault*, ed. J. D. Faubian. Translation R. Hurley et al. New York: The New Press.

———. 1994b. *Ethics: Subjectivity and Truth*. Volume One of *Essential Works of Michel Foucault*, ed. P. Rabinow. Translation R. Hurley et al. New York: The New Press.

———. 1994c. *Power*. Volume Three of *Essential Works of Michael Foucault*, ed. J. D. Faubian. Translation R. Hurley et al. New York: The New Press.

Freedom House Annual Country Reports, available at www.freedomhouse.org.

French, P. ed. 1998. *Individual and Collective Responsibility*. Rochester, Vermont: Schenkman Books.

French, P. 2001. "Unchosen Evil and Moral Responsibility." In *War Crimes and Collective Wrongdoing: A Reader*, ed. A. Jokic. London: Blackwell.

———. 2004. Dis-placing Race: the South African Truth and Reconciliation Commission (TRC) and Interpretations of Violence. Published by the Center for the Study of Violence and Reconciliation, series on *Race and Citizenship in Transition*.

Fullard, M. 2004. *Dis-placing Race: The South African Truth and Reconciliation Commission and Interpretations of Violence*. Race and Citizenship in Transition Series. Braamfontein: Centre for the Study of Violence and Reconciliation.

Galtung, J. 2001. "After Violence, Reconstruction, Reconciliation, and Resolution: Coping with Visible and Invisible Effects of War and Violence." In *Reconciliation, Justice, and Coexistence*. ed. M. Abu-Nimer. Lanham, MD: Lexington Books.

Geis, G. 1976. In *Criminal Justice and the Victim*, ed. W. McDonald. Beverly Hills: Sage Publications.

Gibson, J. and Gouws, A. 2003. *Overcoming Intolerance in South Africa*. Cambridge: Cambridge University Press.

Giliomee, H. 2003. *The Afrikaners: Biography of a People*. Charlottesville: University of Virginia Press.

Glenny, M. 1996. *The Fall of Yugoslavia: The Third Balkan War*. London and New York: Penguin Books.

Gobodo-Madikizela, P. 2004. *A Human Being Died That Night*. Boston and New York: Mariner Book.

Goldberg, D. and Krausz, M. eds. 1993. *Jewish Identity*. Philidelphia: Temple University Press.

Goldstone, R. "War Crimes: When Amnesia Causes Cancer." Speech given at the United States Holocaust Memorial, 2/2/97.

Govier, T. 2003. "What is Acknowledgement and Why is it Important?" In *Dilemmas of Reconciliation*, ed. Prager and Govier. Ontario CA: Wilfrid Laurier University Press.

Govier, T. and Verwoerd, W. 2002. "Trust and the Problem of National Reconciliation." *Philosophy of the Social Sciences*, 32(2): 178–205.

Gowing, N. 1997. *Media Coverage: Help or Hindrance in Conflict Prevention?* Washington, DC: Carnegie Commission on Preventing Deadly Conflict.

Grapard, U. 2001. "The Trouble With Women and Economics: A Postmodern Perspective on Charlotte Perkins Gilman." In *Postmodernism, Economics, and Knowledge*, ed. Stephen Cullenberg et al., 261–285. London and New York: Routledge.

Greenberg, I. 1988. "The Ethics of Jewish Power." *Perspectives*. New York: National Jewish Center for Learning and Leadership.

Gutman, R. 1993. *A Witness to Genocide*. New York: Macmillan Publishing Company.

Gutman, Y. and Krakowski, S. 1986. *Unequal Victims*. New York: Holocaust Library.

Hadot, P. 1992. "Reflections on the Cultivation of the Self." In *Michel Foucault Philosopher*, ed. T. Armstrong. London: Routledge.

Hall, D. J. 1991. "Victims Voices in Criminal Court: The Need for Restraint." *American Criminal Law Review*, 28: 233–256.

Hamber, B. 1998. "The Burdens of Truth: An Evaluation of the Psychological Support Services and Initiatives undertaken by the South African Truth and Reconciliation Commission" *American Imago*, 55(1): 9–28.

Hamber, B. and Kelly, G. 2004. "A Working Definition of Reconciliation." *Democratic Dialogue*.

Hamber, B. and Wilson, R. 2002. "Symbolic Closure Through Memory, Reparation, and Revenge in Post-Conflict Societies." *Journal of Human Rights*, 1(1): 35–53.

Harris, P. and Reilly, B. eds. 1998. *Democracy and Deep Rooted Conflict: Options for Negotiators*. Stockholm, Sweden: International IDEA.

Hayden, R. 1992. "Constitutional Nationalism in the Formerly Yugoslav Republic." *Slavic Review*, 51(4): 654–673.

———. 1996. "Imagined Communities and Real Victims: Self-determination and Ethnic Cleansing in Yugoslavia." *American Ethnologist*, 23(4): 783–801.

———. 2005. "Democracy Without the Demos?" *Eastern European Politics and Societies*, 19(2): 226–259.

Hayner, P. 2001. *Unspeakable Truths: Confronting State Terror and Atrocity*. New York: Routledge.

Herbert, T. and Dunkel Schetter, C. 1989. "Negative Social Reactions to Victims: An Overview of Responses and Their Determinants." Published as part of proceedings from *Victims Conference* 1989, 497–518.

Hentig, H. 1948. *The Criminal and His Victim: Studies in the Sociobiology of Crimes*. New Haven: Yale University Press.

Heuvel, W. 1996. "America, Franklin D. Roosevelt, and the Holocaust." Keynote speech given at the Franklin and Eleanor Roosevelt Distinguished Lecture, Roosevelt University, October 17, 1996.

Hilberg, R. 1992. *Perpetrators, Victims and Bystanders*. New York: Harper Collins.

Holbrooke, R. 1998. *To End A War*. New York: Random House.

———. 1999. Senate Confirmation Hearing, testimony, 6/24/1999.

———. 1999. *Frontline* interview.

Horowitz, D. 1985. *Ethnic Groups in Conflict*. Berkley: University of California Press.

———. 1991. *A Democratic South Africa? Constitutional Engineering in a Divided Society*. Berkley: University of California Press.

Human Rights Dialogue. 2002. "Introduction" Winter, 1.

Humphrey, M. 2002. *The Politics of Atrocity and Reconciliation: From Terror to Trauma*. London: Routledge.

———. 2003. "From Victim to Victimhood: Truth Commissions and Trials as Rituals of Political Transition and Individual Healing." *Australian Journal of Anthropology*, 14(2): 171–188.

Huyse, L. 2002 "Victims." In *Reconciliation After Violent Conflict* eds. D. Bloomfield, T. Barnes, and L. Huyse. Stockholm, Sweden: International Institute for Democracy and Electoral Assistance (IDEA).

Ibanez, A. 2001. "El Salvador: War and Untold Stories—Women Guerrillas." In *Victims, Perpetrators, or Actors?* ed. C. Moser and M. Clark. London: Zed Books.

Ignatieff, M. 1996. *Articles of Faith*. Index On Censorship 5, 110–122.

———. 1997. *Varieties of Experience*. Index on Censorship 3:29–12.

———. 1998. *The Warriors Honor: Ethnic War and the Modern Conscience*. New York: Owl Books.

Institute for Democracy in South Africa. 2004. "Lived Poverty." *Afrobarometer Briefing*, Number 11, April 2004.

International Crisis Group Report on Bosnia, 1999. Available at www.crisisgroup.org.

Jakobsen, P. 2000. "Focus on CNN Effect Loses the Point: The Real Media Impact on Conflict Management Is Invisible and Indirect." *Journal of Peace Research*, 37(2): 131–143.

Johnson, J. 2000. "Maintaining the Protection of Non-combatants." *Journal of Peace Research* 37(4): 421–48.

Jokic, A. 2001. *War Crimes and Collective Wrongdoing: A Reader*. London: Blackwell.

Jong, L. 1989. Erasmus lecture at Harvard University.

Jorgenson, K. 2001. "Four Levels and a Discipline." In *Constructing International Relations*, ed. Fierke and Jorgenson. New York: M. E. Sharpe.

Judah, T. 1998. *The Serbs: History, Myth and the Destruction of Yugoslavia*. New Haven: Yale University Press.

Kaplan, R. 1993. "A Reader's Guide to the Balkans." *New York Times Book Review* 4/18/1993.

———. 2005. *Balkan Ghosts: A Journey Through History*. New York: Picador.

Karmen, A. 1990. *Crime Victims: An Introduction to Victimology*. Belmont, CA: Wadsworth Publishing.

Kelly, L. 2000. "Wars Against Women: Sexual Violence, Sexual Politics, and the Militarized State." In *States of Conflict: Gender Violence and Resistance*, ed. S. Jacobs, R. Jacobson, and J. Marchbank. London: Zed Books.

Kelman, H. 1973. "Violence Without Moral Restraint: Reflections of the Dehumanization of Victims and Victimizers." *Journal of Social Issues*, 29(4): 25–61.

Krahe, B. 1992. "Coping with Rape: A Social Psychological Perspective." *European Journal of Personality*, 13(1): 15–26.

Kreisberg, L. 2001. "Changing forms of coexistence." In M. Abu-Nimer, ed., *Reconciliation, Justice and Coexistence*. Lanham, MD: Lexington.

Kritz, N. 1995. *Transitional Justice: How Emerging Democracies Reckon with Former Regimes*. Washington, DC: United States Institute of Peace.

———. 2001. "The Rule of Law in the Post-Conflict Phase: Building a Stable Peace." In *Turbulent Peace*, ed. C. Crocker, F. Hampson, and P. Aall. Washington, DC: United States Institute of Peace.

Krog, A. 1998. *Country of My Skull*. South Africa: Random House.

Kubalkova, Onuf, and Kowert. 1998. "Constructing Constructivism." In *International Relations in a Constructed World*, ed. Kubalkova, Onuf, and Kowert. Armonk, NY: M. E. Sharpe.

Kushner, H. 1996. *How Good Do We Have to Be? A New Understanding of Guilt and Forgiveness*. New York: Little Brown and Company.

Laclau, E. and Mouffe, C. 1985. *Hegemony and Socialist Strategies: Toward a Radical Democratic Politics*. Translation W. Moore and P. Commack. London: Verso.

Laqueur, W. 1965. "Footnotes to the Holocaust." *New York Review of Books*, November 11, 1965.

———. 1979a. *The First News of the Holocaust*. New York: Leo Baeck Institute.

———. 1979b. "Rereading Hannah Arendt." *Encounter*, 52(3): 73–79.

Lederach, J. 1997. *Sustainable Reconciliation in Divided Societies*. Washington, DC: United States Institute of Peace.

Lenin, V. 1993. *The State and Revolution*. Translation R. Service. New York: Penguin.

Levi, P. 1996. *Survival in Auschwitz*. New York: Simon and Schuster.

Lipstadt, D. 1986. *Beyond Belief: The American Press and the Coming of the Holocaust 1933–1945*. New York: The Free Press.

Lodge, T. 2002. *Politics in South Africa: From Mandela to Mbeki*. Bloomington: Indiana University Press.

Lukes, S. 1987. *Marxism and Morality*. Oxford: Oxford University Press.

Maloka, E. 2001. "The South African 'African Renaissance' Debate: A Critique." *Africa Institute of South Africa*.

Marshall, D. 2000. "Women in War and Peace: Grassroots Peacebuilding." *Peaceworks* 34. Washington, DC: United States Institute of Peace.

Marx, K. 1967. *Capital: A Critique of Political Economy*. New York: International Publishers.

Mawby, R. I. and Walklate, S. 1994. *Critical Victimology*. London: Sage Publications.

Mazurana, D. and Mckay, S. 1999. *Women and Peacebuilding*. Montreal: ICHR.

Mbkei, T. 1999. Speech given at the launch of the African Renaissance Institute, 10/19/1999.

———. 2003. Statement made to the House of Parliament, 4/15/2003.

Mendehlson, B. 1956. "The Victimology." *Etudes Intrenationales de Psycho-Sociologie Criminelle*, July–Sept: 25–26.

Meredith, M. 1999. *Coming to Terms: South Africa's Search for Truth*. New York: Public Affairs.

Mertus, J. 2001. *Wars Offensive on Women: The Humanitarian Challenge in Bosnia, Kosovo, and Afghanistan*. Bloomfield, Connecticut: Kumarian Press.

Miall, H., Ramsbotham, O. and Woodhouse, T. 1999. *Contemporary Conflict Resolution*. Cambridge: Polity Press.

Milliken, J. 2001. "Discourse Study: Bringing Rigor to Critical Theory." In *Constructing International Relations*, ed. Fierke and Jorgensen. New York: M. E. Sharpe.

Minson, J. 1986. "Strategies for Socialists: Foucault's Conception of Power." In *Towards a Critique of Foucault*, ed. M. Gane, 106–148. New York and London: Routledge.

Minow, M. 1998. *Between Vengeance and Forgiveness*. Boston: Beacon Press.

Moeller, S. 1999. *Compassion Fatigue: How the Media Sells Disease, Famine, War and Death*. New York and London: Routledge.

———. 2002. "A Hierarchy of Innocence: the Media's Use of Children in Telling of International News." *Press/Politics*, 7(1): 36–56.

Montville, J. 1993. "The Healing Function in Political Conflict Resolution." In *Conflict Resolution: Theory and Practice: Integration and Application*, ed. Sandole and Van der Merwe. New York: Manchester University Press.

Morphet, S. 2002. "Current International Civil Administration: The Need For Political Legitimacy." *International Peacekeeping*, 9(2): 140–162.

Morris, B. 2001. *Righteous Victims*. New York: Vintage Books.

Morrissey, M. and Smyth, M. 2002. *Northern Ireland after the Good Friday Agreement*. London: Pluto Press.

Moser, C. and Clark, P. ed. 2001. *Victims, Perpetrators, or Actors?* London: Zed Books.

Mouffe, C. 1992. "Feminism and Radical Politics." In *Feminists Theorize the Political*, ed. J. Butler and J. W. Scott, 369–384. New York and London: Routledge.

Moya, C. 2000. "Introduction." In *Reclaiming Identity: Realist Theory and the Predicament of Postmodernism*. eds. C. Moya and M. Hames-Garcia. Berkeley, CA: University of California Press.

Nietzsche, F. 1968. *Will to Power*. New York: Vintage.

Oberschall, A. 2000. "The Manipulation of Ethnicity: From Ethnic Cooperation to Violence and War in Yugoslavia." *Ethnic and Racial Studies*, 23(6): 982–1001.

O'Donnell, G. 1986. "On Fruitful Convergences of Hirschman's Exit: Voice and Loyalty and Shifting Involvements: Reflections from the Recent Argentine Experience." In *Development, Democracy, and the Art of Trespassing: Essays in Honor of Albert O. Hirschman*, ed. Foxley, McPherson, and O'Donnell, 249–268. Notre Dame: Notre Dame University Press.

Oren, M. 2002. *Six Days of War: June 1967 and the Making of the Modern Middle East.* Oxford: Oxford University Press.

Orr, W. 2000. "Reparations Delayed is Healing Retarded." In *Looking Back, Reaching Forward: Reflections on the Truth and Reconciliation Commission of South Africa,* eds. C. Villa-Vicencio and W. Verwoerd. Cape Town: University of Cape Town Press.

Osiel, M. 1997. *Mass Atrocity, Collective Memory, and the Law.* New Brunswick, London: Transaction Publishers.

Palmer-Fernandez, G. 1998. "The Targeting of Civilian Populations in War." In *Encyclopedia of Applied Ethics Volume One,* 509–525. San Diego: Academic Press.

Pankhurst, D. 1999. "Issues of Justice and Reconciliation in Complex Political Emergencies: Conceptualizing Reconciliation, Justice, and Peace." *Third World Quarterly,* 20(1): 239–256.

Parsonage, W. ed. 1979. *Perspectives on Victimology.* Beverly Hills: Sage Publications.

Philip, D. 1986. *Contending Ideologies in South Africa.* Cape Town: Erdmens Publishing.

Posel, D. and Sampson, G. ed. 2002. *Commissioning the Past: Understanding South Africa's Truth and Reconciliation Commission.* Johannesburg: Witwatersrand University Press.

Power, S. 2002. *A Problem from Hell.* New York: New Republic Book.

Quinney, R. 1969. *Crime and Justice in Society.* Boston: Little Brown and Company.

———. 2000. *Bearing Witness to Crime and Social Injustice.* New York: State University of New York Press.

Rabinow, P. 1994. "Introduction." In *Ethics: Subjectivity and Truth.* Volume One of *Essential Works of Michel Foucault,* ed. P. Rabinow. Translation R. Hurley et al. New York: The New Press.

Ramet, P. 1996. *Balkan Babel.* Colorado: Westview Press.

Ramet, S. 2002. *Balkan Babel: The Disintegration of Yugoslavia: From the Death of Tito to the Fall of Milosevic.* Boulder, CO: Westview Press.

Robinson, J. 1965. *And the Crooked Shall Be Made Straight: The Eichmann Trial, The Jewish Catastrophe, and Hannah Arendt's Narrative.* New York: Macmillan Press.

Rooney, E. 2003. *Feminisms and Fundamentalisms—Women in the North of Ireland.* Public Panel Presentation: Gender, Sexuality and Family Project, Cornell University Law Faculty, April 2003.

Ropers, N. 1995. Peaceful Intervention: Structures, Processes and Strategies for the Constructive Resolution of Ethnopolitical Conflicts. Berghof Report No. 1. available at http://www.b.shuttle.de/berghof/eng/ind_pub.htm.

Rosenberg, T. 1995. "Overcoming the Legacies of Dictatorship." *Foreign Affairs,* 74 May/June, 134–153.

Rubin, J. Z., Pruitt, D. G., & Kim, S. H. 1994. *Social conflict: Escalation, Stalemate, and Settlement* (2nd ed.). New York: McGraw-Hill.

Rudolph, C. 2001. "Constructing an Atrocities Regime." *International Organization,* 55(3), 655–691.

Salzman, T. 2000. "Rape Camps." In *War's Dirty Secret,* ed. Anne Barstow. Cleveland: The Pilgrim Press.

Sank, D. and Caplan, D. ed. 1991. *To Be a Victim.* New York: Plenum Press.

Sawicki, J. 1994. "Foucault and Feminism." In *Critique and Power,* ed. M. Kelly, 347–365. Cambridge and London: MIT Press.

Schafer, S. 1977. *Victimology: The Victim and His Criminal.* Virginia: Reston Publishing Company.

Schirch, L. 2004. *Ritual and Symbol in Peacebuilding*. Bloomfield, CT: Kumarian Press.

Schmidt, J. and Wartenberg, T. 1994. "Foucault's Enlightenment: Critique, Revolution, and The Fashioning of the Self." In *Critique and Power* ed. M. Kelly, 283–314. Cambridge and London: MIT Press.

Scholem, G. 1978. Correspondence with Hannah Arendt reprinted in *The Jew as Pariah: Jewish Identity and Politics in the Modern Age*, ed. R. Feldman. New York: Grove Press.

Schulhofer, S. 1998. *Unwanted Sex: A Culture of Intimidation and the Failure of the Law*. Cambridge, MA: Harvard University Press.

Sgarzi, J. and McDevitt, J. ed. 2002. *Victimology: A Study of Crime Victims and Their Roles*. New Jersey: Prentice Hall.

Simms, B. 1996. "Bosnia: The Lessons of History?" In *This Time We Knew: Western Responses to Genocide in Bosnia*, ed. T. Cushman and S. Mestrovic. New York and London: New York University Press.

Smith, M. ed. 2001. *Sex Without Consent*. New York: University Press.

Stiglmayer, A. ed. 1994. *Mass Rape: The War Against Women in Bosnia Herzegovina*. Lincoln: University of Nebraska Press.

Strozier, P. 2001. *Foucault, Subjectivity, and Identity*. Detroit, MI: Wayne State University Press.

Suarez-Orozco, M. 1991. "The Heritage of Enduring a Dirty War: Psychological Aspects of Terror in Argentina." *The Journal of Psychohistory*, 18(4), 469–505.

Tadic, T. 2000. "Ten Years of Ethnic Parties in Bosnia and Herzegovina." *Alternative Information Network*, 8/14/2000.

Teitel, R. G. 2000. *Transitional Justice*. Oxford: Oxford University Press.

Thomas, L.M. 1999. "Suffering as a Moral Beacon: Blacks and Jews." In H. Flanzbaum, ed. *The Americanization of the Holocaust*. Baltimore, MD: Johns Hopkins University Press.

Trunk, I. 1972. *Judenrat*. New York: Stein and Day.

Truth and Reconciliation Commission Report available at www.doj.gov.za/trc.

Turshen, M. 1998. In *What Women Do In Wartime: Gender and Conflict in Africa*. ed. M. Turshen and Twagiramariya. London: Zed Books.

U.N. Economic and Social Council. 1993. *Rape and the Abuse of Women in the Former Yugoslavia: Report of the Secretary General*. Document E/CN4/1994/5 June 30, 1993.

U.N. *Handbook on Justice for Victims*, available at www.un.org.

Underwood, T. and Edmunds, C. ed. 2003. *Victim Assistance: Exploring Individual Practice, Organizational Policy, and Societal Responses*. New York: Springer.

Van Der Merwe, H. 2001. "Reconciliation and Justice in South Africa: Lessons from the TRC's Community Interventions." In *Reconciliation, Justice, and Coexistence: Theory and Practice*, ed. M. Abu-Nimer, 187–207. Lanham MD: Lexington Books.

Vicnecio, C. 1996. *The Spirit of Freedom*. Berkeley: University of California Press.

Vicencio, C. and Verwoerd, W. ed. 2000. *Looking Back, Reaching Forward*. Capetown: University of Capetown Press.

Waever, O. 1996. "European Security Identities." *Journal of Common Market Studies*, 34(1): 103–132.

Walklate, S. 2003. "Can There be a Feminist Victimology?" In *Victimization: Theory, Research, and Policy*, ed. P. Davies, P.r Francis and V. Jupp. New York: Palgrave.

Weine, S. 1999. *When History is a Nightmare: Lives and Memories of Ethnic Cleansing in Bosnia-Herzegovina.* New Jersey: Rutgers University Press.

Wickham, G. 1986. "Power and Power Analysis: Beyond Foucault?" In *Towards a Critique of Foucault* ed. M. Gane, 149–179. New York and London: Routledge.

Wiesel, E. 1985. "A Jew Defends Eichmann." In *Against Silence: The Voice and Vision of Elie Wiesel: Volume Two*, ed. I. Abrahamson. New York Holocaust Library.

Williams, K. 1976. In *Criminal Justice and the Victim.* ed. W. McDonald. Beverly Hills: Sage Publications.

Williams, P. and Scharf, M. 2002. *Peace with Justice: War Crimes and Accountability in the Former Yugoslavia.* New York: Rowman and Littlefield.

Wilson, R. A. 2001. *The Politics of Truth and Reconciliation in South Africa: Legitimizing the Post-apartheid State.* Cambridge: Cambridge University Press

World Health Organization, 2005. *Report on HIV/AIDS in South Africa*, available at www. who.org.

Zaccaria, G. 1994. *We, Criminals of War: True History from the Former Yugoslavia.* Milan: Baldini and Calstodi.

About the Author

Dr. Erica Bouris is an assistant professor at Rollins College in the department of political science. Her teaching and research interests center on political victimization, postconflict societies, and the ethical dimension of international engagement with these issues.

Index

accountability:
    reconciliation and, 20–21
    war criminals, 18–19, 51–52n6
adaptive preferences, 82–84
"Africanism," 152
African National Congress (ANC), 144–53
African People's Organization, 148
"African Renaissance," 175–79, 184n22
Afrikaners, victimized, 183–84n11
agency of victims, 79–80, 84, 119–21
aggressors:
    as victims, 67–69
    versus victims, 15, 24–27, 30, 63–64, 100–105, 131, 147–48
    See also war criminals; specific event
Ahabah Israel, 60–61
AIDS. *See* HIV
Albin, 16
Alcibiades, 130
Alliance for Change, 93
amnesty, 166–68
    as Christian forgiveness, 167–68
Amnesty Committee, 142
ANC. *See* African National Congress
anti-Muslim rhetoric, 94–98
anti-Semitism. *See* Holocaust, the
apartheid:
    Africanist solution to, 149–52
    government responsibility, 146–47
    ideal victims, 154–55
    liberation movement, 149–51
    reparations, 164–66
    subjectivation under, 127

victimization under, 7, 47
    See also South Africa, post-apartheid
APLA. *See* Azanian People's Liberation Army
appeasement, 14
Aquinas, Thomas, 37
Arabs, 54–55
Arendt, Hannah, 10, 51–52n6
    opposition to, 60–62
    on victim responsibility, 54–55, 60–72
    See also "banality of evil"; totalitarianism
Argentina, 174
assistance resources, 31, 188–89
    See also healing, postconflict
atrocities:
    images of, 4–5
    as justification for rape, 95–96
    victim participation in, 60–62
    See also journalistic coverage
Auschwitz. *See* Holocaust, the
Azanian People's Liberation Army (APLA), 147

Babic, Mirko, 95
bad deeds, 38
    See also demonization
Balkan conflict. *See* Bosnian conflict
"banality of evil," 62–64, 87
BCM. *See* Black Consciousness Movement
Beck, Gregory Edmund, 162–64
Bernstein, Richard A., 65
Biehl, Amy, 151
Biko, Steven, 166

 Also from Kumarian Press . . .

Peacebuilding, Conflict Resolution, and Humanitarianism:

Ritual and Symbol in Peacebuilding
Lisa Schirch

War's Offensive on Women: The Humanitarian Challenge in Bosnia, Kosovo, and Afghanistan
Julie Mertus

Aiding Violence: The Development Enterprise in Rwanda
Peter Uvin

Non-state Actors in the Human Rights Universe
Edited by George Andreopoulos, Zehra Arat, and Peter Juviler

New and Forthcoming:

Humanitarian Alert: NGO Information and Its Impact on US Foreign Policy
Abby Stoddard

A World Turned Upside Down: Social Ecological Approaches to Children in War Zones
Edited by Neil Boothby, Alison Strang, and Michael Wessells

NGOs in International Politics
Shamima Ahmed and David M. Potter

Invisible Governance: International Secretariats in Global Politics
John Mathiason

Visit Kumarian Press at **www.kpbooks.com** or call
toll-free 800.289.2664 for a complete catalog.

green press
INITIATIVE

Kumarian Press, Inc. is committed to preserving ancient forests and natural resources. We elected to print *Complex Political Victims* on 30% post consumer recycled paper, processed chlorine free. As a result, for this printing, we have saved:

  5 Trees (40' tall and 6-8" diameter)
2,280 Gallons of Waste Water
  917 Kilowatt Hours of Electricity
  251 Pounds of Solid Waste
  494 Pounds of Greenhouse Gases

Kumarian Press, Inc. made this paper choice because our printer, Thomson-Shore, Inc., is a member of Green Press Initiative, a nonprofit program dedicated to supporting authors, publishers, and suppliers in their efforts to reduce their use of fiber obtained from endangered forests.

For more information, visit www.greenpressinitiative.org

Kumarian Press, located in Bloomfield, Connecticut, is a forward-looking, scholarly press that promotes active international engagement and an awareness of global connectedness.